Community and Class in American Education, 1865-1918

Studies in the History of American Education Series

Henry J. Perkinson
and Vincent P. Lannie
General Editors

Sheldon Cohen
A History of Colonial Education, 1607–1776
David Madsen
Early National Education, 1776–1830
Frederick M. Binder
The Age of the Common School, 1830–1865
Patricia Albjerg Graham
Community and Class in American Education, 1865–1918
Edgar Gumbert and Joel H. Spring
The Superschool and the Superstate:
American Education in the Twentieth Century, 1918–1970

Community and Class in American Education, 1865-1918

Patricia Albjerg Graham
Barnard College, Columbia University

John Wiley & Sons, Inc., New York · London · Sydney · Toronto

Library of Congress Cataloging in Publication Data:

Graham, Patricia Albjerg.
   Community and class in American education, 1865–1918.

   (Studies in the history of American education series)
   Bibliography: p.
   1. Education—United States—History. 2. Social classes—United States—History. I. Title.

LA205.G68   370′.973   74–562
ISBN 0–471–32090–0
ISBN 0–471–32091–9 (pbk.)

Printed in the United States of America

10 9 8 7 6 5 4 3 2 1

For Loren

acknowledgments

The debts one incurs in writing a book are always considerable and in the nature of the debt, cannot be entirely repaid. In order that the default in payment not be total, I would like here to thank a number of persons from whose assistance I benefited. Clearly none of them is responsible for the interpretations or factual matter presented here.

The list of those who have given generously of their time and energies in reading the complete manuscript and commenting most helpfully on it includes Joseph Brennan, my colleague at Barnard College, and Robert Wiebe of Northwestern University. Others whose contributions have been to specific sections are John J. Newman, State Archivist, Indiana State Library, Indianapolis; Sterling Haltom, Assistant Superintendent of Schools, Franklin, Indiana; Mrs. Montrew Gross of the Franklin School Board staff; Robert Coward, Librarian of the Franklin College Library; James Hendricks and William Farley and their students at Northern Michigan University; Ernest Rankin and Mrs. Richard Weesen of the Marquette County Historical Society;

Father Alaric Wolf and Father Lawrence Gauthier of the Roman Catholic Diocese of Northern Michigan; Mr. and Mrs. Laurence Barnett, formerly of Marquette County and now of Hastings, Michigan; Myra Ware Crenshaw of the Butler County, Alabama, Historical Society; Milo Howard Jr., Sarah Anne Warren, and Alice Berta of the Alabama State Archives and History; President David Mathews, Charles Summersell, and Robert McKenzie of the University of Alabama, Tuscaloosa; Frances Honour of the Auburn University Library; Sheldon Hackney, Provost of Princeton University; and Frank Cook of the University of Wisconsin Archives. My late mother, Marguerite Hall Albjerg, read and commented on the chapter on Johnson County, where she was born in 1895 and spent her childhood. My late father, Victor L. Albjerg, prepared an illuminating essay on his early education as a non-English speaking child in rural Minnesota.

Funds for travel in connection with the research on this project came from the Faculty Research Fund, Barnard College and from the Divisional Research Fund, Teachers College. When the book was nearly completed, I also received a fellowship from the John Simon Guggenheim Foundation and from the Radcliffe Institute. Each of these was most helpful.

Inevitably the family of the author become additionally involved with the project as a manuscript progresses (or, especially, fails to progress), and mine is no exception. For their willingness to tolerate cheerfully monologues on various main themes and minutiae of this book I am grateful to my husband, Loren, and our daughter, Meg.

Patricia Albjerg Graham

New York City, December, 1973

series preface

This series provides new interpretations of American educational history based on the best recent scholarship. It contains five volumes that present, chronologically and topically, the history of American education from the beginning to the present day.

Each volume gives an original analysis and interpretation of the development of formal and informal agencies of education during a particular period.

Henry J. Perkinson

contents

Community and Class in American Education, 1865-1918

chapter one
the school triumphant

Writing of the nineteenth century, Arthur M. Schlesinger once observed, "The closing decades of the century saw an educational renaissance comparable in many respects to the great days of Horace Mann and Henry Barnard." That so-called rebirth has impressed many observers by the number and variety of its progeny. Historians have sought to explain the phenomenon by emphasizing the emergence of the high school, by describing the plethora of urban educational problems, by relating political and social progressivism to events in education, and by recounting the growth of colleges and universities. Nearly all have stressed the expansion of formal education and the more and more important role it had come to play in the society.

"The great days of Horace Mann and Henry Barnard" to which Schlesinger referred were the middle years of the nineteenth century when public school systems were being instituted by Mann and Barnard in Massachusetts and Connecticut. This period has often been called "the age of the common school." For Massachusetts and even for Connecticut that is indeed an appropriate appellation, but for much of the rest of the country it was not. This New England reform reached the remainder of the nation after the Civil War.

The Horace Mann-Henry Barnard period in the history of American education had a regional focus that subsequent periods lack. In the early years of the nineteenth century it was possible to speak of New England, the Middle Atlantic states, to except the South, and to have covered adequately educational activities in the nation. In the period from 1865 to 1918 such an approach is insupportable. Westward migration, variations in social structure, and ethnic and religious differences combine to make a regional examination necessary. An example of the importance of a regional analysis can be seen in the school attendance figures for children between the ages of six and fourteen. In 1910 the national figure was 81 percent, but it approximates the percentage for only a miniscule portion of the country, the mountain and Pacific regions, which together accounted for less than one half the number of students in any other single section. The three southern regions were all clustered around 70 percent, and the remainder of the nation was clustered at nearly 90 percent. Thus the use of national figures, alone, can be misleading.

The "educational renaissance" to which Schlesinger refers can best be seen by studying communities and colleges and noting the changes that occurred in them during these years. By viewing closely areas selected because they illustrate the diversity of America in those years, it is possible to develop a clearer picture of what educational opportunities actually were available to Americans in various regions and circumstances. Too often, history of education concentrates on reform, what was new, instead of on what was typical. By looking at the communities one can put the reforms into perspective. Change is certainly visible in these communities and colleges during this period; evidence of it abounds.

The most striking change of all is the establishment and extension of school systems, a reform of the pre-Civil War period but a reality of the postwar era. None of the four communities we discuss in later chapters had, in fact, effective school systems before the war, but each developed them between 1865 and 1918. Most were not the "common" schools idealized by Mann and Barnard, but they were comprehensive. Similarly, vocational education was introduced to the United States in a highly visible fashion in 1876 at the Philadelphia Exposition, but none of the communities discussed here developed vocational education programs until after the turn of the century. The lag between enunciation of a reformer's ideas and widespread implementation of them is considerable.

Each of the counties and colleges illustrates the dominant characteristic of education in late nineteenth-and early twentieth-century America: the preeminent position in which educational institutions, that is, schools, colleges, and universities, moved. In education, as in other facets of American life, it was a time of institution-building, and the enormously expanded roles of the schools were the result.

The expansion occurred for several reasons. First, knowledge grew enormously during this period, the range and depth exceeding all expectations. This was reflected in the altered curricula of the colleges and universities. Much more important for the ordinary citizen, however, was the increase in what it was necessary to know in order to function effectively in society. Between 1865 and 1918 a watershed was passed in America; literacy became an economic necessity.

In the midtwentieth century societies have used radio, television, and other molders of public opinion in campaigns to eradicate illiteracy. In the less pressured times of late nineteenth-and early twentieth-century America such advertising techniques were neither necessary nor available. Literacy for the younger generation was enough, and naturally the institution supposedly equipped for this was the school. In a society in which religion no longer demanded learned study of the Bible for salvation, the churches could not be expected to carry the major responsibility of a literacy campaign. Similarly, in the non-English immigrant society that America became between 1865 and 1918, parents could not be expected to instruct their children in English. In these circumstances the responsibility fell to the schools. Old Yankees were eager to use the schools instead of the families to initiate immigrant children to the American way of life.

Imperfectly and inarticulately Americans grasped this transition, this preeminence of educational institutions. If one were to have asked an American to define an "educated man" in 1865, the reply would likely have been in terms of a man with knowledge of the classics. By 1918 the definition would be, "a man who had been to college." The essential change was in an assumption that what one knew was based on where one had studied. Informal education was in a decline between 1865 and 1918.

The functions of the schools grew in several ways. First, by 1918 all states had passed compulsory education laws. These laws required that children attend a school until they either reached a certain age or completed a certain grade. Compliance with the law necessitated school attendance, but not necessarily literacy. Usually there was a positive relation between school attendance and literacy, but the law did not demand literacy, only school attendance. Thus, an underage child who could read, write, and calculate creditably was required to remain in school while one who had passed the magic age of school-leaving and who was illiterate could leave school with society's blessings. The effect of the law was to increase immensely the significance of formal educational institutions while diminishing the importance of learning acquired outside schools.

Second, schools, particularly in cities but gradually in rural areas and small towns, assumed many of the functions formerly handled informally through families, churches, and small homogeneous communities. Expectations of what the schools could and should do rose to extraordinary heights, and much of the subsequent criticisms of the schools has been a result of the schools' inability to perform adequately these many tasks. In kindergarten programs, schools were expected to prepare children for the separation from their homes and the discipline of formal classes that regular school attendance would entail, a task formerly believed to be that of the family. Schools sponsored a variety of activities, many social, involving both young and old, supplementing the family gatherings and church socials that had been possible in smaller and more stable communities.

Finally, in the more complicated and technical society developing in the United States, it was becoming necessary to have formal preparation in many subjects previously learned either informally in the family or, more formally, through various kinds of apprenticeships. The necessity of detailed and measurable instruction of the sort given by and certified to by schools and colleges was evident both in the trade fields, where vocational training was introduced into the elementary and high schools, and in the professions, which began to require the completion of a carefully ordered curriculum. The demand for this regulated instruction immensely increased the significance of the schools. For example, to be a farmer in early nineteenth-century America one simply hung around a farm, preferably one's family farm, and picked up the lore and practice of successful farming from its exemplars in the neighborhood. By the end of the nineteenth century in the leading farm regions, state universities were telling the farmers that they should send their sons to the campus for 4 years to be taught in classrooms and on model farms how to be good farmers. Such a notion seemed ludicrous to many, who believed that the 4 years would be wasted. The most that many would accept was that a particular "short course," given by the staff of the state agriculture school in the slack winter season, might be of some value to a farmer. The scoffers were unable to go against the tide of the time, which favored formal instruction, and by 1918 undergraduate instruction in agriculture was a major component of Morrill Act universities.

Much the same phenomenon occurred with young women for whom the state universities established departments of home economics to train them to become better housewives. Formerly training of this kind was limited to that provided by the home but, by the second decade of the twentieth century, instruction in cooking and sewing (generally more ostentatiously termed "food preparation" and "textiles") was an important element of the state university's curriculum.

In the professions, too, formal instruction replaced apprenticeships and looser preparations for careers in law, medicine, and teaching. Formerly, what you knew, often as was demonstrated by an examination, determined whether you were qualified to enter the ranks of a profession. The shift in the early twentieth century was to completion of a set program at designated and approved places, sometimes coupled with an examination at the end. On that basis one was certified as a professional. In teaching, for example, throughout much of the nineteenth century one could become licensed simply by passing an examination, but with the further development of normal schools in the early twentieth century, certification became possible only with completion of a series of courses. Such a shift in licensing procedures vastly enhanced the role of the educational institutions.

The higher educational institutions themselves during this period also came to stress accomplishment in an institutional setting instead of in an individual one as prerequisite for admission. During the last third of the nineteenth century both Princeton and Wisconsin actively sought students who had completed an approved high school or preparatory school program instead of students who could simply pass the entrance examination. Both universities moved actively to support the faltering secondary schools. Princeton established a private "feeder" school (Lawrenceville) in its neighborhood. The University of Wisconsin sent its faculty touring the state to determine which high schools were doing work satisfactory for accreditation so that their graduates could be admitted without examination. Marquette High School sought college acknowledgement of its work so that its graduates might be accepted by "diploma and without examination" into college freshman classes. The development of regional accrediting associations at the end of this period further testifies to the increasing role of institutional sponsorship of individual academic efforts.

In the late nineteenth century, then, an immense educational burden fell to the schools, probably more then than at any time previously, and more than today when other agencies and the media perform vital, if less systematic, educational roles. Since these institutions were critically important in the late nineteenth and early twentieth centuries, educational opportunity could be assessed largely by the access of individuals to them and to the quality of the ones that were available.

Whether the schools were public, parochial, or private probably was not very important, much as it has concerned educators of the past. The myth of the public schools as democratizing agents for all segments of society rested mainly on the assumption that one school would, in fact, serve children of diverse social, economic, and ethnic backgrounds. Actually, most schools, based as they were on residential patterns and before widespread school transportation was possible, served children in their immediate neighborhoods, and most neighborhoods were relatively homogeneous. In Marquette the poor children attended the school in South Marquette and the rich ones, the Ridge School. In Butler County, of course, the schools were rigidly segregated by race. In New York City the schools were located in ethnic ghettos so that the children of Little Italy attended school together while the school a few blocks south and east served the Jewish families in the Lower East Side. In Johnson County the white town children did all attend the same school, although the blacks were in a segregated school through the eighth grade. Only in the high school were all children taught together, and by then many had dropped out of school.

Many parochial schools were also ethnically homogeneous, just as many parishes were heavily Irish, Italian, or Polish, and in that respect quite similar to the public school. Their distinctive feature, their instruction in Roman Catholic doctrine, differed only in kind from the pervasive Protestantism of many public schools. The more general rule seems to have been that when there was widespread agreement on religious questions, as presumably there was in parochial schools and also in Protestant Johnson County, religion entered the curriculum.

Private schools, as Horace Mann noted early in his career in Massachusetts, were chiefly important in lessening the commitment of the wealthy and influential leaders of the community to support the public school. For example, in Butler County, as long as the strong Methodist and Baptist schools existed. leading white citizens did not patronize the public schools, which languished from lack of attention but even more from lack of funds. In New York the major reform of the schools was brought about by socially prestigious (and often wealthy) Yankee leaders who feared the consequences for the city if the schools were not improved to educate and Americanize the immigrants more effectively.

In nineteenth-century America, an important determinant of educational quality was the amount of money spent on education. Appropriations from state and local sources for public schools and from the parish for parochial ones were basic, as their inadequacy in Butler County testifies to so bitterly; but given a certain modicum of support for the essential educational services, private benefaction became crucial. The contrast was immense between Marquette, where the wealthy residents of the county were concentrated, and the nearby towns of Ishpeming and Negaunee. Although nearly comparable in size, they lacked the cultural facilities of Marquette, such as a public library, a manual training program, and an elaborate high school building, all made possible by gifts of members of the community. The public library in Johnson County also resulted from community beneficence, augmented by Andrew Carnegie's gift. Butler County, on the other hand, had very little local wealth, and the tiny public library there was not opened until 1970. In New York City, the extensive public library system developed from private donations of collections, Andrew Carnegie's gift for construction of library buildings, various social settlements' and religious groups' contributions, and the city's contribution of land. All but the last were the direct result of individual affluence. Libraries, of course, are the primary source of materials for self-education, which formal schooling was supposed to initiate.

Money, then, was crucial to educational opportunity in two ways. First, the lack of it might limit one's possibilities for extensive schooling by forcing youngsters into full-time jobs at an early age. Secondly, and more important, the resources available to a community significantly influenced the quality of the educational institutions serving the citizenry. Therefore, if a child were born to a relatively poor family but in a more prosperous community, his educational advantages might be considerable. This was often the case in Franklin, New York and Marquette. Conversely, a more affluent white child growing up in Butler County might, in fact, have more spartan educational fare than the poor one in New York or Marquette because of the relative impoverishment of the Alabama school. Obviously, the poor black child in Alabama had the bleakest educational outlook of all.

One danger of stressing the role of schools and colleges is that their significance may be overestimated simply because institutions of this kind leave records on which the historian can rely. Informal educational activities, such as those occurring between parents and children or among youngsters on the street, are much more difficult to determine. Diaries often seem indicative of isolated experiences, not the testimony of group activity, as are school board minutes. The result is that any group and, to a lesser extent, any individual that leaves a record becomes more significant to the historian than circumstances may warrant.

The problem becomes particularly acute in judging the educational activities of blacks in Butler County, many of whom were illiterate throughout much of this period and, therefore, were not inclined to leave detailed written accounts of their education. As a result, knowledge about them is skimpy and largely limited to reports about their schools made to the state or by federal investigators. Furthermore, the education about which information is sought becomes either that which occurs in school or is the heavily verbal kind of which a written record is left, thereby omitting the immense learning that goes on in the home, on the farm, or in the woods. When children in school become familiar with different kinds of plants and trees, we call that the study of botany. When a child learns from his parents in the forest to identify the same plants and trees—and may learn much more about them than he would have learned in the classroom—we do not call that education at all, or even mention it. The reason, of course, is that we have tangible evidence (curriculum guides, student tests, etc.) of the former and only conjecture about the latter.

The same problem affects reporting about the range and quality of adult informal education. There the chief sources are likely to be newspapers, which generally report mostly the activities of the middle and upper-middle class. When *The Mining Journal* in Marquette informs its readers that the ladies in the Literary Guild have been reading Thackeray all winter, we may assume only a very few women in Marquette are involved. What of the rest, who do not read books in regular literary clubs, but who may, in fact, have been devouring Shakespeare all winter? Or, perhaps they have not been reading at all. We simply do not know. Similarly, the intellectual quality of the Charlotte Emerson Club or the Hurricane Literary Society in Johnson County is difficult to assess from either the accounts in the *Franklin Star* or the reminiscences of former members.

Despite these caveats about the history of education, some conclusions about the state of education in America between 1865 and 1918 are possible. Most obvious was the extraordinary expansion of the school systems and the consequent decline of the illiteracy rate. That enormous growth occurred in the elementary grades in the last third of the nineteenth century, but the bulge shifted to the high school level after the turn of the century, as all the counties except Butler dramatically attest. Even there the trend was perceptible, but not as striking as in Johnson, Marquette, or New York. Nationally after 1890 the elementary school pupils increased at the rate of 13 to 14 percent per decade, but the number of secondary students almost doubled between 1890 and 1900, increased about 60 percent from 1900 to 1910, and doubled again in the following decade.

One consequence of this increase in school attendance is apparent from the declining illiteracy rate in America during this period. The national illiteracy rate for persons over 10 years of age in 1870 was nearly 20 percent, and it fell approximately 3 percent per decade so that by 1910 for the nation as a whole it was 7.7 percent. The rates, of course, varied enormously among the different sections of the population. By 1910 blacks had a rate of 30.4 percent, a heritage of the pre-Civil War prohibition on teaching blacks in most southern states and of the inadequate provision made for black education in the South after the war.

The white foreign-born illiteracy rate in 1910 was 12.7 percent, reflecting in part the inadequate school systems of much of southern and eastern Europe from which many had come. In 1880, for example, when most immigrants were coming from northern and western Europe, the foreign-born illiteracy rate was lower (12 percent) than the figure for the nation as a whole (17 percent) and was just over 3 percent higher than the overall figure for native-born whites (8.7 percent). By 1910 the literacy gap between foreign-born whites and native-born whites had increased nearly threefold since native-born whites then had an illiteracy rate of 3 percent and foreign-born whites a rate of 12.7 percent. The most startling revelation of the literacy figures, however, are those for the children of immigrants. Beginning with 1890 when they were recorded separately for the first time, the white persons, one or both of whose parents were foreign born, led the categories in literacy. In 1890 only 2.2 percent of them were illiterate, and by 1910 the percent had decreased to 1.1, making them the most literate segment of the population that the Census recorded. Southerners accounted for the principal white, native-born illiteracy.

The literacy figures varied considerably regionally, the sections of the country with the most blacks (the South) and the most rural areas (also the South) having higher rates of illiteracy than the predominantly white and urban areas. The exceptions were the cities in which heavy concentrations of recent immigrants lived, many of whom were illiterate. In 1910 the rural illiteracy rate was 10.1 percent and the urban illiteracy rate was 5.1 percent. Thus, New York state had an illiteracy rate of 5.5 percent in 1910, but New York City's rate was 6.7 percent, higher because of the higher proportion of foreign born in the population. In Indiana and Michigan the state illiteracy figures in 1910 were both just over 3 percent, but in Alabama, the 1910 rate was 22.9 percent, accounted for both by the large number of blacks and the heavily rural quality of the state. Perhaps most striking about the Alabama figures, though, is that they represented a decrease of more than 11 percent during one decade.

The most telling evidence of the effect of the increased school attendance in the late nineteenth and early twentieth centuries was the discrepancy between the overall illiteracy rates and those for children aged ten to fourteen, who presumably had been in school. In 1910 the illiteracy rate for everyone over age ten was 7.7 percent, but for that group, aged ten to fourteen, who should have learned to read and write in the newly expanded schools, the rate was only 4.1 percent. The highest rates of illiteracy were in the segment of the population over sixty-five years of age, where the proportion of illiteracy was nearly double the national average.

The school attendance figures point to the increasing literacy of the younger members of the population, as the following table illustrates:

Percentage of Children Six to Fourteen Attending School in 1910

New England Region	91.9
Middle Atlantic Region	88.4
East North Central Region	89.1
West North Central Region	87.5
South Atlantic Region	70.3
East South Central Region	70.2
West South Central Region	69.3
Mountain Region	81.7
Pacific Region	86.3

The most startling conclusion about the figures is that they illustrate the wide discrepancy of educational opportunity available in America in 1910. More than one half the children in the country lived in one of the first four sections, roughly the northeastern quadrant of the nation. There nearly 90 percent attended school, but in the South, accounting for more than one third of the American children and almost all the black ones, only about 70 percent were enrolled in school. At a time of increasing importance of formal schooling differences like these had profound effects on the opportunities of the children in the different regions.

The new emphasis placed on school attendance, plus the population increases, put an incredible burden on existing school systems to provide the necessary facilities for their new pupils. The professional wisdom of the day pointed to one solution for the growing schools: the elimination of the small, one-room schoolhouses of an earlier time and the replacement of them with graded schools. It was widely held that by arranging the children in separate classes, according to their age level or by their demonstrated educational accomplishments, much more carefully planned curriculums could be followed and the learning of the children could be considerably enhanced. The assumption was that in the ungraded, one-room school, the teacher's responsibilities were too divided among the many children at the various grade levels. It was hoped that if the teacher could concentrate all her attention on only one grade level, much more rigorous and effective instruction could occur. Such an option was not possible, of course, until the numbers of children attending a school were great enough to divide the school into grades.

Such a necessary concentration of children obviously occurred much earlier in urban areas than in rural ones, accounting, many contended, for the reputed inferiority of rural education. The problems that rural teachers faced were immense, beginning with lack of funds. Their difficulties, such as those of a Marquette County teacher who had to contend with a balky stove for heating, outside toilets, and a classroom of 50 or 60 children of assorted nationalities and ages who were to be instructed in all subjects from the primary through the elementary grades, were immediately obvious to everyone concerned with educational policy. An eminently reasonable solution seemed to be to bring the children together in large enough numbers so that an adequate school with heating and plumbing facilities could be constructed and the children could be divided into grades. The marvels of the graded school and, later, of school consolidation were preached throughout the American educational establishment at normal schools, at summer institutes, at Chautauqua, and in the universities. In these schools each teacher would only have to master the curriculum of one grade. Her classes each day could do the same subjects, each child presumably doing what every other child was doing. How much easier for the teacher! The problem was solved!

But was the problem really solved? Had it not simply been transferred to the students, to whom educational leaders have generally been much less responsive than they have been to teachers? Both these efforts, grading of classes and school consolidation, pointed toward establishing a more rigid classroom organization than was ever possible in the inevitably chaotic one-room school. Furthermore, the grade isolation emphasized the problems of those children who were not promoted and thus were forced to remain in the primary grades with children much smaller than they. In the one-room school the assortment of ages and sizes varied, and a nonreading ten-year-old could, at least, mix with his age mates in the classroom and at recess, possibilities that were not open to him in a school in which all nonreaders were left with the six-year-olds in the first grade. Similarly, an immigrant child who knew no English might be absorbed into a rural, one-room school at age nine and permitted to move at his own rate through the curriculum, an accomplishment that was much more difficult in most graded schools where promotion came semiannually and few allowances were made for children doing work ahead of that prescribed for the entire class.

Undoubtedly there was a multitude of problems with the one-room schools, many of which concerned the teachers, who were poorly paid and often equally poorly educated. For the child, however, there were at least more opportunities for permitting him to progress through the schoolwork at his own rate instead of at a rate determined by a curriculum guide. A few voices protesting the "academic lockstep" began at the end of the nineteenth century and reached a crescendo about the time of World War I with the development of the progressive education movement. The common theme running through the attacks on the schools was that schools should take account of children's individual differences, that flexibility and not rigidity should characterize classroom practices. Each of these criticisms reflected a concern with the increased bureaucratization of education that occurred first in cities and later in towns and rural areas, substantially as a result of the increased numbers of schoolchildren and the conviction that the most efficient way to educate them was in large, graded schools.

That many children found the schools dreary is confirmed by Susan Kingsbury's study in 1905 to 1906 in which she reported that most students who dropped out at age fourteen did so because they were "dulled by the inactive school life." The exceedingly high attrition rates in schools in all the counties attest to the same phenomenon.

The children and their parents wanted the schools to provide literacy, but beyond that the usefulness of formal education was dubious. Gradually the minimum educational requirements of the population began to shift, from simple literacy to completion of the eighth grade, and by the end of the period, high school was no longer a novelty. By 1918 college entrance demanded completion of high school, although in 1865 most colleges were accepting for admission any white male (and even a few white females and blacks of both sexes) who could pay the tuition and pass a rudimentary examination.

The vitality of the high school movement in the late nineteenth century illustrates the widespread commitment to building more extensive educational institutions. Although it is easy to point to the longer formal schooling available to the populace, it is dangerous to argue that the increase in school attendance meant an equivalent rise in learning. Nonetheless, the growth of the high schools, indicating as it did the pervasive concern with extending educational institutions, put severe pressures on communities to establish and to support high schools. After the Kalamazoo decision in Michigan in 1874, the argument that public funds could not be used for postelementary schooling was quashed. Both Johnson and Marquette counties established public high schools in the 1870s, but both, reflecting the national trend, underwent their principal growth after the turn of the century. New York was slow in organizing public high schools, most coming after the mid-1890s, but predictably, Butler County was even slower in providing widespread high school instruction at public expense. It offered none at all to more than half its school population, black children, and the public high school for whites was a creation of the 1890s after the public funds could be diverted heavily to white schools. Even then it was limited to the town, with none available to the majority of the white children, those who lived in the country.

All four counties illustrate the principle that local public funds were more likely to be concentrated at the lower educational levels than at the upper ones. In each of the counties the high-school-level work was more likely to be under private auspices and, therefore, intended for a more limited and affluent segment of the population than was the elementary. In Manhattan, secondary education was almost entirely in private hands until the turn of the century, being mostly limited to the single-sex preparatory schools. The only high school work for blacks in Butler County was offered at two separate institutions, one Baptist and the other Methodist. Whites in Butler County had also been limited to either Baptist or Methodist secondary work in the 1870s, 1880s, and early 1890s, until the heavy diversion of public funds to white schools invigorated the public high school movement. In Marquette, high school work was offered after the turn of the century at the state normal school and at the parochial school. Even in Johnson County, where public facilities monopolized elementary education throughout this period, secondary work was presented under both public and private auspices, the latter being the preparatory department at Baptist Franklin College, which generally enrolled more precollege students than college ones. The Franklin public high school, organized in the 1870s, would have been closed in the 1880s if the leading Johnson County editor had had his way, and students seeking postelementary studies would have been sent at public expense to the prep division of Franklin College.

In all three of the predominantly rural counties, the high school movement was stronger in the towns than in the country. In Butler County the only high school was located in the county seat, Greenville, which served less than a quarter of the population. In Marquette the major high schools were all in the towns of Marquette, Ishpeming, and Negaunee, which together accounted for about one half the population of the county. Only in Johnson County were there high schools in the rural areas.

Concomitant with the high school movement was the interest in vocational training, and the two phenomena were frequently related. Several recent historians of education have observed that the eagerness of certain nineteenth-century leaders to encourage the schools to include many projects earlier undertaken informally stemmed both from their concern with the inability of the society to assimilate the children of the new immigrants and with the more and more technical demands of the industrialized order. These two interests joined together in placing much heavier responsibilities on the schools to include studies that would be immediately useful in later life in their curriculum. In much of the late nineteenth century the emphasis was on what was then termed "manual training," which theoretically taught children the value of work with the hands and of craftsmanship, both without a specific vocational objective. By the turn of the century, particularly as the immigrant problem became more pressing, the emphasis shifted to vocational training that was geared to teaching children particular trades. The progressive educators of the first and second decade of the twentieth century wrote approvingly about black boys being taught cobbling in an Indianapolis school or white boys (and probably sons of immigrants) metal working in Chicago's Lane Technical High School. Little thought seemed to occur to these publicists, so concerned that education should reflect democratic values that, by providing vocational training in the schools and especially by urging this in immigrant and poor neighborhoods, the options of those children who most needed to benefit from the much-vaunted American opportunities for social mobility through education were being curtailed.

Vocational training, at either the high school or the prehigh school level, was generally found most frequently in those schools and areas in which the poor and the immigrants lived. The centers of the vocational training movement tended to be in the cities, and those of the agricultural education programs, naturally enough, tended to be in the rural areas, but often in ones with large numbers of immigrant farmers. The South, where the largest concentration of white native-born farmers lived, had relatively few vocational agriculture programs until the second decade of the twentieth century, although they were flourishing in much of the upper Midwest by the latter part of the nineteenth century. In the South the early vocational work was geared to blacks, who occupied a somewhat analogous educational position to the new immigrants in the North. Both groups were numerically large and politically weak, and were accustomed to the dominant group's, usually native born whites, making their educational policy decisions for them. The dominant group decided that vocational training would be a good thing for the "others."

In the county with the fewest "others," Johnson County, despite its leading role in most educational activities in this period, vocational education programs languished. Not until the second decade of the twentieth century did the superintendent comment favorably on such curricular additions, and then he stressed their special value for the black school. In the rural high schools some attention was given to the agriculture courses, but in Franklin High School itself, the emphasis remained on the classical curriculum as benefiting a student body who did not need to be channeled into their proper niches in society.

That group for which so many of the additional school programs were included, the children of immigrants, responded enthusiastically to the school programs. In 1910 a higher proportion (88 percent) of white children of immigrant parents were attending school between the ages of six to fourteen, the common compulsory school attendance ages, than any other category. Native white children of native parents were next (83.5 percent), followed by foreign-born whites (82.3 percent), with blacks trailing (59.7 percent). Predictably the children of immigrants also had the lowest rate of illiteracy in the nation (1.1 percent) compared with 3.7 percent for the children of native whites and 7.7 percent for the nation as a whole.

The figures on school attendance for children aged six to twenty, thus including the high school enrollments and some college attendance, show the native-born children of native parents leading the children of immigrants (66.9 percent for the former and 64.7 percent for the latter). These data illustrate the success of the schoolmen's efforts to bring the children of immigrants into the schools, where they might be Americanized as well as made literate. They also demonstrate the firm conviction of many immigrants that their children should benefit from the American educational system, a conviction that apparently was more widespread among this group than among native-born parents.

Considerably less effort was made to attract the children of the immigrants to college. Private colleges were expensive places, and many immigrants simply could not afford them. Private higher education dominated college and university life east of the Alleghenies, an area that included heavy concentrations of immigrants and their families, but on the whole, these institutions made no significant attempt to recruit children of immigrants for their colleges. Exceptions were the Roman Catholic colleges, such as Boston College, which relied heavily on sons of Irish immigrants. The students of non-Catholic private institutions came largely from private preparatory schools, not from institutions geared to attract second-generation Italians. Furthermore, near the end of this period many introduced informal quota systems to limit Jewish students, many of whom were children of immigrants, when they began to apply in significant numbers.

The University of Wisconsin, however, with its stated goal to serve the people of the state, enrolled by the end of the period a high proportion of children of immigrants. There higher education was viewed in the state as a logical outgrowth of the public elementary and secondary schools, not as an exclusive club, an impression that some of the eastern colleges and universities conveyed.

The University of Wisconsin also catered to another important segment of the population that was frequently excluded from elite educational institutions: women. During the Civil War, Wisconsin welcomed them, not on ideological but, instead, on financial grounds. Princeton expressed the dominant view of the leading eastern educational institutions that first-rate higher education was mainly the prerogative of white, Protestant males of multigenerational American lineage. Other groups might seek education at the lower levels, but the finest college training was pretty much limited to the group that led the nation, and in the late nineteenth and early twentieth centuries this did not include blacks, women, or recent immigrants and their children.

In 1910, however, a slightly higher proportion of girls than boys was attending school and, furthermore, the girls increased their lead over the boys in upper age groups. The preponderance of girls was greater in rural areas than in urban ones, and since the majority of the nation resided in rural areas until 1920, the proclivity of girls in those regions to stay in school affected the overall figures. In all three rural counties more girls graduated from high school than boys throughout the nineteenth century and into the beginning of the twentieth. The move to keep boys in high school began seriously in the early years of this century. In nearly all rural sections of the country more girls than boys between the ages of ten and fourteen were enrolled in school. Throughout the South at all ages to 15, more girls went to school than boys. The higher figures of girls in the South were partially attributable to the decidedly higher rate of black girls than black boys attending school.

The overall literacy figures for men and women in 1910 slightly favored men, an indication that until the last third of the nineteenth century schooling, or at least learning to read and write, had been more widespread among males than females. In the categories of the population, though, that could have been expected to attend school in the last third of the nineteenth century, female illiteracy was lower than male. Only among persons over thirty-five in 1910 was the illiteracy rate for women higher than for men of the same age.

Despite the fact that women were obtaining more formal schooling in the late nineteenth and early twentieth centuries than men, they suffered serious economic discrimination in academic employment, as well as elsewhere. Throughout the

United States, women teachers were paid less than men, even when they were teaching the same grade and with equal qualifications. At least as important for the future of women in education was the fact that the top administrative positions in educational systems, those of principal and superintendent, rarely went to women after the turn of the century. In both Johnson and Marquette counties women had played leading roles in the schools as principals of the high school or as superintendent of schools in the late nineteenth century, a period when relatively few men or women were continuing formal studies into normal schools or college. The scarcity of college-trained or normal school graduates was such that even women could get jobs when they had acquired such educations. By the turn of the century when there were more men available for the jobs and when education had become increasingly professionalized, women were rarely appointed to administrative posts except in the elementary schools. In most systems, separate pay scales applied to the elementary and the high school faculties, and most women were congregated in the former, where the pay was poorer.

In New York City, however, in the second decade of the twentieth century nearly all of the most important educational reformers, although not the leaders of the traditional schools, were women: Margaret Naumburg, founder of the Walden School, Caroline Pratt, founder of the City and Country School, Elisabeth Irwin, founder of the Little Red School House, Helen Parkhurst, founder of the Dalton School, Lucy Sprague Mitchell, founder of the Bank Street College of Education, and Patty Smith Hill of the Lincoln School kindergarten at Teachers College. Similar female leadership occurred in the new social settlements, but as the reformist zeal was vitiated, and as these institutions became academically and socially respectable, men took over the administration.

Despite the increasing importance of educational institutions in the late nineteenth century, the two groups that participated in them most actively were both outside prestige positions in

American society, women, and the children of immigrants. These were the noticeable segments of the society who had higher rates of literacy and who attended school in considerable numbers. Neither was eligible for attendance at the most prestigious colleges, either by decree as in the case of women, or by custom, as in the case of the children of immigrants. Of the two groups, the immigrants' children made much more rapid progress than the women in gaining access to full economic participation in the society. They also won entrance to the elite colleges and universities before women.

Crucial as the educational institutions were in the late nineteenth century, attendance at them did not guarantee full acceptance in the economic or social life of the nation. No one has ever believed that education alone would provide such an entrée, but at least two groups of the society used it as a lever for themselves. One other, the blacks, for a variety of reasons not the least of which was that public officials refused to provide adequate schools in most southern black communities, did not participate nearly as actively in the formal educational institutions, having lower rates of school attendance and of literacy than any other major group in the population.

In the communities in which immigrants made up a sizable portion of the population, there was likely to be a widespread conviction on the part of the leaders of the community that adequate elementary education facilities should be provided. Marquette County and New York testify to this view, one that large numbers of immigrant parents shared for their children. Instead, less sentiment was expressed in favor of educating women, but the girls themselves were more inclined to stay in school, perhaps because they had a greater tolerance than the boys for the drudgery commonplace in many schools. In a community with a homogeneous population of moderate means, however, the school system flourished, illustrating nineteenth-century middle America's belief in the efficacy of education for all. Such was the case in Johnson County, Indiana.

chapter two
johnson county, indiana

$\mathsf{m}$uch recent work in the history of education in the United States criticizes the standard works in the history of education during the first half of the twentieth century. The two leaders of this earlier group were Paul Monroe and his student Ellwood Patterson Cubberley. Both Monroe and Cubberley have been castigated because their work too narrowly focused on problems of public schools. To read Monroe and Cubberley, their critics have said, is to assume that late nineteenth-century America was a Protestant land with no parochial or private schools, where economic and social class differences were insignificant and had no bearing on educational policy decisions. For them an "urban" community had a few more than 2500 residents, and cities were practically unknown. The Americans of whom they wrote were white, male, and usually of multi-generational United States lineage. That women existed was known, but ignored for such serious matters as writing history. That nonwhites and immigrants resided in the United States was not deemed an important enough fact to be included in most historical writing.

The Monroe-Cubberley view of the world was, of course, much too narrow and too naive. A major difficulty with their conception of education in the nation as a whole was that what they envisioned for the nation was what seemed to characterize the communities in central Indiana where they both spent their boyhoods. Perhaps Monroe and Cubberley viewed all American education as radiating from a Hoosier core. Paul Monroe, born in 1869 in North Madison, Indiana, and Ellwood Cubberley, born in 1868 in Andrews, Indiana, spent their boyhood and college days in central Indiana—Monroe attending Franklin College and Cubberley attending both of the state universities, Purdue and Indiana. Monroe was principal of a high school in Johnson County (1890-1891) before accepting a superintendency in an adjacent county. He received a Ph.D. from the University of Chicago in 1897 and joined the Teachers College, Columbia University faculty in 1902, where he remained for 23 years and inaugurated the history of education as a major component of the professional education studies for future teachers and administrators of the public schools.

Cubberley was Monroe's best-known student in the history of education, and he also enjoyed a Hoosier boyhood, later teaching in a district school in his native Huntington County. Cubberley, too, emigrated from the state as an adult, going west with his former mentor, David Starr Jordan, who left the presidency of Indiana University for that of Stanford; but Cubberley returned east to Teachers College, where he received his M.A. in 1902 and his Ph.D. in 1905, the former based largely on work with Monroe. Cubberley's *Public Education in the United States* appeared in 1919, and this became the standard text in the history of education.

These two Hoosiers, who shaped the history of education in the United States for generations of future teachers, came from a state that joined the Union in 1816. Fifty years later, one of its central counties, Johnson, was a well-established center of agricultural productivity with a settled, homogeneously native-born Protestant population. The Delaware Indians, the original residents, were supplanted by Kentuckians, Tennesseans, and North Carolinians, who deserted their former homes beginning in the 1820s, traveling via the Ohio River and moving north through the heavy woodland covering the southern part of the state. These intrepid folk cleared the forests in Johnson County and discovered that the soil was rich. By 1910 more than 96 percent of the county was being farmed, and more than half the farms were between 50 and 175 acres. Indicative of the richness of the land is the report that the average price for land in Johnson County then was $97 per acre.

The residents of Johnson County were almost entirely white, Anglo-Saxon Protestants. The 1910 census reported less than one percent foreign born and 2 percent Negroes. Although the Roman Catholics established two missions in the county, neither had become a full parish by 1918. No Jewish house of worship existed in the county, and there is no record of Jewish families gathering for religious purposes. As was true in many other midwestern communities, however, the proprietor of a county clothing store, A. J. Finegold, was undoubtedly Jewish. Finegold, who was born in Constantinople and was brought up in London, became one of the patrons of culture in the community, and along with two local doctors, the judge, and the editor of a local newspaper, he journeyed on occasion to the state capital, Indianapolis, 20 miles away, to attend performances of Shakespearean plays. Two other dry goods merchants, Mose Levinson and Phil Joseph, may also have been Jewish, thus following the same trade as their ultimately more prosperous confrere, Adam Gimbel, who had begun his nationwide chain of department stores at nearby Vincennes.

Despite the occasional black, Jewish, and Catholic residents of Johnson County, the population was monolithically white Protestant, one in which severe poverty was as absent as extreme wealth. Furthermore, it was a stable population after the Civil War, growing from just over 18,000 to a little more than 20,000 in 1910.

Franklin, the county seat of Johnson County, gained about 500 residents during this period, which gave it a population (including its adjacent townships) in 1910 of almost 5500. The three other small towns in the county, Edinburg, White River, and Pleasant, remained fairly constant with populations of approximately 2000. The rural nature of the county was typical of the state in 1870, when 90 percent of Indiana's residents lived in rural areas. Between 1910 and 1920, however, the balance of the population shifted to a majority of town dwellers.

The dominant Protestantism of the area originally divided itself into three main denominations: Presbyterian, Methodist, and Baptist. Both Franklin and Edinburg had separate Baptist churches for blacks. The Campbellite movement had made strong inroads into this denominational structure in the 1840s. By the mid-1860s the Church of Christ, or the Christian Church, was a strong member of the Protestant quartet.

Franklin Public Schools

The educational history of Johnson County in the years between the Civil War and World War I is dominated by the public schools. After a 40-year history, in which the educational activities in the county can most charitably be termed haphazard, the town of Franklin established a school board in March 1866 that was composed predictably of the ministers of the Methodist, Baptist, and Presbyterian churches. Their stewardship of the infant public schools was intended to resolve some of the rivalries encountered in the previous educational ventures in the county. These had included the relatively prosperous Presbyterian Hopewell Academy, whose graduates were admitted to the sophomore year at Hanover College, thus rivaling the existing Baptist college, Franklin, which closed frequently during the midnineteenth century, generally for lack of funds. The Christian church in another part of the county established an academy that lasted for about 5 years in the 1860s. Private study was provided with the wife of the Presbyterian minister and was indicative of the many ad hoc arrangements that prevailed before the establishment of a public school system.

The Protestant divines were succeeded in 1867 by secular leaders in the community—the doctor, the lawyer, and a leading merchant, who was the first president of the school board and later mayor of the town. It was their job to implement the plans for an educational system that their predecessors had agreed on, and the first step was to plan a new school. These men took their responsibility so seriously and proposed such an extensive school building that they were immediately censured by the irate citizenry. For the school year 1867 to 1868 the superintendent (a man) was paid $75 per month and the teachers, $40 per month for the 6-month year. The New Series McGuffey readers formed the mainstay of the curriculum along with Willson's *Spellers*, Guyot's *Geography*, Feller's *Primary Arithmetic*, Ray's *Intellectual and Practical Arithmetic*, Ray's *Algebra*, Ray's *Geometry and Trigonometry*, Pinneo's *Grammar*, Green's *Analysis*, Quackenba's *History*, Cutter's *Physiology*, and Wells's *Philosophy*.

In 1871 the 11-room new school building opened, and the school board launched a policy it was to continue for more than 10 years of making a judicious appointment of a family to head the school, the husband to serve as superintendent, and the wife as principal of the high school. At least four couples were so named. The initial appointment of the Boyces at a salary of $2150 per annum was paid to Mr. Boyce alone, although it represented payment for the services of his wife as well. Theoretically Mr. Boyce received $150 per month and his wife, $88.88, for the new 9-month school year. Of the 10 teachers in the school, 9 were women, and the salaries for the teachers were $45 per month, considerably above the state average.

In the 1870s, Franklin came into its own educationally. This was the decade of the creation of the high school, of the extension of the school year to nine months, of the establishment of the supremacy of the public school over the various private educational ventures, of the building of the separate school for black children, and of the organization of a graded system in the elementary school. During that decade the dropping and subsequent reinstatement of the McGuffey readers also oc-curred. By the end of the decade the school enumeration showed nearly 900 children between the ages of six and twenty-one, of whom 60 were black. The teaching staff then included, in addi-tion to the superintendent, 12 teachers, 11 for the white and 1 for the colored school. The colored teacher was paid $40 per month, but 8 white teachers were paid $45 per month, and 2 white teachers (including the one man) were paid $55 per month. Two primary classes existed in the white school and one each of grades two to eight. The high school was taught as a unit by the superintendent, his wife (who was the principal), and one other teacher.

The expansion of formal educational activities in Johnson County during the 1870's had generally met with popular sup-port, but by the 1880s the problems concomitant with that rapid growth became more and more evident, particularly to the editor of the leading weekly county newspaper, the *Democrat*. In 1884 Editor Luther Short announced to his readers (to whom it came as no surprise, since he had been critical of the schools for several years), "It is well known that our city schools have fallen far below their former state of excellence. A few years ago the schools of Franklin even ranked among the best in the state and were a pride and honor to our little city. But now go where you may you will hear of the deplorable condition of the Franklin schools and no one posted in the edu-cational matters of Indiana would think of placing them among those entitled to high rank." Although Short's assessment may not be a wholly impartial one, the problems encountered by the Franklin schools in the 1880s were considerable. Not the least of these was dealing with Editor Short himself, who in June 1881, launched an attack on the high school.

Short was an important figure in Indiana Democratic circles, serving as president of the Democratic editors association for several years. Doubtless as a reward for his political loyalty, President Grover Cleveland named him Consul General in Con-stantinople. The paper during his editorship, 1879 to 1892, was an excellent one, excerpting articles from leading periodicals and newspapers, both domestic and foreign. It was undeniably politically partisan, and Short was fond of pointing to what he considered Republican hypocrisy, particularly with regard to blacks. Short maintained that Republicans were interested only in the votes of blacks and were unwilling to support them in any way. Later he reported favorably on the efforts of Edinburg blacks to gain admittance to the white high school. Despite the feverish Protestantism of Johnson County, Short praised the Roman Catholic Plenary Council's meeting and statement, "It was an able and dignified body and the address prepared by this meeting is one of the ablest and most important documents ever issued in this country of a religious nature." He also severely criticized the Bloomington, Indiana Baptist church for its inquisitional attitude toward one of its members, the former president of Indiana University, who was accused of misconduct with one of the women professors.

After summarizing an article in the *North American Review,* "Do Our Schools Educate?" which answered the question negatively, Editor Luther Short examined the local public educational scene. He concluded that the small numbers of graduates of the high school in the past 8 years did not justify the expense of maintaining it. He noted that there had been one graduate in 1874 (he missed the 1873 graduate), four in 1875, nine in 1876, eleven in 1877, six in 1878, four in 1879, two in 1880, and seven in 1881. The cost to the public of the high school was about $200 per graduate or $50 per year. His suggestion was to abolish the high school and to send at public expense those few students who sought a high school education to the preparatory department of Franklin College, where tuition was $21 per year. This remedy, he estimated, would have saved the town of Franklin $5280 over the last 8 years. Short concluded his mathematical calculations: "We have already demonstrated that the city can educate its people, in the higher branches, much cheaper in the preparatory of the college, and there appears to us no good reason why such an unnecessary expense, as that now borne by the people, should be incurred. We do not question the fact that the work, on the whole, would be better done, for the pupils would be under instructors of the very highest attainments, and these are rarely changed. The apparatus is of a better order in the college than in the High School, and in this respect the pupils' advantages are vastly superior. The name of having a High School sounds well, but the luxury is entirely too expensive."

Although the high school survived Short's initial attack, it was not immune from future ones, nor from political controversy. In 1881 the Democratic candidate for County Superintendent of Schools was elected, and this action may have been one explanation for Short's silence on the school issues for two years. By 1883, however, he reported, "The high school is certainly not a prosperous institution." After an acrimonious exchange of letters with the teachers and the superintendent of schools, marred by errors of spelling and grammar on the teachers' and superintendent's side, Short unleashed his attack: "The truth is, we have heretofore preserved silence with regard to the difficulties which have arisen in the schools, even against the expressed wishes of patrons interested in the work and this course was dictated in a great measure, by sympathy for the profession, believing that as a class, teachers are more often sinned against than sinning."

The first issue Short deplored was, predictably, a fiscal one: when the term had been shortened the previous year, the teachers had been given half pay for the unexpired term, and Short found this a misuse of taxpayer's funds. He alluded to several squabbles at the school but only one serious pedagogic matter: the rapid promotion of students beyond their achievement and consequent demotion to a more appropriate grade at midyear. This final matter Short believed was essentially a failure of the administration to recognize the inevitable embarrassment of the children who were being sent back to lower grades during the course of the year after they had been falsely advanced. This was a consequence, of course, of the rigidity inherent in the graded school.

The Republican paper, the *Jeffersonian*, criticized Short for not visiting the school, but it did not deny his charges. While Superintendent Arnold Tompkins was girding his forces for a renewed letter-writing campaign to the *Democrat*, Short attacked again. This time the issue was the singing teacher, whom Short opposed on classic grounds: she cost too much and singing was a frill in the curriculum. The music teacher had been hired originally for 3 months of the 1881 to 1882 school year as a result of a petition signed by 170 Franklin residents. A petition in 1878 for both music and German teachers had been turned down by the School Board. Her time was divided between the white and the colored school. The other part-time special teacher instructed in penmanship, and her duties were also split between the white and colored schools.

Although Short's opposition to the schools was chiefly financial, he was also against the introduction of subjects or pedagogic practices that differed from the time-honored ones. The problems that the Franklin schools faced and with which Tompkins attempted to deal were ones of a steady town population, but with a rapidly growing enrollment and high attrition in the upper grades. Tompkins, who was an energetic and undoubtedly ambitious man, was eager to use the newest educational practices in Franklin, and these additions to the curriculum were likely to be expensive. Short exhibited the usual skeptical stance when new ideas were tried and did not immediately work.

The Superintendent's reply to the *Democrat*, again with egregious errors in spelling, presents the most comprehensive explanation for what he was trying to do in the Franklin Schools. His first principle was to make the system flexible, "adapting it to the pupil, rather than the pupil to it." Implementing that objective had led to moving the children in and out of classes and to the consequent unhappiness of the children who went down a grade instead of up. Tompkins explained the concern with division of children into proper cubicles as based on crowding in the lower grades: "For the past few years the numbers enrolled in the first room was about 100 and this number decreased gradually through all the rooms. This gave to the first three or four rooms a number entirely too large for one teacher while in the upper rooms, and especially in the High School room, the number was discouragingly small. The proper number of pupils being one of the first conditions for a teacher's good work, the pupils were redistributed at the opening of school, giving to each teacher 45-50 pupils. This was effected by employing one more teacher and moving the eighth grade into the High School room, making the present enrollment in the High School room 100 and giving three teachers to the work. At first it was thought objectionable to have so many in this room but the number was no larger than the usual number here in the first primary and many High Schools in the State have a larger number." Although Tompkins may not have been much of a speller, he had certain political gifts for he concluded his statement by pointing out that the present distribution of students accommodated 50 more pupils than the older one, thus avoiding the necessity of building another school house.

Tompkins' interest in new pedagogical practices was expressed in his discontinuance of percentage grading in the schools. In two lengthy letters in February and March 1883, Tompkins explained his views, giving 12 separate reasons for dropping percents in favor of letter grades. Essentially he opposed grading in general and found the relative imprecision of letter grades preferable to the ostensible exactness of percentages, which had the additional disadvantage of breeding discontent and jealousy among pupils who might quibble over 96 percent versus 98 percent, but who could not argue if both received "E" for excellent. Short's editorial response to this novelty was to publish a letter praising the Edinburg schools "for close grading, thorough and earnest work."

Tompkins' final salvo was a denunciation of percentage grading as an inducement to study. He observed, "Children learn rapidly before entering upon school life, and no inducement is needed or offered except what nature furnishes." He then explained to the *Democrat's* readers that there were four natural motives to study, and the school attempted to exploit these: curiosity, love of activity, sympathy with the teacher, and the feeling of satisfaction where work is well done.

The 1882 to 1883 school year ended abruptly with a smallpox epidemic, which necessitated closing the schools, a not infrequent occurrence in this period. Editor Luther Short married and left with his bride for a European honeymoon of three months. Superintendent Tompkins left the following year, but under less auspicious circumstances, where despite some favorable letters from Franklin residents in the newspaper, he received only one vote from the Board of Trustees for rehiring.

Despite the difficulties Tompkins encountered in Franklin, he was responsible for preparing the first graded course of study for the Franklin public schools. This 231-page volume, giving in meticulous detail the program for each class at 15-minute intervals from 9:00 a. m. until 4:00 p. m., was adopted by the school board in June 1883.

Like so many educational manifestos of various ages, Tompkins' effort was long on objectives. He justified in some detail the intricately graded system, with half-year promotions and sections within classes. Since pursuing this course of study would assure that the schoolwork would be "definite, organic, and progressive," Tompkins explained how carefully this pattern was laid out and how essential it was that teachers follow it closely. Apparently fearful that teachers might not heed his explicit direction, and fearing the academic consequences if they did not, Tompkins cautioned, "The aim has been to set forth the steps so that each teacher will know just what to do. Each part of the work will then fit in as an organic part of the whole. To impress the fact that *subjects* and not *text-books* are to be studied, the parts of the subjects have been stated instead of referring to the pages of a book."

One wonders how Tompkins reconciled his previously stated belief in making the school adapt to the child instead of the child to the school with this intensely structured program that teachers were required to follow daily, throughout the year. The explanation probably lies in Tompkins' assumption that by dividing the school into various grades and sections, and by meshing the academic disciplines from one grade to the other, the curriculum would become a seamless web. The issue then became the proper point of entry. With such a panoply of grades and sections surely the right niche could be found for each child, and once that appropriate spot was found, the internal logic of the carefully organized curriculum would inevitably carry the child along.

The problems that Tompkins saw and the solutions he attempted were characteristic not only of Franklin but of most American towns that were making the transition from one-room district schools, which served a relatively small number of children, all under the guidance of one teacher, to the consolidated schools where several hundred children would be brought together in a single building under the supervision of various teachers. Certainly in the one-room school no teacher could be expected to conduct classes for all eight grades in six subjects. In a graded school, however, this did become an option, and educators in the late nineteenth century were concerned about utilizing the new pedagogical possibilities that the graded school afforded. The common result, as in Franklin, was to pay lip service to such notions as "flexibility," which had certainly been a keynote of many one-room schools where children progressed (or failed to progress) at their own rates through the readers but, in fact, in the new graded schools rigidity was more likely to result. Adults had predetermined what the children should learn, in what sequence they should learn it, and at what hours of the day it should be learned. By judicious placement of children in classes, administrators hoped to get a homogeneous enough group so that the children could move through the carefully planned curriculum. Strict placement by chronological age was less common in most nineteenth-century schools than today.

In many respects, Tompkins' plan for the Franklin schools,

in which he attempted to insure "order" in the curriculum, was a precursor of the efficiency movement in education, which reached its apogee in 1914 in another Indiana town, Gary. One measure of the effectiveness of the Franklin plan, which was based on completion of the various studies, can be found in the dropout rates of children in the various grades in the Franklin schools, the 100 or so in first grade and the 100 in the top five grades of the school (8 to 12). Although these rates were by no means unusual at that time, they do testify eloquently that a course of study based on the assumption of completion of the entire curriculum was a dubious enterprise when more than 80 percent of the entering students failed to complete the curriculum.

Despite the fact that few students were availing themselves of the high school facilities, the high school itself persevered. In 1885, however, a suit was brought in Switzerland County in southern Indiana, and subsequently was appealed to the Indiana Supreme Court, seeking an injunction restraining the treasurer of that county from collecting taxes from Mr. Schenck for the purpose of payment of teachers' salaries. Schenck claimed that local communities had no right under the 1851 constitution to tax for school salaries; only the state had that right, and it could not delegate it. This was essentially the same argument that the State Supreme Court had upheld in 1854 and 1857, but in 1885 the Court overruled the Switzerland Circuit Court, which had supported Schenck, and held that local communities could use property and poll taxes for school purposes. This decision firmly committed local communities to providing school systems, and despite critical editors, such as Luther Short, Franklin and other towns expanded their schools.

Short's role in the school controversies is a curious one. By either blood or by marriage he was related to two principals in the debates: to the vice-president of the struggling Franklin College to whose preparatory department Short urged sending potential high school students and to Schenck, who brought the case in Switzerland County attempting to kill the local schools by eliminating local funds for their support. By such inter-locking relationships is much local policy determined. Most of these positions Short took as a young man, before his marriage, and in later years (1891) he threw the support of his newspaper firmly behind an outlying local district's desire for its own high school, "Union Township furnishes as many graduates from the common schools as any other township in the county, and it is not convenient, neither is it to the best interests of the town-ship for these people to be compelled to go to the adjoining township for instruction in the higher branches." Short and his wife never became parents, so his increasing mellowness on the subject of publicly supported education cannot be interpreted as self-interest for his own offspring. More accurately, his atti-tude is evidence of the initial reluctance of many otherwise public-spirited citizens to devote larger portions of their local budgets for school purposes. Gradually these people came to regard support for these schools as inevitable, perhaps even desirable.

The discontent with the state of the schools, and the super-intendent in particular, fostered in substantial measure by Editor Short, was joined by others in 1885. Recognizing the essentially political quality of the post, the Franklin *Jacksonian* noted that there were more than 20 applicants for the vacant position of superintendent. (Ultimately the post went to H. D. Vories, who demonstrated his political nature by successfully running for State Superintendent of Public Instruction on the Democratic ticket in 1890.) "There are strong indications," the *Jacksonian* reported, "that a Presbyterian will be chosen as Superintendent of our schools, and there is more than half concealed kicking from the other denominations." It continued in what it took to be a statesmanlike manner: "The *Jacksonian* takes no stand on creed, or lack of it, or politics but wants a man with good executive ability, with average book learning, and [who] is not wedded to modern, red-tape humbuggery." This final aspersion is doubtless cast at the recently resigned Superintendent Tompkins, whose last address to the local teachers a few months before had been criticized in Short's paper for the "psychological vein" pervading his remarks. Short had astutely noted the shift in pedagogy that Tompkins' talk indicated and had observed that this new emphasis on children thinking and acting for themselves and consequent diminution of attention to formal methods required greater skill on the part of teachers than the older system of methods and plans did.

The concern with the quality of teaching became prominent in the mid-1880s. The need for more teachers for the school and the particular need for ones acquainted with the new methods and the new subjects necessitated more systematic approaches to preparing teachers. Indiana teachers in the 1880s were licensed simply on the basis of an examination, a common practice in nineteenth-century America. In 1884 the examination consisted of sections dealing with subject matter to be taught and with one part on "science of teaching." Satisfactory completion of the 4-year course in "professional studies" of the Indiana Teachers' Reading Circle could be presented in lieu of the examination in science of teaching. The overall average on the examination had to be at least 75 percent, and the candidate could not score below 60 percent in any section. Such a method of certifying teachers remained in effect throughout the nineteenth and well into the twentieth century. These examinations, many believed, were inadequate instruments to gauge a teacher's knowledge, and Johnson County attempted to supplement them by requiring teachers to attend annual and monthly county teachers' institutes, by offering summer normal schools, and by encouraging them to participate in the state Reading Circle.

The annual county institutes for teachers began in the fall of 1879 with a meeting in which all the local teachers gathered to hear demonstration lessons on common fractions, the causes and effects of the Mexican War, problems in parsing and syntax, and the circulation of the blood. As the topics reveal, the first effort was simply to increase the teachers' knowledge of what they were expected to teach. As the institutes expanded in the following years, the range of topics broadened considerably. In 1880 nearly 70 teachers attended the annual meeting, which included both methodological and substantive presentations. The following year a 5-day institute, at which attendance was required for all teachers in the county, was held in the fall before the opening of the school year. In the early 1880s speakers at the institute came from Indiana University, Franklin College, and Terre Haute Normal School in addition to the local talent drawn from the teaching corps in Johnson County. At the end of the decade a special feature was furnished by the local ministers in the teaching of morals in the public schools.

The program at the 5-day institute in 1885 is typical of the matters covered at the institutes. More than 85 teachers were present, and Superintendent Vories proudly declared that all the topics were handled by local teachers. On Monday, sessions were held dealing with arithmetic, geography, sentence structure, physiology, history, penmanship (the speaker urged teaching only one kind in a school, the Spencerian method), and Pestalozzi. Tuesday was devoted to decimals, reading, geography in Indiana, personal appearance of a teacher, letter writing, teaching and understanding diacritical marks, and physiology of the skeleton. On Wednesday the teachers gathered to learn about chemistry, decimals, etymology, penmanship, history, and Horace Mann. On Wednesday night a special public lecture was given by the Deputy State Superintendent of Public Instruction on Howard Payne and Cowper. Thursday the teachers braced for lectures on arithmetic, the science of teaching, the state school journals, reading, characteristics of the best teachers, science of teaching, the history of Indiana, and the War of 1812, all of this followed by an evening lecture on Lucy Larcum. The final day, Friday, was spent on arithmetic, grammar, Froebel, and plans for the township institutes to be held periodically during the year. The township institutes, it was decided, would all deal primarily with the issue of establishing graded schools, instead of the one-room ones then common in the districts.

Such a program was beneficial in several ways. First, it exposed, if not instructed, the teachers to a broad range of material that could inform their teaching. Both subject matter and what would later be called "professional" questions were discussed, thus simulating the curriculum of a good normal school of the period. Second, this intensive 5-day session, by nature of its being required, brought together the teachers from both the town and the rural schools, thus lessening the status distinctions between them and hopefully giving both groups a sense of common purpose. Finally, by encouraging the local teachers to make the presentations, the superintendent guaranteed that many of the teachers would be forced to work up a topic about which presumably they would learn a great deal, and this kind of enforced in-service training was expected to improve the quality of teaching in the school. Undoubtedly Vories was not ignorant of the degree of competition among various teachers to give the best demonstration lessons, and he fostered this to the end of more active professional development on the part of the teachers.

Beginning in 1880 the county sponsored an annual normal school for teachers in the local area. Although the admissions requirements for the "normal" are not clear, presumably most students had graduated from the eighth grade or a district school. The curriculum of the normal school in 1881 consisted of study of the common branches, that is, how to teach reading, printing, and arithmetic, plus penmanship and algebra. Typically the normal school was conducted by a local educator, often a principal, for a fee for a few weeks in the summer. Although these "normals" never attained the formal status of a college, as did the state school in Terre Haute, they did furnish additional training for teachers.

The third pedagogical assist to teachers in the 1880s was the Reading Circle. Begun as an activity of the ubiquitous Chautauqua enterprises, the Reading Circle was introduced at the

Methodist Church in Franklin in 1884. Known then informally as the "people's college" with an advertised enrollment of more than 60,000, the Circle began as an organization to encourage people to read in a variety of literary and scientific sources. Its particular strength was in the Protestant, small town, Midwest. The Teachers' Reading Circle was an adaptation of this with reading divided between general materials and specified pedagogic ones. The Reading Circle was another of Superintendent Vories' causes for the teachers, and he secured passage of a motion at the autumn, 1885 institute that all Johnson County teachers join it. This Circle, sponsored by the State Teachers' Association, provided books at reduced rates for teachers to read and discuss together during the year at regular meetings. For 1889 to 1890 the "professional" book was Compayre's *Lectures on Pedagogy*, available to teachers at $1.25, and the one in "general culture" was Steele's *Popular Zoology*, for $1. The state board, which made the selection, noted in choosing the zoology volume, "in science we shall find a field as full and fruitful as in literature." Teachers were examined on their reading in the fall and received credit for passing the tests.

Vories' effort to invigorate the Franklin schools in the late 1880s was revealed in the growing senior classes and also in the higher proportion of boys remaining in school. Like most other American high schools, in their early years girls predominated in the upper grades, and school administrators, recognizing that it was indeed a man's world, were eager to persuade more boys to graduate from high school. In 1888 all 6 graduates of the high school were girls; in 1890 of the 12 graduates, 6 were girls, and in 1891, of the 8 graduates, 7 were girls, including 1 black girl. The following year the first 3 students in academic ranking in the senior class were girls, although boys outnumbered girls in the class 5 to 3.

The table below gives the number of students in each high school class from 1892 to 1893 through 1895 to 1896. The figure in parentheses following the number for the class is the enrollment in the class the previous year.

Franklin High School Attrition, 1892 to 1893 Through 1895 to 1896

	1892 to 1893	1893 to 1894	1894 to 1895	1895 to 1896
Senior class	8	16 (24)	14 (23)	14 (19)
Junior class	24	23 (32)	19 (33)	24 (36)
Sophomore class	32	33 (44)	36 (62)	24 (52)
Freshman class	44	62	52	41

Thus, the 44 freshmen in 1892 to 1893 became the 33 sophomores of 1893 to 1894, the 19 juniors of 1894 to 1895, and the 14 seniors of 1895 to 1896.

The enrollments in the grades show even more dramatically the large number of students who simply did not pass beyond the primary grades, a fact often forgotten today when the schools are accused of failing to teach all children to read on grade level. In the 1890s often the children who did not read on grade level simply did not return for future grades.

The most serious overcrowding occurred in the primary grades, the place where children were expected to learn to read. In 1893 to 1894 one teacher was responsible for 66 children in the morning, divided into 1B and 1A classes (the first and second semester of first grade) and 69 children, also divided between 1B and 1A in the afternoon. She had sole responsibility for these 137 children's entry into the academic world. Only the primary grade was on double session. By grade two the enrollment was down to 57; in grade three, also 57; in grade four, 59; in a split grade four and five, 53; in a full grade five, 47; in a split five and six, 58; in grade six, 40; in another grade six, 41; in a third grade six, 42; in grade seven, 34; and in grade eight, 55. The same pattern appeared the following year, 1894 to 1895, when the morning primary class included 62 children and the afternoon session, 61: a total of 123. Grade two had an enrollment of 56; grade three, 57; grade four, 60; grade five, 58; grade six, 53; grade seven, 57; grade eight, 43; and the two combined grades seven and eight, 34 and 22.

Clearly the two major bulges in the system came at the

primary grade where less than half made the transition from grade one to grade two after 1 year and at the upper elementary grades or what today would be called junior high school. Between 11 and 12 percent of the children who entered first grade were graduating from high school. This percentage applied also to the entire county by 1908 to 1909.

By 1893 to 1894 the black school was theoretically operating as a graded school but with only one teacher for 58 children divided among the eight grades, it is difficult to imagine the extent to which strict grade lines were maintained. The pattern of high loss immediately after grade one was also characteristic of the black children. In 1893 to 1894 the enrollment figures there were grade one, 20; grade two, 8; grade three, 8; grade four, 1; grade five, 7; grade six, 6; grade seven, 4; and grade eight, 4. By 1898 the colored school had been divided between two teachers, a practice that continued through 1918. Generally a black woman taught the primary grades, and a black man taught the upper grades and served as principal of the school.

In 1904 the Franklin public schools prepared an educational exhibit for the Louisiana Purchase Exposition. The materials included the weekly plans for the fall term of most of the regular teachers on the staff. Although one cannot assume that the children learned everything that was taught, the plans do give a comprehensive idea of what the teachers expected the students to study. Most striking about the work in the first grade is the absence of any study in arithmetic and the concentration on the acquisition of language skills. The weekly program throughout the fall included reading (in two sections), phonics (in two sections), stories, memory work, rote songs, and nature study.

By the second grade "numbers" had joined the curriculum, but language skills still dominated the children's study. Again in two reading groups, they divided their time between Ward's *First Reader* and phonic studies, with the second group about five lessons behind the first by Christmas. The remainder of their time was spent on spelling words taken from the reading lessons, "language" (stories and dictation), rote songs and "memory gems," history (a mixture of study of the Egyptians and the American Indians), nature study, and physical culture.

The third grade added geography to its studies, but continued to concentrate on language skills with two reading groups, spelling, and language (primarily grammar and composition). Two sections of arithmetic also dealt with the mysteries of addition and subtraction. In history the children studied the Greeks and Alexander the Great. Nature study and physical culture completed their program.

The fourth grade essentially continued the work of the previous year without the addition of any new subjects. Nature study included work on the human body, occasionally termed "physiology," and the history course moved forward chronologically to the Romans. Multiplication tables entered the arithmetic study. The term ended early because of the death of one child in the class from diphtheria and the consequent quarantine of the entire class.

The principal changes in the fifth grade were the multiplication and division of fractions in arithmetic, and the continued chronological progress into the medieval period in history. The sixth grade was the last one in which the children had only one teacher who taught them all subjects except music. There, long division occupied the children in arithmetic and early English history brought them to the beginning of the modern era. Separate sections in reading no longer existed, possibly an indication that the classes were smaller and that the poorer students had dropped out.

Three sections of grade seven were taught during 1904, although only two sections of each of the other grades one to eight existed. Only one section of each high school class was necessary to accommodate the smaller number of students at those levels.

In the seventh grade the children read classics such as Charles Dickens' *Nicholas Nickleby* and Washington Irving's *Rip Van Winkle*. The eighth graders perused Irving's "The

Legend of Sleepy Hollow," John Greenleaf Whittier's "Snow-bound," and selections from Sir Walter Scott and Henry Wadsworth Longfellow. There was considerable overlap in the readings of one seventh-grade section and another eighth-grade section, presumably the better readers in one of the three seventh grades were on a par with one of the eighth-grade sections.

The seventh- and eighth-grade arithmetic classes dealt, again with some overlap, with percentages, bank discounts, tables of English money, ratios, commissions, and compound interest. Grammar, physiology, geography, and history made up the remainder of the seventh- and eighth-grade subjects.

Music was taught to all the children, both white and black, in grades one to eight, with occasional instruction in particular songs for the high school. Most of the classes concerned note reading and singing of simple songs. As with all the other courses, considerable attention was given to relating the work to the seasons so that from mid-November turkeys, snowflakes, Santas, and Christmas carols dominated the music and art programs.

The program of Marie Porter, the teacher of grades one to four in the black school, seems to be almost identical with that of the graded school except that she made no grade distinctions in either history or nature study. Furthermore, she introduced arithmetic to the first graders, although in the white school this was delayed beyond the first term. The black and the white schools used different textbooks, since the white teacher referred to Ward's *Primer* for the first graders, and the black teacher used Bass's *Primer*. As a result, it is difficult to compare the relative progress of the two first grade groups at the end of the first 18-week term.

Although there was a music teacher, there was no separate instructor in art. Instead, Franklin organized an Art League, which was loosely affiliated with the public schools. The Art League was an outgrowth of the earlier City School Art Carnival and represented the efforts of 68 of "the most thoughtful and influential citizens of Franklin" in bringing art to Johnson County. In 1904 this group brought the Horace K. Turner Art Exhibit from Boston to the Lecture Room of the Presbyterian Church for a 4-day showing. The program was complete with lectures explaining the pictures and musical selections (presumably if one were introducing one kind of culture to the citizenry, one might as well provide another). Admission was charged: season tickets (for Wednesday to Saturday) were 50 cents for adults and 25 cents for children. Single admissions were 15 cents for adults, 10 cents for children.

In many ways the most distinctive element of the school programs in Franklin in 1904 was the pervasive religious tone, which was intensely Protestant as befit such a homogeneously Protestant community. Although this was many years before the Supreme Court's decision outlawing school prayers, more religiously diverse communities might well have reduced the amount of daily religious activity in the public school classrooms. In Franklin, however, where nearly everyone had been reared in the Presbyterian, Methodist, Baptist, or Christian church, Bible stories, prayers, and discussions of Christ's life were not thought objectionable. These teachers had, after all, asked the three leading Protestant ministers of the community to lecture to their annual Teachers' Institute on the teaching of morals from a Protestant point of view.

Miss Dungan, an active Methodist, the first-grade teacher, provided the fullest testimony to the religious content of her class. Although all teachers had daily "opening exercises" in their classes, not all were as careful as Miss Dungan to be sure that these were always religious occasions. Miss Dungan invariably included devotional songs, morning prayers, and scripture verses. In the third week, for example, the children were all required to learn the scripture verses, "Suffer the little children to come unto me." In the fifth week Miss Dungan began the story of Abraham, following the next week with Jacob. By the eleventh week she dealt with Joseph, and by the fourteenth, she was talking about Jesus' birth. In the final two weeks, the seventeenth and eighteenth, she discussed Christ's boyhood and His later work. In addition to these daily opening exercises, Miss Dungan also had the children memorize various religious songs for their "rote work," including "Jesus Loves the Little Children."

Although no other grade teacher recorded her biblical texts as carefully as Miss Dungan, the remaining teachers included biblical materials regularly during the year, presumably all from the King James version of the Bible and generally from the New Testament. In grade three Bible stories alternated with readings from "Hiawatha" as opening exercises during the year. In grade four the openings included prayers, Bible readings, celebrations of birthdays of such well-known Americans as Eugene Field, Henry Ward Beecher, and Helena Hunt Jackson, and examinations of familiar paintings including the *Sistine Madonna,* the *Song of the Lark,* and *The Gleaners.* In grade five the Old Testament predominated in the fall term with readings from the Story of Solomon, Elijah, Elisha, Daniel, and Joseph and his Brethren. In the following grade the *Young Folks' Bible History* provided most of the opening exercises with particular emphasis on Moses and on the life of Christ.

In a community with as general agreement on religious questions as Franklin, such pervasive religious instruction was understandable, particularly as familiarity with the Bible was considered not just devotionally desirable but also indicative of wide-ranging literary familiarity. The problem that immediately developed, however, was the leap from textual analysis of Biblical passages to the religious interpretation of them. With an extensive religious education program being conducted in these schools, to which there is no recorded objection in the Board of Education minutes or in the newspapers, the plight of Catholics, Jews, and free thinkers in communities with similar religious programs is obvious.

Franklin here again illustrates the strength of the public school system. Where diversity was minimal, numbers small, and only bare literacy essential, the public schools as in Franklin were supremely successful. When any of these factors changed, that is, when the population no longer was over-whelmingly Protestant, or when several schools were necessary to serve all the children in the community, or when the demands of the society were such that proficiency beyond the primary grade level was necessary to earn a living, systems like Franklin's were required to change. What changes were needed to meet the new conditions effectively were generally not evident.

The high school curriculum in 1904 most pointedly revealed the limited group of students for whom it was designed. Then more than 30 years old, the high school program included 4 years of English, 4 years of Latin, 4 years of mathematics, 3 years of history (ancient, medieval, and American), 2 years of science (botany and zoology, the latter with laboratory work), and German. The emphasis on Latin was particularly heavy with two and three sections in the ninth, tenth, and eleventh grades. That course of study prepared students well for college, but one wonders what proportion of those Franklin youngsters in grade eight, who were considering additional formal education, dropped notions of high school when faced with such a classical curriculum.

The faculty who presided over these classes in 1904 included 25 regular teachers and three "supervisors." The high school group included six persons plus the principal. Five of the high school teachers were women, and all but one had graduated from college. Neither of the men was a college graduate, although the principal had graduated from the state Normal School. Two of the high school teachers had spent summer terms at Harvard, and another had studied a year at Boston University. The two nongraduates had spent some years in college-grade work, the woman at Franklin College for 4 years and the man at the University of Michigan for 3 years.

Educational records of 16 of the 18 elementary school faculty members reveal that all but one had spent some time at either normal school (7), college (5), or both (3). One had graduated from college and one from normal school (the male principal of the black school). Only one had ceased his education before graduation from high school without either normal school or college work—the male principal of the white school. Eight were high school graduates. At this time high school graduation was not a requirement for entrance at either normal school or Franklin College. The most common preparation for these elementary teachers was a year or two of high school work plus two or three terms in college or normal school, often attending summer sessions at the latter. Franklin College led the colleges, and Indiana State Normal led the normal schools, although a number of teachers had also attended the Francis Parker's Cook County Normal School in Chicago and Winona Lake Summer School. Several teachers included their work either at Chautauqua sessions or Chautauqua home study as part of their educational backgrounds.

The two black teachers ranked high in educational attainment and experience. The woman responsible for grades one to four had graduated from high school and attended several terms of normal school. She had taught for 20 years in Indiana and 5 in Franklin. The man had taught nearly 30 years in Michigan and Indiana and was in his first year at Franklin, teaching grades five to eight and serving as principal of the black school. He had graduated from Michigan State Normal School and had also attended Indiana State Normal School.

The salaries of the teachers in the elementary schools averaged $50 to $55 per month and in the high school, $70 per month. The superintendent's annual salary was $1600 and the high school principal's was $1000. By 1904 all the principals were men and all the elementary teachers were women; the departmental grade teachers (grades six to eight), were divided evenly between men and women. As noted previously, throughout most of the 1870s and 1880s the principal of the high school was a woman, the wife of the superintendent, but in 1887 Miss Kitty Palmer was named principal of the high school, a post she held for 12 years, the longest term of anyone during this period. She left the principalship in 1899 but remained as a teacher of history in the high school for several years. Her replacement by a man illustrates the decline in numbers of women holding major administrative positions in the schools, a decline that has also characterized twentieth-century American schools.

In December 1906 the Franklin Board of School Trustees appended to their minutes an informal survey they had done of school conditions in comparable Indiana communities. Like Franklin, each of these towns was a county seat and two others (Bloomington and Greencastle) also were the homes of colleges. What is most striking about these figures today is the extent to which Franklin is representative of other small cities and towns in the state. A summary of these findings appears in the table on pages 54-55.

Although the number of children eligible for school in Franklin remained essentially static through the late nineteenth and early twentieth centuries, partly as a result of the trend toward smaller families, the school enrollments grew in the early years of the twentieth century. This expansion is largely attributable to two factors: the greater persistence through the grades of the children and the increasing number of transfers to the Franklin schools from outlying areas. This latter group constituted 96 children in 1907 to 1908, 104 in 1908 to 1909, and 114 in 1909 to 1910. The tuition rate was about $20 per child per year. The influx of these transfer students is a good indication of the high regard in which the Franklin schools were held in the surrounding community in those years.

In 1910 the school adopted the pattern of organization that was dominant until after 1918. Two sections of each grade in the white school were established except for the primary room, which had three sections. The colored school continued to be divided into two sections, the first covering grades one to four and the second, grades five to eight.

Since 1871 the Franklin schools had been alternating between an 8- and a 9-month school year, the changes largely determined by the tightness of the school budget. In 1871, the real beginning of a public school system in Franklin, the ambitious board

Town	Value City Property	Males and Females Ages 6 to 21	Males and Females Enrolled (Total)	Males & Females in High School	Teachers Total / High School		Special Teachers	Monthly Teachers' Salaries Grade / High School		Principals' Salaries Grade (Month) / High School (year)	
Franklin	$ 2,673,865	1185	896	203	29	7½	Music Art Writing	$ 55-60	$ 60-80	$ 60-65	$1000
Bloomington	2,979,455	2000	1626	326	43	10	Music Drawing Manual Training	Min. wage	70-90	55-70	1000
Columbus	45,00,000	2077	1770	330	49	9	Writing Drawing Music	45-60	55-80	70-80	1000
Connersville	4,070,000	1821	1225	152	33	7	Music Drawing	60-65	85-100	75	1200
Covington	980,000	824	600	125	17	7	Music Drawing	43-54	50-60	52-54	70/mo.
Delphi	1,500,000	600	500	160	15	5	Music	51-60	65-	None	800

Frankfort	4,300,000	2199	1788	293	51	9	Drawing Writing Music	375-480/ year	720-810/ year	650-900/ year	1050
Greenfield	12,353,230	1271	1291	181	28	6	Drawing Music	50-55	65-90	65-70	90/mo.
Greencastle	2,122,000	920	777	211	21	7	Drawing Music Calisthenics	51-55	65-70	50-65	100/mo.
Madison	4,014,575	2500	1290	229	42	9	2	Min. wage	65-100	—	900
Martinsville	2,300,000	1266	1062	150	28	5	Music Writing	Base license	675/ year	525/ year	900
Rushville	12,353,320	1289	850	170	27	5	Music Drawing	Min. to 60	70-85	50-75	85/mo.
Shelbyville	5,000,000	1990	1750	202	43	6	Music Writing Drawing	41-58	85	55-85	1000
Bedford	3,000,000	1923	1836	193	40	8	Art Music	Legal base	70-80	60	1000

started with a 9-month school year, but this was shortened in 1882 to an 8-month school year. In the 1890s they went back to a 9-month year, only to return to an 8-month year in 1898. In 1907 Franklin returned to a 9-month year of 180 school days, where it remained through 1918. The average length of the school year fluctuated throughout the state during this period as well, the shorter terms generally existing in the rural schools, and the longer ones existing in the towns and cities.

One aspect of the increased enrollments that particularly pleased local observers was the substantial rise in the number of boys in the high school. Between 1907 and 1910 the high school enrollment increased from 221 to 287, and the number of boys rose from 94 to 144. The girls still dominated most of the graduating classes, although in 1907 there were 16 male graduates and 17 female ones. In 1908 the more characteristic ratio returned with 9 male and 28 female graduates, and in 1909 with 5 male and 32 female graduates. But in 1910 the boys came into their own with 25 male graduates and 21 female.

No doubt one important reason for the larger high school enrollment in the first decade of the twentieth century was that the high school was moving from the excessively classical and limited curriculum that had characterized it through 1904 to one designed to attract a wider group of student interests. In 1906 the School Board signed a contract with the American Manual Training School for them to begin providing instruction in manual training in the Franklin schools. With the opening of the new high school building in 1910, which provided considerably more space than the cramped old one, instruction in commercial subjects began. A sewing teacher was also hired that year. In January 1912 typewriters arrived for the use of the commercial students. That same year the state lowered standards for high school graduation so that only 30 credits instead of 32 were necessary for graduation, and mathematics was no longer required. Other activities at the high school in 1913 included an orchestra, a debating club, a senate, oratorical contests, a Corn Club of 65 members, and a girls' sewing and cooking club of 80 members.

By 1914, Superintendent Paul Van Riper reported that one of the most pressing needs was for more materials for the commercial courses in the high school, which had proved very popular. That same year 105 girls beyond grade seven were studying sewing and cooking as part of the regular curriculum, and 35 boys were in the practical agriculture classes, although Van Riper added that the agriculture course in the high school needed improvement. The superintendent noted also, "The colored children take readily to manual training and domestic science and we hope to do more in these lines for them another year."

Van Riper is the only superintendent between 1865 and 1918 to report to the Board in the extant minutes about the non-classical subjects that Franklin should consider for its schools. A 1907 graduate of Franklin College, Van Riper taught in the Franklin schools before becoming superintendent. In 1912 he received an A.M. from Columbia University's Teachers College, where new ideas such as vocational education and "tieing the school to life" were much in the air. He left Franklin to become superintendent of schools in LaPorte, Indiana in 1916, and after World War I went to Lebanon, Indiana as superintendent.

The influence of town residence on educational opportunties is indicated graphically by comparing the enrollment of the Franklin schools with others in the county. In 1910 Franklin constituted 22 percent of the Johnson County population. The school enrollments for 1907 to 1908, the closest year for which comparable figures are available, show that the Franklin schools were enrolling just over 20 percent of the Johnson County children who were in school, a figure consistent with the population of the town and county. The discrepancy appears, however, in looking at the high school figures. There were 591 high school students in Johnson County in 1907 to 1908, and 240 of them were at Franklin High School. The same proportion holds for the high school seniors, 91 in Johnson County of whom 37 were at Franklin High School. Thus, 40 percent, or double the overall enrollment figure, of the high school students were coming from Franklin. The calculations were complicated by the transfer students who came to Franklin from other schools in the county. They constituted about 10 percent of the Franklin enrollment at that time.

General enrollment figures must be used with caution for this period, since state aid was partly determined by the numbers of children in school. Superintendents and principals were always eager to appear to have the largest possible number of children on the rolls, and often, particularly in rural schools during harvesting and planting times, the number of children actually in class bore little relation to the number on the roll. Furthermore, the state wished to show a high proportion of children in school, and thus rates such as the 83.7 percent figure given in the 1910 census for the number of children attending school in Johnson County, ages six to fourteen, is based on rolls and not on average daily attendance, a much more realistic figure that was not computed regularly until later in the twentieth century. The 1910 census data reported one percent of the Johnson County population over age ten as illiterate.

County Schools

The schools serving the 80 percent of the Johnson County schoolchildren not attending the Franklin schools were scattered throughout the county. By 1908 consolidation was beginning to occur, and the one-room district schools were being rapidly replaced by township graded schools, which included high schools. Schools included in their costs the construction of wagons to bring the children from distant homes. Here, again, the increase in the high school enrollments were most dramatic. Although one of the townships had preceded Franklin in the establishment of a high school (Nineveh in 1872), the high school movement did not take firm root in the townships until the, beginning of the twentieth century. The aggregate high school enrollment in the county increased 68 percent between 1903 and 1908. The school year was shorter in the rural schools, generally 6 to 7 months through the first decade of this century.

The township high schools moved more rapidly than Franklin to add subjects destined to attract the interests of their rural students. Although Nineveh had begun as a high school as a result of a court action by parents who were seeking instruction for their children in Latin, it was one of the first schools to utilize school gardens as a means of teaching both nature and agriculture. Agriculture began to be widely taught in these schools about 1905. Hopewell, whose high school had evolved in the 1880s from the successful Presbyterian academy, began instruction in agriculture in 1908. The year before art had been introduced into the curriculum, and 2 years before music had been included. In 1909 sewing and manual training became part of the regular offering.

In the rural schools the pattern of a man as superintendent and a woman as principal of the high school persisted longer than in Franklin. For example, in 1913 a male graduate of the state normal school was superintendent of the White River Township Graded School and a young woman graduate of Franklin College was principal of the high school, which was then graduating between 10 and 15 students a year.

The most firmly established of the township high schools, Hopewell, graduated 46 girls and 37 boys between 1888, the first graduating class, and 1911. The largest of these classes was in 1910 with six girls and one boy. Another of the townships, Hensley, offered high school work sporadically through the 1880s and 1890s. Between 1885 and 1899, four girls and eleven boys completed the high school course of study despite the short 6-month school year. Union Township began offering high school work in 1888 with three students joining 44 children in grades one to eight, all under the direction of one teacher who was responsible for all the instruction in the school. The following year a two-room building was opened with one room for the high school, and in 1906 a new graded high school building was completed. In Clark Township temporary high school work was offered in one room of the two-room building from 1897 until 1911, during which time 27 students graduated.

Franklin College

The one remaining educational institution of significance in Johnson County between 1865 and 1918 was Franklin College. Founded in 1837 through the efforts of the New Englanders active in Baptist Home Missionary Society work in Indiana, Franklin suffered all the tribulations common to impecunious denominational colleges in the Midwest in the nineteenth century, including the threatened competition of an "Old Side" Presbyterian college being founded in the same community. Although the Presbyterians did not establish a competing college, they did organize an academy, which had the same effect, since neither Franklin College nor Hopewell Academy had many collegiate grade students in the middle of the nineteenth century. In 1847 Franklin awarded its first B.A.

Franklin's principal institutional indebtedness was to Brown University, the first Baptist college in America. Silas Bailey, Franklin's second president, from 1852 to 1862, was a graduate of Brown where he had been influenced by Brown's innovative president, Francis Wayland. Bailey attempted unsuccessfully to introduce some of Wayland's ideas about an expanded curriculum, including science, modern languages, civil engineering, and agriculture. In 1864, however, the college closed, partly as a result of the disturbances resulting from the Civil War and partly because of competing Baptist institutions in the state.

Franklin reopened again in 1869, still with grave financial problems, and in 1870 H. L. Wayland, son of Brown's former president, was named president. Wayland called himself a "Christian Socialist," and brought Congressman William Holman, an early student at Franklin in the 1830s, to give the commencement address in 1871. Holman's address, "Capital and Labor," was completely consistent with Wayland's Christian Socialism. Holman recalled the institution's founding name,

Manual Labor Institute, and reminded his audience of the institutions' alignment with the working man. Arguing that the standards of human progress in every age could be measured by the success of the struggle against injustice for the worker, he added, "The true test of greatness of a nation is the condition of its laboring people." Holman explained that the contest of the future would be between the comparatively few men of wealth who controlled the means of production and the working classes. He argued that the government must intervene on behalf of the workers in order that they might secure "the just rights of labor." "Against this tendency to give wealth an unjust preponderance," Holman concluded, "must be arrayed the intelligent judgment, the best public opinion of the whole people. I question the soundess of a system of political economy which enlarges facilities for unbounded opulence."

Such a speech was not likely to win support where Franklin then needed it most, from wealthy Baptists who would contribute a bit of their "opulence" to save the institution. Without their help the college closed again in January 1872. Through that year local residents worked to reopen the college, and in the fall they did so, under the leadership of a much more conventional Baptist than Wayland, W. T. Stott. In 1888 the faculty included six men and one woman. Three of the six men, including the President, Vice-President C. H. Hall, and Professor of Chemistry and Physics Arthur Chaffee, were ordained preachers. One of the seven, Professor Francis Brown of Latin, had a Ph.D. The woman, Miss Rebecca Thompson, joined the faculty in 1872 and remained for 38 years, most of them as professor of mathematics.

The enrollments gradually increased in the 1880s and 1890s. In 1881 to 1882 only 23 of the 114 students were in the collegiate program; a decade later 76 of the 273 were enrolled in the college program. The enrollment declined again in the 1890s and dropped almost 100 students between 1898 and 1901, most of them in the college department. In the early years of the century the enrollments averaged less than 200, the majority still in the preparatory department.

President Stott was succeeded in 1905 by Professor Elmer Bryan, who had been a professor of education at Indiana University. Bryan's ties with the Baptist were considerably less firm than Stott's, and Bryan attempted to put the college into the mainstream of small colleges in America. One effort to do this was to affiliate Franklin with the Carnegie retirement plan for faculty, and this meant certification that there were no denominational tests for faculty, students, or trustees, or in the curriculum. Bryan was quite willing to do this to get the relatively generous pension for the traditionally underpaid faculty, but his action won him enmity from the state Baptist association, whose direct financial contributions to the college had already severely declined but whose good will in recommending Franklin to potential students was crucial. Unlike Princeton, Franklin had neither academic eminince nor isloation from inexpensive higher education. It was difficult to know why Franklin parents should pay $75 tuition per year plus fees for laboratory, library, and athletics when their children could attend the state university at either Bloomington or West Lafayette where the curriculum was much broader, the faculty more distinguished and, most important, the tuition cheaper. The main advantage that Franklin offered was Baptist orthodoxy, and if this were diminished in the eyes of the Baptists in Indiana, the college's viability was seriously threatened.

Bryan left to become president of Colgate in 1909, and enrollments, chief harbinger of financial stability for the college, immediately declined. His success, Elijah Hanley, a Baptist minister from Providence, Rhode Island, took another unpopular step; in 1915 he attempted to regulate the fraternities, which dominated undergraduate social life. He left in 1917 to be succeeded by Charles Goodell, who recognized Franklin's historic tie to the Baptists and attempted to make it stronger. One way to do this was to drop the Carnegie pension plan with its required pledge of no denominational tests, since this had so infuriated the Indiana Baptists. The effect of Goodell's decision was to lose the younger faculty, who refused to remain at the low Franklin salaries without the pension guarantee.

Franklin's role in the county is difficult to assess. The impact of the mere physical presence of the college in the community, providing tangible evidence that formal education beyond the high school level was available, was incontrovertible. Undoubtedly the college's presence also contributed to the locale a pool of young people who had taken work at the college who could be called on to teach in the neighborhood schools. Sometimes a student at the college would teach high school while completing his college work, as did Elmer Davis, who taught Latin in Franklin High School while finishing his college program and before going to England as a Rhodes Scholar. On the other hand, the faculty was so small, rarely more than a dozen, that its influence on the community of more than 20,000 was limited. The curriculum remained so traditional in its offerings that there were few subjects of general interest that could be offered to the community. There again the state universities with their avowed policy of outreach to the community made their educational contributions much more visible than a denomination college possibly could. Franklin was unable to reach the outlying communities with agricultural extension agents, home demonstration agents, traveling displays, and special courses for adults as Purdue and Indiana Universities did.

Informal Education: The Library

Another institution that had undoubted educational influence on the community was the library, which opened in Franklin in 1911, the result of the agitation of local women's clubs. Abortive efforts to establish township libraries had been made in Johnson County in the last half of the nineteenth century, although the chief historian of the county estimated that no more than 1500 books were ever involved in this enterprise and no effort was made by the township trustee, who controlled them, to circulate them. Unlike the other local libraries, which required membership, the Franklin library was open to the residents of the town of Franklin and, soon after its founding, to those living in the outlying townships. By 1912 the library had nearly 2000 books and regularly received 20 periodicals. The annual circulation was 18,589 among nearly 1400 patrons. Major gifts of books to the library had been received from the Daughters of the American Revolution (who gave classic works in American history by Parkman, Fiske, McMaster, and Hart), the ladies of the Shiloh Church, and the Franklin Baptist Young Peoples' Union.

Like many other midwestern communities, Franklin was offered funds from the Andrew Carnegie estate for a public library building if the community was able to raise a specified amount of money. Also, like many other communities, local private gifts were also necessary. The Carnegie fund gave Franklin $17,500, and a Franklin woman gave $2000 so that the new library could be built. It opened in 1916 with 5000 volumes and that year had an average daily circulation of 100 volumes, nearly double what it had been 4 years before. The new library building also contained an auditorium that was large enough to seat 300 people and could be used for public meetings.

Other Informal Education

An earlier alternative to the library, which served the children of the county well in the late 1880s and 1890s, was the Young People's Reading Circle. Related to the adult Chautauqua movement and the Teachers' Reading Circle, the one for youngsters functioned on the same principle of providing good literature at low cost for children either to keep themselves or to circulate through the school. Participation was widespread in Johnson County for a few years and then withered away by the turn of the century.

The most generally available reading matter was the newspaper. Johnson County residents had an abundance of these to choose from between 1865 and 1918. The leading paper in the 1880s and 1890s was the *Democrat*, largely because Johnson County was heavily Democratic in its political persuasion, and also because it was an unusually good paper. A weekly, it excerpted from many of the familiar national magazines and newspapers, thus giving readers secondhand access to major publications. The *Jeffersonian*, also a weekly, was less interested in national news, but like the *Democrat*, held a strong political partisanship, in this case, Republican. The *Star* came to dominate the county newspapers by the twentieth century. A daily paper, it carried much more local news of Franklin and relatively less national and international. Furthermore, as a daily, it had a great obligation to present stories of immediate interest and was less inclined to the more speculative and reflective pieces found in the weekly *Democrat*.

Other quasieducational activities that engaged the populace of Johnson County in the late nineteenth century were Sunday School Conventions, which met annually, and whose large attendance demonstrated their popularity. They were Protestant ecumenical gatherings to which, usually, each Sunday School sent one delegate per 50 members of the Sunday School. At this period the Sunday School was a vigorous institution primarily for adults, not the tepid Sunday morning hour for children that is common today. The conventions included lectures as well as devotional activities.

A number of secular activities also involved substantial numbers of members of the community but, until 1883 when the 600-seat opera house opened, these were generally held in the churches, since they had the greatest seating capacity. Often the lectures in the churches dealt with religious topics, such as the periodic lectures on Mormonism and the perils of polygamy. More often, the topics would be entirely secular, such as an East Indian lecturing on his country or a professor at Wabash College discussing Darwinism. Later lectures with an international emphasis included Swiss mountain climbing, complete with pictures, and a Japanese educated at Columbia University talking about his native land. Attendance at these lectures was open to the entire community, and a small admission fee was sometimes charged.

With the opening of the opera house, Franklin organized a Free Lecture Course that offered monthly programs during the winter. Most of them were light entertainment, as were most other programs at the opera house. The program for 1885 included Professor Tompkins on "Morals, the Work of the Public Schools"; J. L. White, "Row"; a recitation by Emma Turner; Professor Moncrief, "Little Facts"; Dr. Andrews, "Slices out of London"; and a band concert that included selections from the *Barcarole* and *Tannhauser*.

In the early years of the century a somewhat more exclusive version of the Lecture Course existed in the form of the Lyceum, which invited persons to attend its regular meetings that took place in members' homes and were open to both men and women. Musical programs, including the compositions of Mozart and Puccini, alternated with presentations on literary topics, such as the art of William Makepeace Thackeray. Membership tended to be limited to the professional men in Franklin and their wives.

Three other clubs with cultural pretensions existed in the early twentieth century, a Ladies' Musicale, the Charlotte Emerson Club, and the Hurricane Literary Society. The former, as its name implies, was limited to musical programs, but the two latter had more general cultural interests—the first having programs such as a discussion of Italian art, while the second ran heavily toward the reading of original poems. All three were limited to women.

Of more direct educational benefit were the traveling agricultural exhibits prepared by the Purdue University School of Agriculture. These came through on train cars in the winter and attracted large groups of farmers to see displays on preventing hog cholera, spraying apple trees, and encouraging corn germination. One winter day in 1912 more than 400 people waited several hours at the Franklin railroad station to see the exhibit. During this period Johnson County farmers also took advantage of the slack winter activities to attend short courses at Purdue for a week or longer on topics such as feeding the dairy cow, the horticultural awakening, and lime-sulphur as a winter and summer spray.

Although the evidence for noninstitutional educational activities is sketchy, the conclusion is inevitable that the most efficient educational agencies in the county were the schools, inadequate as they were. In an era before widespread information dissemination by radio and television and when national newspapers and magazines were not widely available outside major cities, the schools and the churches remain the two institutions beyond the family where educational matters were intentionally pursued. But the churches in a community like Johnson County where Protestantism was so strong had educational commitments of a much lower order than their inspirational, missionary, or moral ones. One of the major denominations, the Baptists, even had had major fights over the wisdom of educating their clergy at all in the midnineteenth century. The churches, presumably recognizing the greater effectiveness of the schools in reaching the children, lamented the public schools' move toward secularism. The Johnson County public schools, then, were left with the principal burden in the late nineteenth and early twentieth centuries for education of the citizenry.

chapter three
marquette county, michigan

Marquette County, located on the southern shore of Lake Superior in the center of the upper peninsula of Michigan, was a newly populated and rapidly growing region in 1865. By 1918 it had undergone a serious economic depression, expended most of its major natural resources on which nearly all its economy depended, and was losing its population, both urban and rural.

Composed of more than 1800 square miles, the county in its first census in 1850 reported a population of 136, of whom 105 were men and approximately one third were foreign born. These settlers accepted the rigorous conditions of life in the unexplored north woods with its inhospitable climate in order to exploit the natural resources the area then possessed in abundance: iron ore. After the mines became exhausted, timber, the other principal short-term natural resource, was cut until it, too, was eliminated. Not until well after World War II did mining and lumbering return to the area and then only after significant changes in technology and the economics of the market made exploitation of the existing reserves possible.

Iron ore was first discovered in the Marquette area in the 1840s and mining began at the end of the decade. In 1855 the

St. Mary's Canal opened at Sault Ste. Marie, providing a link between Lake Superior and the other Great Lakes and thereby making ports on Lake Superior accessible to major industrial centers. For 20 years the town of Marquette, which had an adequate but not outstanding harbor, was the leading iron ore port on Lake Superior.

The iron industry spurred the development of this area, and its early successes had immediate effects in the community. Blast furnaces quickly replaced "puddling" as the preferred method of smelting iron. When the Civil War broke out in 1861, the demand for iron vastly increased. In 1862, the year after the opening of the railroad, the main iron company paid its first dividend to stockholders, and the residents looked to a prosperous future.

By 1870 the population boom had struck Marquette County, and it had grown to more than 15,000 residents. By then three towns had been organized: first, Marquette city, which was the port, the most economically stable community, and crucially for educational developments, the home of the wealthy. The other two communities, Ishpeming and Negaunee, reputedly named for the Indian words for heaven and hell, were located adjacent to each other about 15 miles inland from the lake and from Marquette city. Their fortunes fluctuated with the vicissitudes of the mining and lumbering industries. In some years Ishpeming had an even larger population than Marquette, but by 1910 it had fallen behind Marquette and never caught up again.

The depression of the 1870s hit the mining industry hard, the price of iron per ton dropped from $12 in 1873 to $5.50 in 1878, and these changes in the economy were immediately apparent in the county, particularly in the two smaller towns. By the late 1880s prosperity was returning with exploitation of the second natural resource. Lumbermen then began the wholesale cutting of the magnificent stands of virgin timber in the region.

The population of the county passed 40,000 near the end of the century, reaching a maximum for the period of over 46,000 in 1910. The Marquette city population reached 10,000 at the turn of the century and gained 2000 more in the next decade. By the second decade of the century, however, the population decline set in as both mining and lumbering operations ceased or were substantially reduced. Since the land was poor and the growing season short, farming was not an altogether satisfactory alternative. Marquette city experienced some small population gains, but both Ishpeming and Negaunee lost approximately 2000 residents each between 1910 and 1920. This was the second consecutive decade that Ishpeming had undergone a population loss. In Marquette County one suspects that the population shift was not the characteristic one from farm to city, but was instead the more and more common one of town to city. Although the rural population had grown rapidly in previous decades, it now remained stable.

Immigrants and their children dominated the population of Marquette County. In 1900 less than 10 percent of the population were native-born and of native-born parents. Nearly half the population were native born with one or both parents born abroad. About 40 percent were foreign born. By 1920 the proportion of foreign born was still nearly 40 percent of the population. Blacks constituted less than 1 percent of the population, with American Indians and Orientals counting even less.

The preponderant nationalities represented among the foreign born changed in the area over the years. In the 1860s, 1870s, and 1880s the Germans, Irish, and French-Canadians predominated. Significant numbers of Cornish also arrived, chiefly to work in the iron ore mines. Later Scandinavians, especially Swedes, came in large numbers. By the 1890s Finns were immigrating to the area. By 1910 the leading countries of origin of the foreign born in the county were (in order) Finland, Sweden, England, and French Canada. For those residents of the county with one or both parents born abroad, thus indicating the earlier immigration, Sweden led, followed by England, French Canada, Ireland, and Germany.

The religious affiliations of the Marquette populace reflected their national traditions. A survey in 1916 revealed that nearly half the county residents were members of churches. Of those who were members 62 percent were Roman Catholics and nearly 20 percent were Lutherans.

Well over half of the Lutherans belonged to the Suomi (Finnish) Synod. The remaining church members were distributed among the Methodists (nearly 9 percent) and the Episcopalians, Presbyterians, and Baptists, each with less than 3 percent. No Jewish members were listed.

Despite their small numbers, however, the Presbyterians and the Episcopalians included in their congregations most of the leaders of the community. The early leaders of the county had not been foreign immigrants, but New Englanders and New Yorkers, and they brought their churches with them just as the Irish and Finns did. They also brought to the Michigan frontier considerable entreprenurial skill, and some of them either brought or developed a sense of responsibility for their community. They settled in Marquette city, and the town would soon benefit by their presence. In contrast to Ishpeming and Negaunee, where most of the wealth of the towns was controlled by nonresident investors, Marquette was home to some of the men who made their fortunes there. Some who prospered in Marquette followed the examples of more successful entrepreneurs of the era, such as Andrew Carnegie, and made substantial investments of their own funds to improve the cultural and educational facilities in their community. Peter White, probably the leading citizen of Marquette during the last half of the nineteenth century, provided funds for the public library and for a manual training program in the high school. John Longyear assisted the normal school, an early high school, the manual training program, and the local historical society. A son of a Jewish clothing merchant, Louis Kaufman, whose father had married Juliet Graveraet, a daughter of an early state senator from Marquette, deserted the family business, joined Peter White's bank, and later moved to New York. Before doing so, however, he provided funds for the purchase of the land of the new high school, which was given his mother's maiden name, Graveraet.

Philanthropic generosity was a necessity in Marquette. Like many other communities built largely of wood, fire was a constant danger. Almost the entire downtown area burned in 1868, and skeptics doubted if the struggling community would rebuild. Later fires destroyed schools in 1875, 1882, and 1900. Only in the last one of these, which ruined the combined elementary and high school, was there appreciable insurance.

The educational opportunities in Marquette County between 1865 and 1918 varied tremendously from the rather considerable efforts in the towns to the much less concerted ones in the tiny rural settlement. During most of the period a majority of the county's population lived in one of the three towns and thus could enroll in the more systematically organized schools, either public or parochial, and benefit from other cultural amenities, such as the library. Obviously the child living on a farm, in a shack in the woods, or in one of the tiny and ephemeral mining sites lacked the option of selecting which school he would rather attend, a public or a Catholic one, or of deciding whether he would continue for a high school program. The rural child who persevered beyond the one-room school on to a high school course did so at great personal effort and some financial cost. Arrangements had to be made too for him to room and board in town in order to attend the high school, and transportation had to be arranged to join his family on the weekends. In short, it was easier for the child living in one of the towns to have formal schooling than it was for one in the country.

In Marquette county as in so many other mixed rural and small town counties in America in the late nineteenth and early twentieth centuries, the chief educational opportunities of the area were found in the schools. In this era before the widespread circulation of books and magazines, before radio and television, and before the increased leisure time that enabled ordinary citizens to give some of their attention to these diversions, the schools largely determined educational and cultural facilities in the community.

Marquette exemplified those communities in which the common school ideal for education of all the children of the community in a single school or school system was not achieved. This was so in Marquette, as it was in many other communities, primarily because of a large concentration of Roman Catholic families who preferred to send their children to parochial schools. From the town's earliest years Catholic education had been available to the children of Marquette. The Marquette Catholic schools were among the first in the area and were established as a direct result of the Bishop's conviction that formal education, preferably in Catholic schools, was essential for the children of his diocese. In Marquette, then, the parochial schools came from the Catholic commitment to education *per se*. They preceded the public schools and were not organized in protest against the public schools' Protestantism or agnosticism, as some parochial schools were.

Like many other towns Marquette was also host to a variety of very small, private, nonreligious schools, which operated chiefly in the 1860s, 1870s, and 1880s. These short-lived educational efforts subsided as the public schools became more firmly established, leaving the equally well-organized but smaller parochial school the only alternative to the public schools. By 1900 another option became available to Marquette families with the opening of the private elementary school at the normal school and later with the addition of a high school in 1914. This tuition-charging institution ostensibly offered the most modern facilities in the community. Marquette clearly deviated from the Johnson County norm of the public school monopoly of elementary education. In Marquette County the public schools dominated the formal and informal education, but did not have sole responsibility for it.

Like so many other facets of education in America in the nineteenth century, the history of the schools of Marquette is one of extraordinary growth. The earliest schools, Catholic and

German-language ones, date from the 1850s, the decade of the earliest settlement in the area. By 1865 the "public" schools had dropped their $1 per child per term tuition charge and enrolled several hundred children predominantly in the primary and grammar grades (roughly equivalent to grades one to eight). The total county school population in 1870 was nearly 2200 children, and by 1910 it had grown to over 14,500. In 1910 nearly 92 percent of the children between six and fourteen were enrolled in school, of whom the native-born children with one or more foreign-born parent had the highest percent of enrollment, followed closely by the native born of native parents and the foreign born.

The schools were, in fact, teaching the children to read, or at least they were learning to read somewhere, for the illiteracy rate in 1910 for persons aged ten to twenty was less than 1 percent. For all persons in the county in 1910 the illiteracy rate was just over 4 percent. The illiteracy rate was higher for men (6 percent) than for women. This was partially attributable to the higher proportion of foreign-born men than women in the country, and the greater likelihood that the foreign born will be illiterate. An exception was the Finns, of whom it has been estimated that less than 2 percent who left Finland between 1898 and 1910 were illiterate.

Marquette Public Schools

By 1877 the Marquette city public schools were enrolling nearly 900 children, but like most other schools in the United States at that time, the children were clustered in the lower grades, shown in the following table.

Enrollment, Marquette Public Schools, 1877

High school	57
Second grammar (grades seven and eight)	54
First grammar (grades five and six)	194
Second primary (grades three and four)	283
First primary (grades one and two)	275

Sixteen teachers were employed to instruct these children, an average of one for 54 students. Twenty-eight of the 57 high school students were boys, a higher proportion of boys than occurred later in the century. The high school did not begin to graduate regular classes until 1879. Between 1879 and 1900 almost twice as many girls graduated from high school as did boys.

The child who attended school in one of the three towns in the county in the 1870s participated in a program where children were already roughly divided according to grades and where boys and girls attended together. In the district schools in outlying parts of the county throughout the 1890s and well into the new century the boys and girls were frequently taught separately. A principal stimulus to organizing the Marquette city schools into graded classes was the influx of children beginning in the 1870s. In 1882 a young woman who had completed her high school work the previous spring began teaching 103 pupils in the first three grades in one of the older schools. By 1884 only one of the three city schools was not crowded. In the newest school 95 children of various nationalities were packed into one first-grade room with one teacher. Predictably the numbers declined in the upper grades, 69 in the third, 65 in the fourth and fifth, and 63 in the sixth. By 1887 the number of children enrolled had nearly doubled from that of the previous decade, and the schools now had student-teacher ratios of nearly 90 to 1. Since some of the children were listed as "irregular" in attendance, no doubt most teachers did not actually face 90 youngsters daily, but even so their task was staggering. The crowding became steadily worse, and some children were denied entrance to the schools in the 1890s. The growth slowed after the turn of the century, although the high school classes expanded steadily.

By the 1870s the Marquette schools were organized in three four-year segments, although only a fraction of the students finished the total program. Texts were prescribed throughout the grades and teachers expected to reach specific pages by the end of the year. The first, the primary department, initiated children into the literate world, providing their first and for many their only contact with formal education. At the end of the primary sequence children were expected to be well acquainted with reading and spelling, arithmetic, writing, and even a little geography. In the grammar department students continued their primary studies, beginning formal study of English grammar in grade seven, and adding United States history in their final year. The teachers of the sixth grade were urged in the "general remarks" to "cultivate a spirit of observation and point out the structure and uses of plants, and peculiarities of animals." This introduction to science had become an integral part of the curriculum by the 1890s when eighth-grade students presented papers in science to the Columbian Exposition Educational Exhibit for Graded Schools at the Chicago World's Fair in 1892–1893. Also in the 1890s some of the Marquette teachers began to share the interest of others of their colleagues throughout the country in the study of geography and one reported, "It is in the spirit of the new education that our teachers are trying to present the subject of geography."

By the 1890s other Marquette teachers had become interested in the "new education." Preeminent among them was the primary teacher who wrote, "No department of teaching has undergone such a change in the last ten years as the primary work. The child is beginning to be recognized, not as a fraction of the school but as an individual. This is due in large measure to the new feature of the work, Child Study." She regretted bitterly the lack of kindergarten facilities in Marquette but recounted with enthusiasm the introduction of nature study and story reading and telling in the early grades. The concern for both child study and kindergarten was reflected in naming the new elementary school, built in 1901, for the German educational pioneer and popularizer of kindergartens, Friedrich Froebel. Froebel was a popular name for schools as evidenced by the fact that it was also selected for the new school built in 1896 in Munising, the county seat of the adjacent county.

When the Froebel school opened, the teachers of Marquette

had won their campaign for a kindergarten but on grounds different from those on which they had made their case. A state normal school had opened in Marquette in 1899 and soon began operating jointly with the city schools a model school that included a kindergarten. Gradually in the early years of the century all the city schools with primary departments added a kindergarten.

That the kindergarten should come with the Normal School but not with the city Board of Education's initial blessing was indicative of the ways in which educational policies were established in Marquette and in many other communities. The dynamic and controversial superintendent of schools appeared before the five-man board in 1899 to argue for appropriations for a kindergarten. Appealing first to their civic pride, she observed that Marquette was the only town in the Upper Peninsula of Michigan of any considerable size without provisions for a kindergarten. She then moved to the argument that apparently she and her teachers, like so many educators of that period, considered critical. She urged the immediate establishment of a kindergarten at the South Marquette school "since there was such a large proportion of children there whose parents were working people and who have not had the time and attention given to them they should have." In short, her argument for a kindergarten was essentially a remedial one for the children of the poor. Such an approach did not win favor with the affluent board, who pointed out that other Marquette families would feel their children were being neglected if the only kindergarten were established in South Marquette. Thus the first kindergarten was not for the poor but for the wealthy who could afford tuition to send their children to the Normal School's special primary school.

Another example of the influence of the business and professional community of Marquette on its school board was the decision about the turn of the century to return to teaching Spencerian handwriting in the schools instead of the vertical method. A petition signed by 133 Marquette residents was presented to the board requesting it to return to the Spencerian method, since the vertical method was too slow and destroyed individuality in penmanship. With the advent of widespread typewriting, penmanship would not be such a burning issue, but at this time interest in handwriting illustrated the influence of the business and professional community on the schools that trained the local work force.

The high school was an object of considerable pride in the Marquette community, and difficult as educational quality is to assess, most historians would undoubtedly share some of the local enthusiasm for the high school efforts in Marquette. Certainly Marquette offered public high school work earlier than many other communities. For the small proportion of youngsters who persisted in the program, and as late as 1903, only seven graduating classes had exceeded 15, a number of options was available. From its earliest years the high school offered students a choice of four courses of study, which varied principally in foreign language requirements: Classical (requiring both Greek and Latin), Latin-Scientific (Latin but French or German instead of Greek), Scientific (either French or German but no ancient language), and English (no foreign language and only a 3-year course). By 1890 the high school had won the accreditation of the University of Michigan for the graduates of all but the English course, and graduates were also admitted "by diploma" to Smith and Wellesley Colleges. During the 1890s the Latin-Scientific course was the most popular with the graduates and the Classical extremely rare by the end of the decade. The English program, a full 4-year course in the 1890s, grew steadily in enrollment.

The 1892 course of study is very similar to the one followed in the 1870s, but in the following decade substantial changes occurred in the high school program. Just as their colleagues in the primary departments in Marquette were becoming interested in "the new education" with its emphasis on child study, the high school faculty were becoming involved with national movements in secondary education. The accession to national interests is noticeable in two major developments: the introduction of electives into the high school curriculum and the inclusion of a variety of vocational subjects. The new course of study in 1901 specified nine of the required fifteen units for graduation (three in mathematics, three in English, two in history, and one in physics) and left the balance for election. Students who wished to follow a college preparation program could select among Greek, Latin, French, German, and Spanish. Biology, botany, chemistry, and "physiography" were also available for the scientifically inclined.

Once the principle was recognized that a nonprescribed course was acceptable for high school graduation, the step to the inclusion of vocational education subjects was not so difficult. In this respect Marquette joined the national movement for vocational subjects, and it was peculiarly appropriate for Marquette to do so. In much of its early period the high school had served the children of the middle and upper-middle classes and had thought of its program as either college preparatory or as terminal general education. Marquette had always had a small aristocracy for whose children attendance at an Eastern college was not out of the question, but most Marquette children were not college bound; in fact, not even high school bound. For this substantial group the educators argued some more appropriate curriculum was necessary. Furthermore, the local merchants welcomed new personnel who were equipped with business techniques, and as evidenced by the petition to restore the Spencerian handwriting instruction to the curriculum, their influence was felt. Two of the most prominent local citizens, Peter White and John Longyear, agreed in 1900, after the burning of the Ridge Street School, which housed the high school, to donate $1000 each for the creation of a special manual training building to be attached to the new high school. This insured the full development of a substantial vocational program, and indeed the autonomy provided by the grant permitted the manual training department to operate quite independently of the high school, a fact the principal and board of education later lamented. Private beneficence providing vocational training supported the notion that the elites wanted this training available for immigrants' children.

Even in 1901 the range of offerings in vocational subjects was considerable. Among the commercial subjects available were bookkeeping, commercial arithmetic, stenography and typewriting, business correspondence, and commercial law. In manual training students could study mechanical drawing, woodwork, ironwork, pattern making, and reflecting the dominant industry of the region, advanced ironwork. This emphasis on ironwork also exemplifies a common problem of school vocational education programs, teaching skills that are obsolete. By the time that Marquette High School began extensive training in ironwork, mining was seriously declining throughout the Upper Peninsula. A testimony to the low caliber of the nearby farm land and probably also to the unavailability of Marquette High School to rural children was the absence of any work in agriculture. In domestic science, however, a variety of subjects was taught: cooking, sewing and design work, dressmaking, household economy, and, in keeping with the early twentieth-century fetish of scientism, laundry science.

Undoubtedly another reason for introducing the vocational subjects and for the particular emphasis on manual training was to entice the boys to remain in school. Throughout the nineteenth century boys had been dropping out at an earlier age than girls, so that two thirds of the high school graduates through 1903 were girls. The high proportion of girl graduates was also characteristic of the other two high schools in the county, Ishpeming and Negaunee. Negaunee's first graduating class (1879), for example, included ten girls and two boys. Although the primary and grammar school rolls reflect the ethnic distribution of the community, the high school enrollment is dominated by children of Irish-English-Scottish descent. Noticeably absent are the French-Canadian youngsters.

Marquette's efforts to attract more children to remain in high school were successful and coincided with the national experience of rapidly increasing high school enrollments in the first two decades of this century. From a high school enroll-ment of 175 in 1901 on which an increase of 25 was projected, so that the new high school building that opened in 1903 was planned for 200, the enrollment jumped to 396 in 1915. The problems of extreme overcrowding, which had characterized the elementary schools in the 1880s and 1890s, had shifted to the high school in the second decade of the twentieth century. In 1916 to 1917 the total public school enrollment was about 1750, an increase of roughly 650 in 40 years. The jump was largely in the high school enrollment, since the earlier figure had in-cluded only a very few high school students whereas the later one included nearly 400. The gain in the elementary school en-rollment, therefore, had been only about 250 between 1877 and 1917.

The teachers who presided over these changing classes were frequently young women who had graduated from Marquette High School, and after its opening in 1899, from the Normal School. The school board had in fact passed a resolution in 1899 "giving the preference to young ladies in this city" for new teachers. The teachers, especially the elementary ones, thus reflected the ethnic concentration of the local school enroll-ment, and a high proportion of them were of Irish descent. Not until the 1920s did the Finns begin to enter the teaching force in large numbers. Although men apparently taught with some frequency in the district schools, women dominated the faculties of the Marquette city schools where presumably dis-cipline problems were not as acute since teachers were usually not alone to cope with all the students as they were in the isolated, one-room schools. At the turn of the century 26 of the 32 Marquette public school teachers were women; 10 years later, 56 of the 62 teachers were women. Of the 66 teachers in the Marquette system in 1917 to 1918 (46 in the elementary grades), only eight were men, and seven of them were in the high school, concentrated in such subjects as manual training, physical education, and science. This had been roughly the male-female distribution throughout the history of the system.

In Marquette there was a higher proportion of women on the staff than either the state or national percentage. One important reason was salary.

In salary the high school teachers were substantially better off then the elementary ones, partially because of the greater educational attainment expected of most of them and partially because of the greater demand for them nationally. Only three of the 20 high school teachers earned less than $925 annually in 1917 to 1918, but only two of the 46 elementary teachers earned more than that. That year the average elementary teacher's salary was $726, although the high school average was $996. Nonetheless, this represented a considerable increase from 1894 when a woman had been hired to teach 58 children aged six to fourteen, at the standard beginning salary of $350. In 1906 the minimum salary for grade teachers was raised to $450. Obviously a married man could not support his family on such an income, but a single woman, often living with her parents, could survive. Furthermore, employment opportunities were much more limited for proper young women than for comparably educated men, and until World War I schoolteaching was one of the few vocations open to them.

The educational attainments of the Marquette teachers were quite respectable for this period, and the board insisted that these standards be maintained or improved. In the 1880s teachers not having diplomas from the state normal school or "other first class educational institutions" were required to pass "a thorough examination and to maintain an average of at least 75 percent." In 1897 26 teachers (only one a man) took the examination in spelling, grammar, reading, arithmetic, and geography or music while eight presented diplomas from either a state normal school or the university. All were teaching in the system at the time of the examination, and five failed the spelling test and were required to retake it until they achieved a score of 80 percent. There were no failures on any of the other tests that year. The examinations were limited to subjects taught and did not include a section on pedagogy.

The preponderance of women in the Marquette schools was

highlighted by the fact that the single most significant super-intendent of schools between 1865 and 1918 was a woman, Miss Anna M. Chandler, who came to the superintendency from a teaching position in the city schools in 1888 and left the super-intendency and Marquette in 1900. Both the expansion of the high school and the acceptance of the kindergarten as well as rigorous standards for teachers were largely the result of her insistence. She was not, however, a unanimously popular figure in the community. Her appointment as superintendent caused a group of citizens to petition the board to reconsider its de-cision to select her. She left in 1900 when the board voted not to rehire her after considerable discussion and several split votes. At the time of her departure a group of Marquette citi-zens (presumably different ones from the group 12 years before) again petitioned the board asking it to reconsider, this time to rehire her, but again the board did not yield to com-munity pressure and stuck with its original decision.

Among the actions that alienated Miss Chandler from her faculty and from some of the community was her survey of the effectiveness of the teachers. Miss Chandler had been asked by the Board to rate all the teachers in the system for the purpose of salary readjustment and reappointment. She evalu-ated the 33 teachers (31 women and 2 men) and found 17 "excellent," 9 "fair," 2 "incapable," 1 "dull and tiresome," 1 "lost interest," and 3 "teaching with the wrong motive." On the basis of this the Board lowered several salaries and threatened to cancel their contracts after January 1 if the weak teachers did not improve. This prompted at least one representation and protest to the board from a resident and mother of one of the teachers concerned, one whom Miss Chandler had listed as "teaching with the wrong motive."

The tremendous growth of the Marquette public schools from the Civil War to World War I illustrates the evolution of that community and of so many other similar American settlements, which in the nineteenth century were on the fringes of the frontier but by the twentieth century were no longer isolated and indeed were extremely responsive to developments throughout the nation. The attitudes of the teachers, so many of them long-time residents of the community and often entirely locally trained, express the view that educational practice in Marquette should reflect what is being discussed nationally.

The question of how these discussions of educational questions reached Marquette is an important although difficult one. It is never easy to trace the flow of an idea. Teachers did begin attending regional and, later, state educational associations and teachers' institutes in the 1880s. Miss Chandler made at least one extended visit (at the Board's expense) to observe a large city school system, Minneapolis, in 1895. According to Joseph Mayer Rice, the physician turned muckracking journalist, Minneapolis had one of the few good school systems in the country in the 1890s. It was also a logical choice for a Marquette superintendent to visit. Although it was considerably larger than Marquette, it was on the edge of settlements and also had a hearty immigrant population. Later in the period the Board paid for the superintendent to attend national meetings of the National Education Association where many of these kinds of questions were discussed.

The concern for kindergartens, for the child study movement, for geography in the grammar grades, for vocational education in the high school—all were indicative of Marquette's efforts to follow what was considered new and best, or the word that was often used as a synonym for new and best in national pedagogic circles, "progressive." Similarly the appointment in 1908 of a special teacher for deaf children and the establishment in 1914 of a regular health officer for the school with a detailed plan to keep the children healthy both illustrate the acceptance by this quite isolated school system of broader responsibilities for its pupils, a characteristic of many schools in the early twentieth century. Here schools assumed obligations and concerns formerly thought quite alien to them. More and more the schools' functions were seen to be not simply training for literacy but much broader preparation for all of life itself.

Roman Catholic Schools

Although the public schools of Marquette made substantial efforts to broaden their curricula beyond mere literacy training during this period, another set of educational institutions in Marquette traditionally had seen their responsibilities in considerably more expansive terms. These were the Roman Catholic parochial schools, which by the end of this period were enrolling well over 25 percent of the schoolchildren in Marquette. In addition to the customary subjects, these schools took instruction in Christian doctrine and the catechism seriously. Perhaps what is most striking about the public and the parochial schools is the extent to which their courses of study were similar instead of different. As one would expect, the elementary grades were nearly identical except for the religious instruction in the Catholic schools. The high school programs were also very similar, although the public school had a more extensive manual training program after the White-Longyear gift. The parochial schools, however, had a highly regarded commercial course.

The success and the difficulties of the Catholics in Marquette in establishing their schools is similar to that of American Catholics throughout the United States in this period, a critical one for Catholicism in this country. Marquette was peculiarly fortunate in becoming the seat of the new diocese of Sault Ste. Marie and Marquette in 1866 when the first bishop, Frederic Baraga, moved the seat of his episcopacy from the Sault in order to locate it in a more accessible place. The development of the diocese as a whole, and of its educational commitment in particular, was largely the result of the indefatigable Bishop Baraga. Born in 1797 in Krain, a Slovenian province in Austria, Baraga came to the United States as a missionary priest in 1830. His great interest was working with the Indians, and he was remarkably successful with them, first with the Ottawas in lower Michigan and later with the Chippewas farther north. Unlike the Protestant missionaries in the same areas, Bishop Baraga did not insist that the Indians learn English. Instead, Baraga, himself fluent in German, French and English, began the study of the Indian languages, first publishing a hymnal and prayer book in Ottawa and in the 1850s completing prayer book, hymnal, catechism, grammar, and dictionary in Chippewa. The Chippewa materials remain useful today.

Baraga's concern with the Indian languages is indicative of his overall commitment to education as an aspect of religious development. When Baraga moved to a new community, invariably he provided first for a church, then a place for himself to sleep, and then for a school. These priorities were so inextricably linked in his mind that these three facilities often came at the same time and sometimes were, in fact, all the same building.

Baraga's emphasis had been on providing instruction for Indian children, but on arrival in Marquette, where very few Indians lived and the Catholic children were primarily of Irish and French-Canadian families, he began to seek assistance from women's religious orders to open a school in Marquette. Instruction for Catholics in Marquette had begun in 1857 with the arrival of Father Sebastian Duroc, who had come at Bishop Baraga's request to establish a mission and, also at Bishop Baraga's insistence, had organized a school in connection with it. Like many educational efforts of that period, Fr. Duroc's school never became fully developed, and not until the arrival of the Ursuline Sisters from Chatlam, Ontario, in 1867 did a regular Catholic school open in Marquette. St. Anne's Academy offered girls a traditional elementary curriculum of that time with such additional subjects designed to bring a little refreshment to the primitive area as "embroidery" and "grace and charm." Instruction in religion was also provided, of course.

The Ursulines' understanding of refinements apparently was greater than their grasp of economics, and in 1872 they were forced to give up their academy in Marquette, just as they had 12 years before at the Sault. Financial problems troubled all facets of the diocesan work, and the new bishop, who like his predecessor was also a native of Krain, Austria, found another order to buy the Ursulines' property and to reopen a Catholic school. The Sisters of St. Joseph of Carondolet renamed the school St. Joseph's Academy and began in 1872 with a staff of five nuns, four of whom were Irish-Americans. St. Joseph's prospered and weathered such diocesan storms as the burning of the Cathedral in 1879 by supporters of its pastor, a man who was unacceptable to the new bishop. Within a decade of its founding St. Joseph's had been forced to expand its teaching staff to 13 to accommodate the increased enrollment. The growth was a reflection of the tremendous expansion of the community, one that was seen in public school enrollments as well.

By the early 1880s Bishop John Vertin, again an Austrian, began to state publicly the diocesan necessity to promote parochial schools for all Catholic children. His pastoral letters on Christian education were a direct outgrowth of the Third Plenary Council in Baltimore in 1884, in which the ideal of every Catholic child in a Catholic school was announced. Bishop Vertin and the entire Marquette diocese apparently were not much influenced by Archbishop John Ireland of Minneapolis and the Americanism controversy then shaking the Catholic church. Archbishop Ireland spoke eloquently as late as 1890 on the advisability of educating Catholic children in the public schools with additional instruction in religion at the Catholic churches. Archbishop Ireland's chief opponents in this debate within the church were other Irish prelates in New York and the German faction within the American church, all of whom rejected Ireland's effort at accommodation. The Marquette diocese, whose first three bishops had all been born in Austria and whose fourth was born in Germany, apparently yielded to its national ties despite its relative proximity to Ireland's own diocese of Minneapolis where the Stillwater-Faribault plan of cooperating with the public schools was tried.

The response to Bishop Vertin's pastoral letters in his own diocese was rapid, all three major communities in Marquette County having parochial schools by the end of 1884 (Marquette beginning in 1867, Negaunee in 1882, and Ishpeming in 1884). The second Marquette Catholic parish, St. John the Baptist, organized in 1872 by the French-Canadians, had great difficulty in establishing a school, partly because of the poverty of many of its parishoners. With 400 families in 1905 it began to talk of a school. The parish priest announced that he was "acting under the orders of the Right Reverend Bishop, who enforces wherever possible the law of the Council of Baltimore which declares that every parish shall maintain a school." None was organized until the fall of 1911. Originally staffed by the Franciscan Sisters of Canada, a French-speaking order, the nuns had much difficulty with the children, many of whom were not fluent in French.

By the turn of the century Catholic education in Marquette was thriving. About 3000 Catholics lived in the city, and they filled St. Joseph's Academy with its new wing for boys with more than 300 students. At the peak of this prosperity a fire destroyed the school, and the Catholics fell victim to the same disasters that befell the public schools. The question of who should rebuild the parochial school was a thornier one than for the public school, which was not divided between an order that owned the school and the parish that provided the students. After considerable debate the parish rebuilt the school and hired the Sisters of St. Joseph to teach in it. The new school was called Baraga School in honor of the first bishop of Marquette and opened to both boys and girls in grades one through twelve in 1905.

By the end of this period the Baraga school was enrolling 625 students, of whom 80 were in grade one, but only 37 in grade eight. The dropout rate continued in the high school, which enrolled 84 students, including 12 seniors. These declining numbers of students in the upper grades were consistent with the pattern of public school enrollments in Marquette as was the preponderance of girls in the high school grades. Twenty-two of the 29 sophomores and 7 of the 12 seniors were girls. The tuition at the Baraga School was officially stated as $1 per child per month, but this was not a necessary condition of attendance. All but two of the seniors paid this, but only 13 of the 29 sophomores did.

The determination of Irish Catholic families to educate their children in parochial schools, although frequently these children later taught in the public schools, is apparent from the families who had more than four children enrolled in the Baraga School in 1917: Deegan, Falandeau, Mahoney, Maloney, Quilliam, Crowley, Conlin, Cleary, Haley, Hogan, Murk, O'Neill, Robinson, Siegel, Stickney, and Yeshinsky. The French-Canadians are no doubt under-represented on such a list, since their children who attended parochial school did not enter Baraga until grade nine.

Private Schools

Although the Catholic parochial schools were the major institutional alternative to the public schools in Marquette, several other private schools existed largely in the early years of Marquette's development. One of the earliest of these was organized in the 1850s for children of German settlers in Marquette, and its explicit purpose was to provide as nearly as was possible in the remote American community a German primary education. About 20 children attended the school, whose history was relatively short since assimilationism triumphed over cultural separatism among the German families of Marquette.

Three other private-venture schools existed in Marquette in these early years. All were designed for very young children and were a cross between a kindergarten and primary school. Spinsters and widows conducted them, and each attracted children of Marquette's wealthy families. None survived long nor had a large enrollment. In one early one a fee of $3 was charged for each 14-week term, and in this one, which enrolled little girls, the two headmistresses frankly stated they hoped their experiences in the school would teach the girls "first, moral excellence; second, intellectual improvement; third, physical well-being; last, worldly thrift and prosperity that they may attain the blessings promised [for] Christian nurture."

In addition to the schools, Marquette also boasted various institutions of higher learning. By 1891 two "colleges" were located in Marquette, neither of which met even the lax definition of a traditional college of that day. They were "colleges" in the sense that they enrolled adults. One of them, the Upper Peninsula Business College, had a student body of 92 men and 51 women who were distributed among four departments: commercial, penmanship, shorthand, and typewriting. The business college also had an evening division that had courses of various lengths (a "full six month course" and a "thirty lessons course") and that enrolled adults at all levels of educational achievement, including some who were illiterate. The other institution was a more short-lived one, the Marquette Music and Art College, which in 1891 attempted to bring culture to the area with its staff of six instructing in art, vocal and instrumental music, and "thorough" French and German. The very fact of the existence of these institutions, however fragile their claims to academic excellence, bespeaks the quest for institutional learning among even the isolated Americans.

The most significant of the higher educational institutions to develop in Marquette at this time, however, was the Normal School. Despite the efforts of downstate legislators to block its formation, the Normal School opened in 1899 with 61 students (23 of whom were from Marquette) and a faculty of three men and two women. Originally offering a 2-year program to prepare teachers for elementary schools, it became a college in 1902, reflecting in part the demand for high school teachers. The training school, where future teachers could observe children in classes, was an integral part of the institution.

Named John Pierce for an early leader of public education in Michigan, it opened in 1900 with grades one to six, and it began a high school program in 1914. By 1918, then, a Marquette child had a choice of three school systems from grade one to twelve, the public one, the parochial one, and the training school. The latter two charged tuition.

Education Outside the Schools

One of the perennial problems with which the historian of education wrestles is the extent to which nonschool agencies educate. It is so much easier to recount the number of schools and what the officials said was studied in them and to call this "education" than it is to evaluate the influences on children and adults from other sources. This is a problem in contemporary analyses and an even greater one in historical assessments. Since histories depend heavily on documents, those activities that have left records are inevitably emphasized at the expense of those that have not. The nonschool educational forces, then, must be recognized as extremely important, although one is not always sure what they were.

Local newspapers provide an important although slanted source of information about some of the community activities in which individuals learned in rather structured ways. They recount events of interest to the community, but frequently these are found on the equivalent of the social page and include only those activities that would attract the ruling social set of the community. For example, extensive coverage was given to a lecture on Ireland at the Presbyterian Church, the house of worship of many of Marquette's most prominent families, but little attention was given in the city paper to the activities of the much larger Catholic community. Presumably the Baraga School, which was officially built to house community events for Catholics, did indeed sponsor various programs of general interest, but these do not find their way into the pages of the daily paper.

Near the turn of the century the local newspaper dealt at length with various clubs to which some of the ladies of Marquette belonged. In a panegyric to its city the paper rhapsodized in 1897, "Intellectual recreations and the keen joy which comes from the pursuit of knowledge are not unknown to her. She counts among her people many an educated man and woman, many a student, many a traveler, and those who are not unknown in the world of letters, and with such a society would we not expect to find many literary clubs flourishing in her midst. Separated as she is from the advantages of city life, lacking the opportunities of theater, lectures and music, her men and women are obliged to depend upon their own resources and work at their own literary salvation and clubs are a means to that end." The paper then recounted some of these clubs and their activities, including the 26-year-old Circulating Book Club, which had purchased over 800 books, chiefly in travel and biography. The Monday Night Club was then 21 years old and its emphasis over the years had been on art, history, and literature. During the winter of 1897 the ladies were studying the works of Thackeray, Ruskin, Eliot, Carlyle, and Tennyson. The same winter 75 members of the music association were preparing a production of "Fra Diavlo."

In this pre-McLuhan age the library played an important role in the lives of the fraction of the population who were members. In the history of the library the discrepancy between the minority of the residents who attempted to be well read and the majority who had nothing to do with such cultural matters is especially apparent. In 1896 the library had over 2300 members who could borrow books and an average monthly circulation of almost 2200 volumes or an average of almost one book per member per month. The reading room reported that an additional 1200 magazines or newspapers were read in the library each month. Although the librarians were rather pleased by the use of the facilities by the members, they lamented that about 70 percent of the residents had never entered the library, and they hastened to assure these nonborrowers that a high school education was not necessary to use the library. Furthermore, the $3 membership fee could be waived if a resident taxpayer would act as a guarantor. Undoubtedly this community *noblesse oblige* did not encourage impecunious and independent nonusers to seek library patrons.

The small but culturally awakened Marquette aristocracy was responsible for many of these literary amenities. The library building was the gift of Peter White and was itself a handsome edifice. The existence of the literary clubs depended on the leisure time of ladies not beset either by domestic demands or by necessary employment. All these activities were possible in Marquette, which had such a nascent leisure class, but they were not likely to be available in the nearby communities.

Nearby Communities

Two communities also located in Marquette county, Champion and Humboldt, illustrate the boom-bust economy of the area. Both of these began, as did Marquette, as iron ore mining towns, but both had considerably heavier concentrations of immigrants than the larger city. The Cornish came in the 1870s and 1880s to work in the mines, and the French-Canadians came a little later to cut the timber. Scandinavians, Irish, and Germans also came in significant numbers, but the massive movement to the area was that of the Finns, who began arriving in the early 1890s and soon became the dominant immigrant group.

Champion, which had one of the richest iron ore veins in the Upper Peninsula of Michigan, reached its apogee in the 1880s with a population of over 2500. By the second decade of the twentieth century, when the iron ore was exhausted and the virgin timber cut, the population had dropped to 300. The school population reflected, although somewhat less starkly, the population shifts. With an enrollment of 379 in 1882, the beginning of the boom, the attendance jumped to 528 the following year. Three years later a town hall was built with a modern library and in 1889 a newspaper was started. Also in 1889 a separate adult school was organized for men and boys who worked and could not attend regular classes. The special school charged $3 tuition per month (probably not an exorbitant fee for well-paid miners) and taught reading, writing, spelling, and arithmetic. The work there paralleled efforts in a number of communities to extend the offerings of the school beyond the traditional bounds. Disasters also struck in the boom decade, the schools closing for a substantial period of time in 1885, 1886, and 1889 for diphtheria epidemics.

By 1915 the corps of teachers had dropped from nine in 1889 to eight despite the fact that outlying schools in neighboring areas had closed and these children were sent to the remaining open schools. Truant laws were also in effect by then, unlike the earlier years. The following years indicate further construction of the school program, including the closing of the kindergarten immediately after World War I.

The tale of Humboldt, just a few miles from Champion, and also within Marquette county, is remarkably similar. The population dropped there from a high of 3000 toward the end of the nineteenth century to 325 at the time of World War I. Five very small one-and two-room schools were established there between 1880 and 1912. The children attending the first and largest were English (chiefly Cornish), French-Canadian, and Finnish. The four remaining schools had almost entirely Finnish student bodies, although the teachers were not. By 1928 the school age population had become so small that all five schools were closed, and the remaining children attended the Champion schools.

The salaries of teachers in the county schools were roughly equivalent to those in the city. Typically the teachers boarded with the families of their students. The necessity of such arrangements tended to keep the staff young and unmarried; therefore, the salaries could also be low.

The curriculum below the high school in both the county schools and Marquette was quite similar. Champion offered the only other high school work besides that of the three towns, Marquette, Ishpeming, and Negaunee, and here the difference in curriculum was great, Marquette's being much more extensive than Champion's. In recognition of the rural children attending their schools, however, Champion did include instruction in agriculture, which Marquette did not. Commercial courses and domestic and industrial arts did not penetrate the Champion curriculum until the 1920s.

The educational experiences of other Upper Peninsula communities tend to confirm that of Marquette city and county as being representative, or at least, not unique. In Baraga County (named for the first bishop of Marquette) which, unlike Marquette, had a substantial Indian population, the first formal educational offerings were in two back rooms that the missionary priest added to his church 2 years after his arrival in 1861. The arrival of teaching nuns in 1866 put the school, which chiefly enrolled Indian children, on a regular basis.

The first public school in Baraga opened in 1867, although the system remained ungraded until 1891, when 10 levels were established. Grades eleven and twelve were added in 1900. There also the period of tremendous expansion occurred in the 1880s when one teacher was responsible in 1885 to 1886 for 77 pupils ranging in age from five to twenty-one. Following the Bell-Lancastrian system (whether he knew it or not), he had the older children listen to the lessons of the younger ones in the hall of the school building while he taught other children in the schoolroom. The following year he employed a young woman from the community to assist him, and the two were able to divide the school between primary and grammar students. Despite the large numbers of students, the two teachers managed to arrange numerous school activites, including plays, concerts, skating, sledding, hay rides, baseball, and an occasional dog sled trip to a local lumber camp. Thirty-five students "graduated" from Baraga schools (from grade ten until 1911) between 1891 and 1911, and only 10 of them were boys.

The history of another Upper Peninsula community located a little farther from Marquette in Gogebic County in the western part of the state encapsulates the peculiar characteristics of a frontier town whose economy depends on its quickly depleted natural resources. Settled in 1882 and rapidly expanding after the railroad went through in 1884, Bessemer took its name from the process that converted its ore into a marketable product. Like the other communities its second major resource was lumber, but unlike Marquette the mining and timber rights to the nearby land were almost entirely owned by nonresidents, many of whom were financiers in New York City. The absence of a small, wealthy aristocracy to oversee the community's development was a particular hindrance in educational matters. Unlike Marquette where the town's leading citizen and philanthropist Peter White served on the school board for more than 50 years, Bessemer had no such local reserves on which to draw. Although the community struggled valiantly to provide good schools for its children, it had very little money on which to rely. The citizens were unwilling to approve heavier taxes for themselves when their sources of employment (the mines and the forests) were rapidly becoming depleted.

By 1885 Bessemer was beginning to assume the characteristics of a boom town, including a large number of residents who came initially without families. By 1888 the population had reached 5785, and these people were served by 18 boarding houses, 15 hotels, 48 saloons, 5 restaurants, 6 lawyers, and only 3 grocery stores. The following year it officially became a "city."

The 1890s were the great decade, and by the turn of the century, the iron and lumber were nearly gone. In 1894 the school enrollment was 255 and 2 years later 455 were attending, although there were seats for only 416. The following year 515 were expected. In 1898 two kindergarten teachers and a special music teacher were hired. Two years later a truant officer was employed at a higher salary than the teachers. Each year brought some new evidence of expansion, including night school for adults in arithmetic, penmanship, and bookkeeping in 1900, and manual training in grades one and two in 1902. Also in 1902 the University of Wisconsin assessed the curriculum and founded it strong enough to admit graduates of its high school without examination. By 1904 the voters had defeated still another bond issue to expand the schools, and although the population had declined by over 1000, the schools were very crowded. The single men who inhabited the boarding houses and hotels left when the mines closed, and the families were less eager to be uprooted.

By 1906 the first-grade children were sent to school on half sessions, since there was no room to accommodate them any other way, and in 1908 when the enrollment had reached over 1200 pupils, a new school could not be put off.

The contrast between the population of 5785 in 1888 and a school enrollment of 255 in 1894 and a population of 4538 in 1910 and the 1908 enrollment of 1249 testifies to the enormous economic problems that these communities faced in educating their children. The towns that were hardest hit were ones like Bessemer in which the population and the financial resources were unstable. Bessemer's problem was further complicated because it was a large enough community that it attempted to provide a number of educational services, besides the minimal literacy training for which the small towns could settle. As late as 1912 the high school curriculum was revised to provide a 2-year commercial course and 4-year industrial one along with the traditional 4-year college preparatory sequence. The following year the schools undertook to examine children for eye disorders and to provide special classes for the "academically deficient." The role the schools played in the community is evidenced by the formation of the "Improvement Association" in 1913 to make the schools the leading social center for the community, since few other institutions existed in the town. An opera presented at the school by 120 students several years earlier had attracted the largest audience ever established.

The varied educational efforts of communities in the Upper Peninsula of Michigan attest to the immense faith these first and second generation immigrant families placed in education. They attempted, sometimes haltingly, to provide their children —and occasionally themselves—with the rudiments of an American education they deemed essential for the twentieth century. The contrast between the efforts of these communities, none of which was really wealthy, with those in the South, dominated by native-born whites, is stark.

chapter four
butler county, alabama

In 1918 one of the earliest American educational statisticians, Leonard P. Ayres, completed a system of "index numbers" to rank state school systems on such criteria as percent of school population attending school, average daily attendance, expenditures per school age child, and salaries of teachers. By such calculations Ayres concluded that Alabama ranked fourth from the last in 1890, second from the last in 1900, fifth from last in 1910, and fourth from the last in 1918. The Carolinas, Mississippi, Georgia, and Arkansas regularly clustered close to Alabama on these lists.

The bottom quarter of Ayres' distribution was principally occupied by the states that had formed the Confederacy, thus doubtless giving rise to the familiar remark in history of education courses that Horace Mann's accomplishments in Massachusetts gradually spread west and became universal throughout the country with the exception of the south. The "exceptional" nature of the South often is interpreted principally in racial terms, namely the South's unwillingness after Reconstruction ended in the 1870s to educate black and white children in the same schools. The obligation, assumed with varying degrees of responsibility, to provide two school systems was expensive, particularly in sparsely settled areas. The rural South, especially, was not interested in investing substantial amounts of money in public education. The value of formal schooling was not apparent to most rural Southerners. Furthermore a tuition-free, publicly supported school system was frequently seen in the South in the late nineteenth century as a Yankee artifact, and as such was inimicable to Southerners, who took pains to maintain their distinctive cultural traditions. The fact that Massachusetts was an early leader in public education was enough to condemn the entire institution in the eyes of some Southeners.

The "exceptional" nature of the South, then, was that unlike the rest of the nation in the last quarter of the nineteenth century, it did not make a massive push to include more of its children in school for longer periods of time. What did happen in the South, and what is frequently minimized, was that its black population was nearly entirely illiterate in 1865 and only one third illiterate in 1910. Credit for the accomplishment belongs primarily to southern blacks, who managed to educate themselves with minimal help from their white neighbors and only a little more assistance from northern philanthropic groups. Mostly did it themselves.

As Ayres's studies showed, Alabama was in many ways representative of its region. Located in the deep South, Alabama had endured the ravages of the Civil War. Troops had marched through the countryside. The economy had been seriously disrupted, both by the inability to plant and harvest crops as well as by the difficulty of reaching markets. The population had been severely disturbed by the loss of young men in the war, by the acute and catastrophic financial reverses suffered by white landowners, and by the newly freed blacks whose economic situation was precarious. For the whites who survived one common way of dealing with the seemingly insuperable problems in Alabama was to move west, just as their ancestors had done before them in leaving South Carolina or Georgia to come to Alabama. In the late 1860s and early 1870s the letters "G.T.T."

scrawled on the door of a decrepit house became increasingly familiar, indicating that the former resident had "gone to Texas" and joined the westward emigration.

The significant emigration out of Alabama during the 1860s, combined with the deaths during the war, reduced the population growth in Alabama between 1860 and 1870 to just over 3 percent, compared with nearly 23 percent for the country as a whole. In the following years Alabama's population grew about 20 percent each decade, slightly trailing the national average except in the 1890s when the two were almost identical.

Most of the people in Alabama, both black and white, lived in rural areas. In 1890 barely 10 percent of the population lived in towns larger that 2500, and 20 years later, ones of rapid urbanization throughout the United States, the increase in Alabama had been only to 17 percent. The proportions for blacks and whites in rural and urban areas were nearly the same.

The Alabama residents in 1910 were nearly all products of the South. Less than 1 percent were foreign born, and nearly 88 percent were born in Alabama. Such a local concentration doubtless helped in the development of unanimity among the whites on such questions as education, particularly of black children. For example, the quite small number of children one or both of whose parents were foreign born led the categories in school attendance in 1910 with 78 percent of these children between ages 6 and 14 in school. The comparable figures for children of native-born whites was 70 percent and for blacks, 50 percent.

Blacks constituted 42.5 percent of the Alabama population in 1910, a proportion that had gradually declined throughout the late nineteenth and early twentieth century. It dropped precipitously around World War I when disastrous natural conditions in Alabama, the boll weevil and floods, combined with job opportunities in the North to spark a major movement of blacks to the North.

Both black and white Alabamians faced one common problem: illiteracy. On this index, as on so many other educational ones, Alabama ranked near the bottom among the states. Illiteracy among blacks had been decreasing steadily since the Civil War when it had been nearly universal. After 1832 it had been illegal in Alabama to teach slaves to read and write. White illiteracy increased after the Civil War, no doubt an indication of the turmoil in which the state found itself, the poverty affecting large numbers of the white community who were no longer able to afford to send their children to private schools, and the inadequacy of the public schools in reaching white children. By 1890 the illiteracy among the population was beginning to recede. The overall illiteracy rate among persons over ten years old in Alabama, both black and white, was 41 percent. Among whites the rate was 18 percent and among blacks, 69 percent.

A report by the Alabama Superintendent of Public Instruction to the Southern Educational Association in 1896 correlated illiteracy rates in the various states with length of the school term and found that Alabama ranked 46 in illiteracy with its 41 percent figure (the New York illiteracy rate then was 5.5 percent, Michigan's was 5.9 percent, and Indiana's was 6.3 percent) and also 46 in length of school term with 81 days (New York had 176, Michigan, 129, and Indiana, 140). By 1900 the illiteracy rate for all Alabamians over ten years old had dropped to 34 percent, and 10 years later, to 23 percent. Alabama's ranking remained roughly the same, however, in 1910, as it had been in 1890, with South Carolina and Louisiana still having higher rates of illiteracy than Alabama. The percentage of illiteracy among Alabama native-born whites was nearly 10 percent in 1910, but it was over 40 percent among blacks. Among Alabama draftees in World War I, 17 out of 100 were illiterate, compared to the national average of 7 out of 100. Perhaps most discouraging among the illiteracy figures was the realization in 1910 that even among the children aged ten to twenty, who should have been benefitting from the improved Alabama schools, 16.4 percent were unable to write. Such testimony provided a severe indictment of the Alabama school system.

One of the reasons, of course, for the poor showing in literacy in Alabama was that until 1915 Alabama had no compulsory school law. Again, Alabama was one of the last states to pass such a statute, Massachusetts having led the nation with its passage of one in 1852, and New York followed in 1853. Michigan passed similar legislation in 1871 and Indiana in 1897. Apart from the difficulty of having no law at all until 1915, the central problem in Alabama was that even after the law was passed, it was not enforced, a failing certainly not limited to Alabama. In 1919 an educational survey of Alabama noted no marked improvement in school enrollment and attendance since passage of the law 4 years earlier. Sixty-three percent of the enrolled children attended regularly, and the average daily attendance represented only 35 percent of those eligible to attend school. The school year in Alabama was 132 days long, and the average number of days attended by each pupil was 85. In all but two other states the terms were longer; in New York, for example, the average term was 190 days, with 154 days attended; in Michigan the comparable figures were 172 days and 140 days, while for Indiana they were 155 days and 127 days. Such discrepancies as these among the states, with even more pronounced differences between rural and urban communities, indicate the necessity of dealing with local or regional conditions in describing educational conditions in America between 1865 and 1918.

Probably the single most serious problem affecting education in Alabama between the Civil War and World War I was that the state was unwilling to spend enough money to create an adequate school system. The reluctance stemmed from several considerations: the concern after Reconstruction that the state and not local governmental units cling to the purse strings for educational expenditures; the belief among rural Alabamians especially that education was of limited value to them, the assumption throughout most of the nineteenth century that free public education for all children was not a southern tradition, but a dubious northern import; and the unwillingness of whites who controlled state and local government to spend significant amounts for education of blacks, particularly after 1890.

The era of Reconstruction in Alabama, like many other southern states, was characterized by profound fiscal mismanagement. Such difficulties encompassed the nascent educational system as well as other governmental activities. In the schools, however, the ramifications of the problems were severe, since Alabama had very little public educational tradition on which to build. Only Mobile, widely considered the most atypical of Alabama's cities, had a fully established school system before the war. The efforts of the "radical" Superintendent of Public Instruction, N.B. Cloud, who served from 1868 to 1870, to establish free public schools throughout Alabama were thus severely hampered by the lack of a local school structure on which to build, by the shortage of qualified teachers and suitable school buildings, and by the misappropriation of the state's school funds. Furthermore, Alabama had not kept her money gained from the sale of federal land in each section, the "sixteenth section fund," but had lost this money between statehood in 1819 and 1851. From then until after the Civil War such money that was available for education (for which only the interest was supposed to be used) was spent, both interest and principal, for current expenses. A conservative, that is, representative of the Bourbon class, took over from Cloud as superintendent of public instruction in 1870, and immediately denounced the financial policies of the Cloud regime. He was followed in 1872 by the last "radical" superintendent, whose initial act was to close the schools in 1873 because all the public money had run out. They remained shut from January to October, when they opened for a brief term. Not till the return of conservative Democratic government, after 1874, did the schools begin to function regularly.

The new constitution adopted by Alabama in 1875 established provisions for public school, and this document remained the base for government in Alabama until the 1901 constitution. The state administration, faced with developing a school system, had little previous expertise on which to draw. The initial efforts, however, were directed toward opening schools for both black and white children to provide minimum literacy training throughout Alabama. Since no local property taxes were applied to educational expenses, nearly all the public money for running the schools came from the state, the only exception being local poll taxes. In 1883 an effort to levy local taxes for school support was declared unconstitutional. (Very limited local funds could be raised, if counties voted to do so, after 1901). The state funds were divided among the counties on the basis of the number of black and white children between the ages of six and twenty-one in the counties. Initially the counties were expected to divide the funds from the state between the two races in roughly equivalent amounts based on their percentages in the population. As a result, it was a common occurrence in many Alabama counties in the late 1870s and 1880s for black teachers to be paid more than white teachers. The principal reason for this was that fewer schools were usually provided for black children and consequently there was a smaller number of black teachers to divide their portion of the allotment.

By the turn of the century the public school financial situation in Alabama was grim. Alabama was then spending about $.50 per school age child for educational purposes in contrast with the national average of $2.84. Furthermore, the white population had gradually come to support the public schools after having preferred private education for their children throughout most of the nineteenth century. The increased numbers of children attending schools and the parental interest in having adequate schools for their offspring put additional strains on the limited funds being made available by the state for public education. Finally the high school movement was beginning to win support among white patrons in towns. The development of public high schools, however, was really a phenomenon of the first two decades of the twentieth century for white students and of the third and fourth for black ones. The state legislature's decision in 1907 to set aside funds for county high schools for whites led 57 of the 67 counties to establish white high schools by 1918.

Alabama's response to these problems was characteristic of that of many southern states in the last decade of the nineteenth century. It limited opportunities for blacks. In 1890 to 1891 the legislature passed revised legislation that no longer made it obligatory to distribute money for school purposes in counties equally to blacks and whites on the basis of their respective populations. The Superintendent of Public Instruction had explained the rationale for the revision: "It is alleged that in portions of the State under our present law the colored race gets well nigh all the school fund, whilst that race pays a very small percent of the taxes that make up that fund." He continued that this was a reasonable disposition of funds since colored children "in general, (are) only capable of receiving and profiting by an elementary education which costs comparatively much less than that suitable for the white race in its more advanced stages of civilization." His advice to county superintendents was that they distribute the state funds (which were apportioned to them on the basis of the total number of children, black and white, of school age) "in proportion to the number of children who will probably attend school." The white county superintendents would assume that more whites than blacks would benefit from schools.

The results of the change in the law were predictable. In black belt countries, where the proportion of blacks was much higher than that of whites (chiefly because these had been the sites of the richest land and hence the largest plantations before the Civil War), white officials were delighted. Now it would be possible for them to divert their considerable state aid, based on their combined black and white population, largely to white schools for the small number of white children. The county superintendent of schools in Wilcox County, one of the black belt counties, reported in 1890-1891, "Wilcox never had such a boom on schools. The new law stimulated the whites so that neighborhoods where no schools had existed for years are now building houses and organizing schools. The attendance for 1892 will far exceed that of 1891."

The Wilcox superintendent's prophecy was accurate, and funds did congregate around the white schools. Although the state average monthly salaries for white and black teachers had been nearly equal in 1889 to 1890 ($23 for whites and $22 for blacks), 20 years later the effects of the new law were painfully apparent. Then the average monthly salary for white teachers was $54 and for blacks, $24. The discrepancy between white and black teachers' salaries grew so that at the end of the period (1917 to 1918), black teachers received less than half that of white teachers. This created a particular hardship for black women teachers, who outnumbered black men. Then white men teachers received an average annual salary of $473 and white women $367. The comparable figure for black men teachers was $196 and for black women, $172. The white school year averaged 132 days in 1917 to 1918, while the black averaged only 102.

In short, the whites had achieved a greatly increased share of the state funds and were now able to establish schools that were reasonably adequately funded for white children although woefully deficient for blacks. This was particularly true in the black belt counties where the discrepancy between what was spent for black and white children was greatest. For example, in Lowndes County, which is adjacent to Wilcox, in 1912 for every dollar spent on education for a black child, $33.40 was spent for a white child.

The state school system for children in Alabama was often called the "free public schools" in the late 1860s and 1870s, but by the 1880s that term had become rare, mostly because the so-called public schools were not in fact free for many children. The system of charging supplemental fees was widespread throughout Alabama well past 1918. Sometimes these additional charges were called "matriculation fees" or "tuition." In some cases they were charged of all children who wished to attend the school; in others a "free" term would exist when no fees were charged, but a "pay" term would follow during which only those children whose parents had paid the supplemental fee would attend. The more frequent occurrence was that a supplement would have to be paid each month, including the period of compulsory attendance. The amount increased considerably in the high school, where it might be as much as $5 per month. The amount of the school budget supplied by these supplements varied in 1917 to 1918 from less than 1 percent in Birmingham to 42 percent in the small south Alabama towns of Dothan and Enterprise. Such supplements were much more common in the town and city schools, which had longer terms and paid teachers more, than in the rural schools.

The lack of funds for schools was reflected in the conditions of the schools themselves. As late as 1918 no provision for bathrooms, either indoor or outdoor, was made in 29 percent of the rural schools. At the same time Mobile was the only public system in the state with a kindergarten.

The curriculum and pedagogical practices in many of the rural schools were apparently often of the same caliber as the physical facilities. Music, drawing, and vocational courses were rarely offered in the rural schools, although the county high schools, which began to be organized gradually after 1907, did often offer vocational agriculture, home economics, and manual training. Industrial and commercial subjects were not available, and the high school curriculum tended to be largely the traditional course, requiring 4 years of mathematics and emphasizing classical languages.

The teaching itself frequently left a great deal to be desired. A national committee visiting Alabama schools in 1918 to 1919 reported, "Modern ideas and methods are quite disregarded and do not apparently enter into the consideration of the majority of the teachers. The recitation is a lesson-hearing process in which the pupil is expected to memorize the material found in the textbook and repeat it. In many cases the teacher is himself unfamiliar with it, and entirely unprepared either as to subject matter or methods of instruction. He merely attempts to follow the text closely enough to find out that the pupil's effort is either successful or unsuccessful. The result is approved or disapproved without much spirit and no incentive to do better or help in ways of doing it are given to the pupil."

Little else could be expected of teachers of whom 80 percent of the white and 95 percent of the black had had no special training for their job. Teachers were licensed on the basis on examinations, which were begun in 1879. Four kinds of certificates were available, life through the third grade. A third-grade certificate could be acquired with the merest rudiments of a primary education. Often persons who had failed the third-grade examination in one county would go from county to county until they passed it in one. Manipulation of test results in favor of the applicant, often for a fee, was not unknown. As a result the educational qualifications of the teachers were minimal, and salaries reflected this. This combination of factors also hindered recruiting efforts to get able persons to join the teaching ranks and remain there. The uncertainties of the pay and supplement budgeting in many counties also discouraged individuals who might find a better livelihood elsewhere from becoming teachers in Alabama. Between 1860 and 1900 average salaries of teachers in Alabama decreased from $175 to $159 annually. Undoubtedly some of this decline is attributable to the fact that in 1900 black teachers were also being counted, and their salaries had begun their precipitous drop after 1891. By 1915 the average annual salary for teachers in the United States was $543; for teachers in the South, $328; for white teachers in Alabama, $356; and for black teachers in Alabama, $159. Broken down by race and sex for Alabama they were:

white men, $444; white women, $367 (the largest category); black men, $169; and black women, $153. Drivers of the wagons that hauled children to rural schools in Alabama then averaged about $350 a year. Such low salaries account in large part for the poor quality of education generally available in the public schools in Alabama during these years. Competent teachers who could find more remunerative positions often did so.

Of the many educational problems that Alabama faced in the last third of the nineteeth century the question of inadequately trained teachers was certainly one of the most difficult. One of the crying needs of the state was for more comprehensive teacher training programs. Given the small amount of money that Alabama appeared willing to spend on education, they were difficult to organize. The source of funds for this enterprise came from a source increasingly important to southern education, from northern philanthropists. The principal outside support for teacher training came from the Peabody Fund, originally from the largesse of George Peabody, a Massachusetts industrialist who wished to extend greater opportunities for training in pedagogy to southern teachers, mostly white. At first he gave grants to communities to assist their public school systems, both black and white, but after 1880 his grants concentrated on scholarships for attendance at normal school, usually the normal school named for him (as a result of his substantial contribution) in Nashville, Tennessee. After 1914 the remaining money in the Peabody Fund was combined with that in the Slater Fund largely through the efforts of J.L.M. Curry, an Alabamian who served as an executive for both groups.

The Slater Fund was established in 1882 through the benefaction of a Connecticut textile entrepreneur. Its money was particularly geared toward providing industrial education for blacks, such as that at Hampton Institute and Tuskeegee, and toward training black teachers. Much of its support went to private black colleges committed to these efforts. After 1911 it played an instrumental role in establishing "county training schools" for blacks. Because of adverse white public opinion to schools for blacks that provided them with traditional educations, they initially emphasized industrial education. Nonetheless, they were the antecedents of the public high schools for blacks that developed in the 1920s and 1930s.

Another philanthropic effort of a northern white to help southern blacks was the Rural School Fund, more familiarly known as the Jeanes Foundation, named for the Philadelphia Quaker woman, Anna T. Jeanes, who endowed it. Both the Peabody and Slater funds were intended for institutions that were already making a beginning on their own, but Miss Jeanes deliberately sought to help the small country schools for blacks, ones that were unlikely to attract support from either of the other two organizations. Beginning in 1909 in Alabama, the Jeanes Foundation provided teachers to work with the rural black schools providing demonstration lessons and advice on teaching, usually emphasizing industrial or vocational agricultural subjects. By 1915 the Jeanes Foundation was supporting 22 teachers in 19 counties in Alabama. Frequently after 1911 the Phelps-Stokes Fund worked closely with the Jeanes Foundation in providing assistance for rural teachers of blacks.

The General Education Board, sustained by Rockefeller money, was organized in 1903 and provided the funds to support projects of the Southern Education Board, which had been an outgrowth of a meeting at Capon Springs, West Virginia in 1898 at which Northerners and a few Southerners had discussed the educational needs of the South. The Southern Education Board, which merged officially with the General Education Board in 1914, gradually attracted support from white Southerners in positions of authority in state school systems. Together the S.E.B. and the G.E.B. provided funds for instructions in practical farming, promotion of secondary education, improving higher education, and for black schools. Unlike the other organizations, the General Education Board had a great many other interests besides education in the South, but its contribution to rural education in Alabama for whites after 1911 and for blacks after 1913 was considerable.

The greatest help to Alabama blacks, however, was the Rosenwald Fund, created by Julius Rosenwald from his Sears Roebuck earnings in 1913 and incorporated in 1917. Initially Rosenwald donated funds, generally varying from $300 to $1000, for construction of school buildings for blacks in rural counties. Rosenwald's idea was to provide a small cash subsidy for a school, and local blacks were expected to raise the necessary additional funds, provide the labor for the school, and win state support for the teacher. The system was immensely successful in providing cooperation between outside capital (Rosenwald's), local contribution from both blacks and whites, and state support. Once the schools themselves were built the problem of finding teachers to staff them, difficult though that was, was not insurmountable. The construction of the majority of these schools in the 1920s coincided with the important growth of black schools, which had struggled for funds since the 1891 decision.

A final source of philanthropy for black education in Alabama was the American Missionary Association, financed largely by northern white Congregationalist contributions. Working jointly with the Freedman's Bureau in the 1860s, the AMA turned its attention to staffing institutions for blacks, ranging from elementary schools to colleges. It supported Talladega College, which offered the only college level work available to blacks in Alabama. Its collegiate program, however, did not develop until the end of this period. In 1894 to 1895 only 6 of its 581 students were in the collegiate or professional program. Twenty years later the number had increased to 55 of the total 668 students. In both years the majority of the students at Talladega were enrolled in the elementary division (509 in 1894 and 382 in 1914 to 1915). The proportion of blacks on the faculty had grown from 5 percent (one person) in 1894 to 1895 to 29 percent (12 persons) 20 years later.

The necessity of outside money, particularly northern money, to aid black education in Alabama was acute, because it was clear from the late 1880s that public officials in Alabama were not going to divert adequate sums of public money to black schools. Two important factors influenced future developments. One was the debate over the proper kind of education for a black child: industrial versus classical, and the other was the secondary school question.

In Alabama, home state of Booker T. Washington's Tuskeegee Institute, the principle that the proper kind of education for blacks was literacy plus industrial training won vocal support from the dominant white leaders. Booker T. Washington towered above all other blacks in the eyes of the white community, and doubtless most of the blacks as well. The W.E.B. DuBois side of the dispute, that classical education was at least as important for blacks as for whites, since only with it would the black ever achieve academic and professional mobility on a par with whites, won little attention among Alabamians. Furthermore, the Washington argument was an immensely convenient one for whites to accept. Given acceptance of industrial training for blacks, whites could cogently argue that blacks did not need as much money to support their "different" type of education. Barnas Sears, the agent for the Peabody Fund, explained in perfect seriousness, "It costs less to maintain schools for colored children than for white." This widely held view was indeed accurate if one accepted the idea that the best kind of education was one that taught black children to till the soil more productively, can tomatoes more efficiently, and develop carpentry skills more carefully. Although Washington never intended his rationale for Tuskeegee to be transformed into a justification for reducing funds for black schools, which he vigorously deplored, the fact remained that the industrial-agricultural model was the one that whites, both northern and southern, accepted as the one best suited to blacks. That it could be used to justify spending less money for black schools was an unexpected but altogether desirable bonus.

Given the public unwillingness to provide adequate funds for black education in Alabama, the small amount of money that was available was devoted to elementary education. In 1879 the financial costs per pupil had been roughly equally divided between whites and black children in the state, with the blacks slightly in the lead because of the lower proportion of black children attending school than whites; the rate was $1.91 per white child and $2.10 per black child. By 1914 to 1915 the rates had become $9 per white child and $1.47 per black child. The following year in two black belt counties, Lowndes and Wilcox, the rates for white children were $35.09 and $27.72, respectively, and for black children, $1.26 and $.54. Furthermore, the state average of pupils to teachers in 1918 was 41.5 children per white teacher and 70 per black teacher. An observer in Alabama in 1919, 4 years after passage of the compulsory education law noted, "No one seems interested in enforcing the compulsory attendance act as far as Negroes are concerned." In such circumstances as these, high schools, which, of course, cost more than elementary schools, were out of the question for Alabama counties to provide for blacks.

A persistent—and totally justifiable—criticism of black schools was that teachers were poorly trained. In 1916 only the lowest-grade teaching certificate, which generally did not require the recipient to have completed a full elementary course, was held by 70 percent of the black teachers. The fact of the matter was simply that the state was not preparing blacks to become teachers for the public schools.

The least expensive type of schooling (elementary), the state provided for blacks, but the more expensive (secondary and college), it offered in steeply declining proportions. For whites, on the other hand, public education was available at the elementary, secondary, college, and university levels. By the end of the period nearly all the white students were attending public elementary schools, the large majority of those in attendance were in public secondary school, and about half the college enrollment in the publicly supported colleges. For black children, whose families ranked at the bottom of the economic scale, the majority of elementary pupils were in public elementary school, the majority of secondary students were in private schools, and all college students were in private institutions. There were no postgraduate programs in the state for blacks, although the state university provided them for whites. Nothing else illustrates more clearly the reluctance of white Alabamians to provide adequate public education for blacks.

In 1916 only two public high schools and normal schools with a full 4-year course open to blacks existed in Alabama. They enrolled a total of 224 students. The remaining 1220 black secondary students attended 72 schools under private control. Over half of these students were in schools with denominational boards. The ones that enrolled the preponderance of secondary students (574) were under white auspices, particularly the American Missionary Association and the American Baptist Home Mission Society. Most of the remainder were in independent schools. By 1918 Baptists controlled 69 percent of the black schools, and Methodists, 28 percent. The AMA had fewer but larger schools.

These figures demonstrate that the ruling whites made no serious effort to improve the quality of black education in the late nineteenth and early twentieth centuries. Doubtless this was not unrelated to the use of literacy tests for voting, which Alabama adopted after 1901. As long as free public education was not accessible to blacks, most were likely to remain illiterate, and thus could not constitute a significant voting bloc.

Butler County

Insofar as Alabama can be said to exemplify many of the characteristics of the states of the deep South, Butler County typifies many of the attributes of Alabama. Located in the south central portion of the state, its county seat, Greenville, is 40 miles southwest of the state capital, Montgomery. On its northern and western edges, Butler County is bordered by Lowndes and Wilcox counties, both distinctively black belt counties. On the eastern side of Butler is Crenshaw County, named for one of the early and still prominent families in the area.

Butler County was one of the earliest settlements in Alabama and was created by the first session of the state legislature after Alabama achieved statehood in 1819. The area had first been occupied by whites in 1815, but bloody skirmishes with the resident Creek Indians discouraged further immigration to the area until decisive white victories over the Indians in 1818. Captain Butler was killed in the Indian battle and gave his name for the county.

After the cession of some land to form Crenshaw County in 1866, Butler County included 763 square miles or 488,320 acres. A ridge runs through the county, and in the northwestern section of the county the ridge divided the land so that west of it creeks flow into the Alabama River. The river played an important role in the commerce of the county during its early history. This section of the county has the richest land and was the most prosperous area prior to the Civil War. Here the plantation economy flourished, but with the economic turbulence resulting from the Civil War, many white families were ruined financially and lost their land. The Crenshaws were one of the few who survived.

The county itself is usually classified as belonging to the "piney woods" section of the state, although just as it is on the fringe of the black belt, it is also on the edge of the "wiregrass" section. Whatever one called the land, its major enterprise was farming. In 1910 almost 70 percent of the county land was in farms, of which the largest number were between 20 and 49 acres. Almost 40 percent of the farms and nearly 65 percent of the acreage was tended by owners, while the balance was farmed by tenant farmers. There were three times as many white farmer-owners as black and nearly twice as many black tenant-farmers as white.

The value of the land in the 1880s in the county ranged considerably, the northwestern section being the most valuable and bringing $10 and in some areas, $35 an acre. In other parts of the county land sold for $2.50 to $3 an acre. Then the principal crop was cotton, with a little less than half the tilled land planted in it. The proportion of corn was increasing, partly because of a vigorous editorial campaign in the local newspaper urging farmers to diversify their crops so that a bad cotton year would not ruin them and so that they would not have to buy feed for their livestock. About 20 percent of the land was in corn and 15 percent in oats. The balance was in fruit trees and truck farming.

By 1910 cotton was still the dominant crop in the county, although corn was advancing as a strong second. Cotton declined through the decade as the boll weevil made its appearance and as labor became more scarce. Then the average price for land per acre was $9.17, one tenth the average price in Johnson County, Indiana at the same time.

The population of Butler County grew steadily but slowly after 1870, at the rate of approximately 4000 per decade, with the black population growing more rapidly than the white. The population of the county in 1860 was just over 18,000. A decade later, however, it was just under 15,000. The decline then was a result of the loss of land of Butler County to form Crenshaw County, the emigration out of the county following the war and the deaths in the war.

By 1910 the total population was just over 29,000. Blacks constituted 38 percent of the population in 1860, 43 percent in 1870, 46 percent in 1880, 48 percent in 1890, 51 percent in 1900, and 52 percent in 1910. The emigration of blacks from Butler County, like the rest of Alabama, began about 1915, and by 1930 the number of blacks declined to just over 48 percent of the population. The number of blacks of school age was higher proportionately than the whites so that school population figures show a slightly higher proportion of blacks than the overall population reports.

One of the most interesting features of the population was the small but significant group of Jewish families in Butler County. Probably never numbering more than two dozen families, they came mostly from Germany, both before and after the revolution of 1848. Generally they went into merchandising, particularly the dry goods business, occasionally going into banking. Their stores were located in Greenville and in the outlying countryside, one of the oldest settlements in the county being "Steiner's Store." These families intermarried to a considerable extent, and in the late nineteenth century the names Flexner, Lichten, Greenhut, Ezekiel, and Steinhart were among the most prominent businessmen in the area. In the 1890s their children dominated the Honor Roll of the Greenville public schools. They maintained a distinct social life in Butler County, often giving an annual Purim Ball in the 1870s. The 1874 ball was described in the local paper: "The Jews of this city had a grand Purim ball on Tuesday night. As is usual with them, neither taste nor energy was spared to make the occasion a pleasant one and the ball successful. We presume that their anticipations were fully realized. The attendance was large, and the enjoyment general. The proceeds of the ball will be sent to the Cleveland orphan asylum." The Jews declined in numbers later in the century, and often the Butler Jews would then join with the Montgomery Jewish community for social occasions and religious observances. The Montgomery rabbi also came to Greenville when necessary for weddings or funerals. Annual notices appeared in the local newspaper listing the stores closed in observance of Rosh Hashanah and Yom Kippur, frequently accompanied with the editor's note wishing a "happy new year." One of the Jews, Abe Lehman, whose family ran a fruit and candy store, was a prominent Populist and editor in the mid-1890s of one of the leading Populist newspapers, *The Living Truth.*

Butler County generally was Democratic in its political alignments until the 1890s when agrarian populism gained a stronghold in the county. Reconstruction government in Alabama, of course, brought Republican control to Butler County from 1865 to 1874, but this could scarcely be called popular among whites in the county. J. B. Little, the historian of Butler County, writing in 1885, reported that during Reconstruction, "Every office was . . . filled by an officer against the will of the majority of the most intelligent citizens of the county."

The intense resentments of the whites to the Reconstruction government often expressed itself in attitudes toward blacks in the community. The *Greenville Advocate,* unswerving in its conservative Democratic loyalties, reported in 1873 the inquiry of a black Congressman from Alabama, Jere Haralson, asking what was being done to stimulate emigration from Africa, as well as Europe. The *Advocate* had been frequently enthusiastic about encouraging Europeans to come to Butler County to augment the population losses suffered by the war and subsequent western migration. The *Advocate's* enthusiasm did not extend to black Africans, however: "So it appears that the Hon. (?) Jere wants a little more African leaven in the Radical lump. He need not give himself any unnecessary trouble about this. White supremacy in this country, now, henceforth and forever is as certain as fate. The present anomalous relation of the races in some portions of the South is bound to yield to a more rational and healthful order of things. The best that Sambo can do is *ease himself down* as comfortably as possible and give way to the race which is bound to rule this earth until a new creation shall have produced a superior one. It is not a spirit of unkindness or prejudice towards the negro which prompts the utterance of this opinion; but a calm view of the whole subject in the light of philosophy, ethnology, and the inexorable logic of historical facts."

The criticism of blacks extended to Northerners as well, as evidenced by the *Advocate's* comment in 1872 about a fire ("the greatest perhaps of the century") in Boston, home of abolitionism. The *Advocate* observed, "We are not glad, but we can not say that we feel sorry *much.*"

When Reconstruction government passed from Butler County, the residents elected to Congress from their district a Butler County native, Hilary A. Herbert, the most prominent political figure to emerge from the county. He served first in the House of Representatives and later as Secretary of the Navy during Grover Cleveland's second administration. Herbert was the son of the couple who established one of the first schools in Butler County before the Civil War. After spending his childhood in Greenville, Herbert spent a brief period at the University of Alabama, where he was expelled as a result of some campus pranks, and then completed his college work at the University of Virginia. He fought in the Civil War, returned wounded in 1864 to practice law in Greenville, and left several years later to establish a law practice in Montgomery. In Montgomery he became well-acquainted with a local banking family, the Lehmans, who named their youngest son, Herbert, for him. The Lehmans, like Herbert, also left Alabama, but settled in New York where Herbert Lehman followed his namesake in a successful career in Democratic politics. From Montgomery Hilary Herbert was elected to national office, and by the end of the century became one of the leading spokesmen on the legitimate role of blacks in southern society as president of the Southern Society for the Promotion of the Study of Race Conditions and Problems in the South. He disapproved the disfranchisement that resulted from the 1901 Constitution, stating that it would give rise to the two-party system in Alabama, an abhorrent notion to a life-long Democrat.

The shattering of the established social order in Butler County by the war distressed some whites, but certain results pleased others, such as J.B. Little, the historian of the county who attended the University of Alabama in the 1880s and returned to teach in the county. He observed in 1885, "Since the late war the higher circles are not controlled by the so-called aristocrats, and any person who is honest and worthy of respect is now permitted to enter the social circles without further restriction."

Such sentiments indicated a nourishing environment for the subsequent populist strength in the county. Throughout the 1890s the populists were strong in Butler County. In 1890 Ruben Kolb, the former state agricultural commissioner and leader of the Alabama populists, had found strong support in Butler County in his candidacy for governor on the Democratic ticket. In the 1892 election, in which Kolb was a candidate for governor on the populist ticket, Butler County supported him, as it did again in 1894. In 1896 when Kolb was no longer a candidate, Butler County again supported the populist ticket.

Greenville, the county seat of Butler County, was a quiet, well-tended small community with a population growing from just over 2000 at the beginning of the period to nearly 3400 in 1910. The surrounding areas of Greenville brought its total population in 1910 to almost 5400, nearly the same as Franklin, Indiana. The Montgomery and Mobile line, which subsequently became part of the Louisville and Nashville Railroad, was the source both of much convenience but also of considerable consternation to local residents, who objected to its exorbitant freight rates. For example, the freight charges for sending 27 cookstoves from Mobile to Greenville was $127 and from Troy, New York to Mobile, $44.62. Since the railroad had a monopoly on service, and since the meager roads of the county were nearly impassable in all but the driest weather, the cotton farmer had little choice but to use it in order to get his product to market.

The community was heavily Protestant, the earliest church being the Presbyterian, established in 1826. The church was never large or prosperous, but always included some of the most influential persons in the community. After 1873 services were held only once a month, but in the late 1890s the church had a spurt of growth and organized a regular Sabbath School.

The two most important churches in the community and in the county were the Methodist and the Baptist, both of which had offshoots, such as the Methodist Protestants and the Primitive Baptists. The Methodists reputedly had the "finest" church in Greenville and 235 members in 1885.

Blacks always attended separate churches, which held separate conventions and were completely isolated from the white churches, although doctrinally very closely related. The African

Methodist Episcopal Zion Church in Greenville was the strongest black church in the county, although many others were scattered throughout the countryside.

In 1885 there were at least 76 functioning churches in the county, both black and white, with the heavy preponderance either Methodist or Baptist. Only the ones in Greenville held services weekly, but the others all had at least monthly gatherings. By 1915 Greenville had regular services in a Christian Church, an Episcopal (established in 1860), and once per month in the Roman Catholic church, built in 1905. The Catholics were never more than a very small congregation, the largest group probably having been the Irish railroad workers resident in the county briefly in the early 1860s. A very energetic Jesuit missionary from Mobile served Greenville irregularly in the early years of the century. He interested a wealthy New Yorker in the community, and when his wife died, he gave funds to build the church and name it for her, thus creating St. Elizabeth's.

One of the leading activities in the community throughout this period were the annual Sunday School Conventions. These were "Union" conventions so that Protestants gathered for several days of hymn singing, Bible lessons, and general frivolity. They were widely publicized and heavily attended.

The churches in Butler County were less likely than those in Marquette or Johnson Counties to sponsor lecturers or to present programs of nonreligious content. These churches emphasized their religious or denominational activities and focused their attention on groups such as the Women's Missionary Alliance or the Sunday School Conventions.

One of the major vehicles for informing the citizens of Butler County was the newspaper, and the *Greenville Advocate,* which began publication in 1865 and continued as a weekly throughout the period, was the leading paper of the area. The editor and founder, J.B. Stanley, was well known among Alabama editors, of whose press association he served several terms as president. In 1883 the *Advocate* was named the best-edited weekly newspaper south of Ohio at the Louisville Exposition. It reportedly had a larger circulation than any other weekly paper in the state by the late 1870s.

Stanley was a Methodist and a Mason, and both his affiliations received prominent treatment in the paper. Very little international news was covered, although Father Gapon and Bloody Sunday in St. Petersburg in 1905 received considerable attention. As a rule, the paper emphasized local Greenville, Butler County, Lowndes County, and other south Alabama events. It commented critically on actions of the state and of the federal governments as they affected local people. During this period the paper did not run official editorials, but unsigned pieces that commented on current issues.

The paper included serialized fiction, of dubious literary merit, regularly throughout the nineteenth century. It also occasionally summarized the contents of such magazines as *Scribner's* and the *St. Nicholas Magazine* (for children). It was much less inclined to print articles or excerpts from other prominent papers, as was the wont of the *Franklin Democrat*. The *Advocate* took local issues very seriously and concentrated on them.

A number of other newspapers were organized in the late nineteenth and early twentieth centuries, but only two were of significant duration, the *South Alabamian* and *The Living Truth*. The former was published intermittently before the Civil War and again afterward. Apparently it could not compete effectively with the *Advocate*, and it closed down in 1876. *The Living Truth* was born of the populist enthusiasm in Butler County in the 1890s, and it presented an alternative to the monolithic conservative Democratic view of the *Advocate* from the early 1890s until World War I.

Butler County residents who sought more information about the wider world than the local newspapers provided were forced to rely on the supply of local bookstores or to order materials from either Mobile or Montgomery bookstores, both of which advertised in the *Advocate*. As early as 1873 the proprietor of the local bookstore proposed that a circulating library of current fiction be established, but again nothing seemed to come of it. In 1886 a local schoolmaster urged the establishment of a public library, but no action was taken. In 1894, the YMCA, which was then a popular local organization, began collecting books to form the basis of a public library, but again the library did not materialize. By 1918, Butler County still had no public library, the only collection of books being the very meager one in the school that state funds had made possible. Finally, in 1932 a local white women's club did establish a circulation library for themselves and their friends, and in February 1970 this collection, increased with the addition of some reference books from the state, formed the first public library in Butler County. It also serves residents of adjacent Lowndes County, which still (1974) has no public library.

The absence of a public library, particularly in a community that was not on the whole prosperous and therefore could not be counted on to buy books and magazines, was a serious limitation on the educational opportunities available to Butler County residents. The newspapers' intensely local emphasis also made it difficult for its readers to extend their horizons through it. The other remaining avenue for cultural enlightenment for adults was likely to be the social activities, but in Butler County these were more likely to be balls than reading clubs. There is no evidence today that any appreciable educational or cultural activities affected significant numbers of adults in Butler County between 1865 and 1918.

Secret organizations for white men, particularly the Masons and the Odd Fellows, were prominent in Butler County in the late nineteenth and early twentieth centuries. White women seemed to concentrate their energies on the United Daughters of the Confederacy and the Temperance Movement. Much of the entertainment in the community was provided by local groups, such as the Greenville Histrionics. An art association was initiated in 1878, but does not seem to have played a long or significant role in the community. In the 1880s the Claytonian Literary Society presented public debates on subjects such as "Is Ambition a Vice or a Virtue?" By the turn of the century the Young Ladies Literary Club was reading Ben Jonson and books dealing with Elizabethan England. The social activities of blacks are difficult to document, since the white newspaper did not record them and Butler County had no black newspaper.

Initially outside lecturers did not draw large audiences. The local paper commented it was "sorry to see so few in attendance" at a lecture on Irish-American humor in 1877. When the circus came, however, a crowd of over 2000 persons appeared.

Greenville apparently became a regular stop on the Chautauqua circuit by 1894 and continued to be until at least 1915. The stops were usually for one week, and $2 admission for adults was charged for the entire series. The extent to which these occasions were distinctly educative or chiefly social, like the Sunday School Conventions, is difficult to ascertain. A similar problem appears in assessing the role of the end-of-year expositions presented by the students in the various local private schools in the 1870s and 1880s and by the public school pupils in the 1890s. At the heyday of these performances in the 1880s the schools would sometimes hold six or seven consecutive nights of programs by the students, all of which would be widely attended. The small children would give musical selections or little plays the first evening, gradually leading up to the oldest students, who would also give musical performances, but in addition would give declamations or speeches of their own authorship. The popularity of these occasions with the local public testified primarily to the age-old interest in seeing one's family and friends perform.

Formal Education in Butler County

In Butler County more than in any of the others the schools assumed responsibility, nearly unilaterally, for the educational activities of the community, and they, of course, concentrated their attentions on the very young. Since the churches, newspapers, and social groups did not engage regularly in endeavors that could be termed "educational," and since the area lacked that crucial institution for self-education, a public library, the schools bore the responsibility for the education of the Butler County populace. Therefore, once a child reached the age of ten or twelve, formal education was likely to cease, and informal education was haphazard at best.

The effectiveness with which the schools performed their mission can be gauged by looking at the literacy figures. In 1900, 37 percent of the adult population was illiterate, and 10 years later the figure had been reduced to 28.5 percent. In both cases the Butler County figures were about four percentage points higher than the state average, a difference that could be substantially attributed to the black population of the county, which was higher proportionally than the state's average, and which consistently ran a higher proportion of illiterates than whites. In 1910 almost 10 percent of the Butler County white population and 43 percent of the black was illiterate. The most direct indicator of the schools' ability to reach students was the percentage of illiterates between the ages of ten and twenty. In 1910, this was 19 percent, compared to the state average of 16.4 percent. These were persons who should have learned to read and write in the schools in the first decade of the twentieth century. In 1913 Butler County ranked 21 among the 67 counties in Alabama in literacy. The ones at the bottom of the ranking were ones with large black populations for whom the county had not provided adequate public schools.

An explanation for the relatively high illiteracy in the county can be found by examining the school attendance figures for the same period. In 1910 only 59.5 percent of the children in the county between the ages six and fourteen were enrolled in school. In Butler County, as in Johnson and Marquette, the urban-rural difference was pronounced, and in Alabama this was particularly true for blacks. In 1910, for example, 60 percent of the black children eligible were enrolled in Greenville, although the overall county figure for blacks was only 47 percent. Unfortunately for blacks' educational opportunities, the majority of them (more than 85 percent) lived in the country. The difference for white children, 20 years after funds no longer had to be divided proportionately among the races, was much less; 75 percent of the whites in the county and 79 percent of the whites in Greenville were enrolled in school. Most startling, however, was the discrepancy between the county-wide and Greenville literacy rates in 1910. Then just over 4 percent of the adults in Greenville were illiterate, although the county figure was 28.5 percent. In towns literacy was relatively easy to acquire and an important enough skill that most people achieved it. In rural areas, on the other hand, it was more difficult to get and not necessary for daily life.

Butler County had had schools of one kind or another since its earliest years. The best-established early school was that founded by Hilary Herbert's parents, Thomas and Dorothy Herbert, in 1846, although a number of other academic ventures preceded and followed it. The 1860 census of Butler County revealed a number of persons who listed themselves as teachers. The war years themselves, of course, severely disrupted formal schooling in the county, but apparently even then the Crenshaw children were attending classes fairly regularly with a local school master. A night school for blacks to teach literacy was also reported in Greenville during the war.

The major educational effort, however, came after the Civil War in Butler County. Throughout the Reconstruction period the schools, like nearly all other social institutions, were in a state of confusion. Until 1874, only two annual reports on public education in Butler County were filed, one for 1869 showing an average school year of 89 days with an enrollment of 103 white children and 10 black children, and a much more complete one for 1870 to 1871. Then, 842 white children and 263 black children were enrolled, with average daily attendance reported of 712 and 185. Teachers were paid an average of $70 per month for whites and $52 per month for blacks for a school year that extended a little less than 3 months. Reconstruction ended in Butler County in 1874, and beginning that year a dramatic increase in school enrollment and attendance occurred. In Butler County, as throughout the rest of the state, teachers' complaints for back pay continued to trouble the county superintendent throughout the 1870s.

By 1874 the school scene in Butler County had become relatively stable. For the next 15 years the school populations remained about the same size, although the number of whites declined slightly and the number of blacks increased. An important characteristic of education in Butler County was a confusion about the distinction between public and private schools.

The lack of clarity in distinguishing between public and private schools in the county appeared in the selection of county superintendnents of schools. Normally such a position assumed an exclusive commitment to the public educational system, since such an officer was responsible for staffing and paying the teachers in the public schools. Generally a county superintendent accepted a responsibility to lobby in his district for support for the public schools and in his state for additional funds for public education in his county. In Butler County, however, the situation was different. There the early superintendents were all affiliated with private educational ventures, and one can only assume that their allegiance to public education was mixed.

The first county superintendent had been the founder of the earliest private school for young ladies. The next taught in the Greenville Male Academy, a private institution. In the middle and late 1870s when the public schools were becoming firmly established in Butler County, the county superintendent was J. M. Thigpen, who had taken over Herbert's school during the war, had directed the Greenville Female Academy (an offshoot of Herbert's) during the 1860s and early 1870s, and by the mid-1870s when he was county superintendent, was also engaged in establishing a new private school for boys and girls, the South Alabama High School. By the end of the decade he had become principal of one of the two leading private schools in the county, the Baptist South Alabama Female Institute, and he was still county superintendent of schools. Teachers seeking positions in the Butler County public schools were notified to seek Thigpen in his office at the South Alabama Female Institute next to the Baptist Church on Saturdays. Since the Baptist school was generally engaged in a fierce rivalry with the Methodists for students, it is difficult to imagine that Thigpen was actively urging prosperous whites to send their children to the public schools. Until that group began to support the public schools they would be severely handicapped by woefully inadequate funds. A local minister, W. H. Morris, succeeded Thigpen as superintendent, and he was followed by J. B. Little, whose primary professional commitment was also to the South Alabama Female Institute, of which he had become principal.

Another element confusing the distinction between public and private education in Butler County was the system of paying tuition to attend the public schools. Apparently this practice was not widely followed in the rural areas of the county, but in Greenville it was universally accepted. In 1898 to 1899 tuition provided 15 percent of the funds for the white schools and 2 percent of the funds for the black schools. In 1900 to 1901 the monthly fee rate ranged from $.50 per month per child in grades one and two to $2 per month per child in grades nine to eleven.

Throughout the 1870s and most of the 1880s discussion of the public schools was conspicuous by its absence from the local newspapers and from the history of Butler County, written by J. B. Little in 1885. J. B. Stanley filled his columns in the Greenville *Advocate* with detailed summaries of events occurring at some of the county and nearby private schools but until the late 1880s he scarcely mentioned the public schools. The scattered extant issues of the *South Alabamian* for that period revealed the same lack of interest in public education. Little, who himself was very much interested in schools as evidenced by his term as county superintendent and by his principalship of the local Baptist school, failed to devote a single section to education in his history, despite the volume's more than 250 pages and 59 chapters on such varied topics as stores, railroads, medical profession, churches, and voting precincts.

What Little did report on the state of education in the County was gloomy: "The people are not as much aroused upon the subject of education as their interests demand, and it is sincerely hoped that they will soon arouse themselves from their apparent lethargy, in order that they may be in harmony with the efforts now being made by the State to advance the cause of education and to extend its enlightening influences to the masses of the people." In his descriptions of the tiny communities scattered through the county Little invariably added a comment about the schools, nearly always critical. In Dead Falls they were "generally poor," "not what they ought to be" in Shackelville, "very poor" in Starlington, "sorry" in Garland, "not near what they ought to be" in South Butler, "very ordinary" in Bear's Store, and "of low order of excellence . . . as they are nearly all over the county" in Sardis. He praised the Methodist and Baptist schools in his home community of Forest Home, one of the most prosperous in the county, and J. M. Thigpen's academy in Georgiana. The single village whose public schools he found reasonably good was the one nonfarm one, Bolling, whose residents mostly worked in the factory there. Possibly there the residents recognized the need for a more adequate education for their children than the farm families did.

Throughout the 1870s and the 1880s the state funds for education were allocated to the white and black schools on roughly the proportion of the two races in the school population as the law required. Therefore, in 1888 to 1889 white schools received $4447 and black ones received $3157 to maintain their schools. Since whites then constituted 54 percent of the school population and received 58.5 percent of the available funds, the distribution was almost equitable. Generally in this period a slightly higher proportion of the black school population enrolled than the whites, but the whites were a little more regular in attendance. The reported percent of attendance was higher for both blacks (62 percent) and whites (73 percent) in 1873 to 1874 than it was in 1888 to 1889 (58 percent for blacks and 61 percent for whites).

Between 1873 to 1874 and 1888 to 1889 the average daily attendance for whites increased by 50 percent and doubled for blacks in Butler County. During this same period the school populations themselves grew by 8 percent for whites and by nearly 25 percent for blacks. The financial plight of the county was apparent from the fact that the average monthly salaries remained approximately the same, $20 for white teachers in 1874 to 1875 and $21 for black teachers then. Fifteen years later the salaries were reversed. The school days per year had dropped from 90 days in the white school and 99 in the black to 63 in the white and 68 in the black. Despite the substantially larger number of children regularly attending school the number of teachers had only increased by 24, of whom 18 were for the black schools. Thus the pupil/teacher ratio increased from 26 per white teacher and 35 per black teacher in 1874 to 42 and 61, respectively, 15 years later. An educational crisis was clearly in the making.

The nature of the crisis was apparent to any alert Butler County observer. More blacks and whites were spending more time in schools than previously. The potential black student population was growing more rapidly than the white. The white Methodist and Baptist schools in the county were in financial difficulty, a problem that would be heightened by the depression of the 1890s, which hit Butler County hard. Should the private schools close, their pupils would naturally expect to attend the public schools. Since funds for the black and white public schools were by law required to be divided evenly between the races on the basis on their school-age population, the amount for black schools would inevitably increase as the number of black children in the county grew, and consequently the amount for white schools, already grossly inadequate, would be even less. To make matters worse, whites in Butler County, led by the editor of the newspaper, were coming to recognize the necessity of improving the educational opportunities (for whites only, of course) in the community as a means of attracting new residents.

Gradually a solution to the dilemma began to emerge, and it lay not in Greenville, but in Montgomery. It was an obvious remedy and one that was coming to white legislators afflicted with similar problems throughout the South: change the law so that the state funds could be appropriated to the white and black schools at the discretion of the county superintendent, always a white. By this means it became possible for counties with substantial black populations, like Butler County, to divert the funds formerly apportioned to the black schools to the white ones. This created an adequate budget for most white schools, thus postponing the unpopular decision to raise additional school funds locally. The results for the blacks' schools were catastrophic.

In Greenville the situation resolved itself absolutely according to the formula. The year after the legislature passed the amended law permitting allocation of funds at the superintendent's discretion, Greenville began to build a large brick public school for whites at the phenomenal cost (for Greenville) of $15,000. In the spring of 1893 the school was completed. The intense rivalries between the Baptists and Methodists remained to be dealt with, but these were resolved in a satisfactory manner. Both schools closed, and the principal of the Methodist one became the new superintendent of schools, now a full-time position. A former principal of the Baptist school became the new principal of the high school. Both the Methodists and the Baptists sold their schools' furniture to the public school and converted their schools into parsonages, all to the general approval of the community. The *Advocate* noted that the formal endorsements of the public school by both the Methodists and the Baptists brought Greenville one large school. "Let us hope," the *Advocate* continued, "that it will ever be so conducted that the utmost satisfaction will result and there may never be cause for the establishment of any sectarian school again." It concluded by noting that the new school had taken for its motto "In union there is strength."

Although the *Advocate* could report with pride the strides made for white public education in Greenville in the 1890s, it could not report similar gains for blacks. In fact, the advances for whites were made largely at the expense of blacks, whose share of public funds steadily declined from the early 1890s. Perhaps the ultimate irony was that after all the denominationally supported private schools for whites closed in the county, largely because the public schools were now providing a satisfactory education for white children, the blacks found it necessary to establish both a Methodist and a Baptist school for their children. Just as in the white community, these schools were established because of dissatisfaction with the quality of education available in the public schools and because the public schools did not offer work at the high school level. At least in the white community there were some families who could afford to pay tuition to send their children to these schools, but in the black community there was no wealth.

By 1898 to 1899 the discrepancy in allocation of funds was readily apparent. Blacks, who then made up 40 percent of the enrollment (and a higher proportion of the school population) received only 23 percent of the funds. Another index of the reduced public money available to Butler County blacks was the average salaries received by teachers. Having been nearly identical in 1888 to 1889, 10 years later white teachers were averaging $28 per month and blacks, $22.

By 1917 to 1918 the gap was enormous. A little more than 5 years after the crucial decision affecting allotments, whites, who were now a minority in the county, were able to pay their teachers substantially more than the state average. Furthermore, the voters defeated by a small majority a proposal to increase local taxes for school purposes, and whites no longer found it necessary for patrons to pay supplemental fees for their children in the schools.

The fiscal vitality of the white schools in the county sharply contrasted with the nearly destitute black schools, where teachers were necessarily being paid considerably below the state averages. Figures reveal starkly the discrepancy between black and white schools in Butler County and their deviation from state averages, to which they had always been quite close in the nineteenth century. In 1917 to 1918 the 24 white male teachers averaged $801 annually; the 86 white female teachers, $456; the 16 black male teachers, $107; and the 30 black female teachers, $141.

Further indication of the limited educational opportunities for blacks in Butler County was the length of the school year. In all but Greenville, it was 60 days, less than half the white school year. The white school year nearly corresponded to the state average, but the black was more than 40 days less. Finally, a public high school was available in Greenville, beginning in the 1890s, but none was open to blacks throughout the county.

One explanation doubtless given by whites in Butler County for the low salaries of black teachers was that they were not as competent as white teachers. On the basis of the kinds of certificates each held, such an argument could be maintained, although the differences were not marked. Both whites and blacks had more teachers with second-grade certificates than any other kind, and the next most common for both whites and blacks was the bottom certificate, third grade. Whites, however, had nearly 40 percent with either first grade or life, while blacks had barely a quarter with first grade and none with life certificates. Adequate qualifications of teachers had been a persistent problem in Butler County. Except for the men, who were generally principals, it was rare to find a college graduate among the teachers, unusual to find a normal school graduate, and common to find someone who had completed a local school (not including high school) and had passed the teacher's examination with a third-grade certificate. In 1918, for example, only 12 of the white teachers had graduated from normal school. Through future study, often sponsored by the Teachers' Reading Circle, which became widespread in Alabama about 1910, or through participation in Teachers' Institutes, which began regularly in the 1880s and were greatly stressed in county superintendents annual reports, teachers gradually advanced through the grades of the certificates. Since teaching was so poorly paid, however, there was little incentive to remain in the field, and many talented persons either left teaching altogether or teaching in Alabama. That left a permanent majority of young, inexperienced, and untrained persons supervising the classrooms.

Integrally related to the shortage of trained teachers was the lack of high schools in the county. Butler County was one of only 10 in the state in 1918 that did not have a white county high school, most of which had been organized after 1907 when state funds became available for that purpose. After the demise of the Methodist and Baptist institutes in 1893, the one high school for whites in the county was in Greenville. By 1895, 300 pupils were enrolled and separate teachers were provided for grades one to four. Grade five was divided between "A" and "B" sections, doubtless evidence that this was a cluster point where children who were not making satisfactory progress through the school were retained. One teacher took care of grades six and seven, and another (the only male teacher) was responsible for the high school.

Predictably the high school was small, the result of high attrition rates in the elementary grades. In 1900 there were six graduates, all girls, and in 1910 four girls received diplomas and two others received certificates. In 1913 seven girls and two boys completed the course and were awarded diplomas. Two years later the previously totally classical curriculum was amended to include manual training and domestic science. By 1917 to 1918 the Greenville public schools provided a separate teacher for each of the first seven grades, but the high school was still small enough to be supplied by only an assistant and the principal. The superintendent probably did some teaching in addition to his administrative duties.

The extremely small number of young people who graduated from Greenville High School, although indicative of the educational attainments of the Butler County population, did not include those youngsters whose parents sent them away to private boarding school for their high school course. Although these probably never amounted to more than a dozen or so a year, they did reflect the southern preference for private education when possible.

The Methodist institution, Greenville Collegiate Institute, was founded in 1872 and almost immediately attracted strong support. By 1874 its enrollment was 110, and it offered work, theoretically, from primary through "collegiate" grade. Tuition for the 40-week session was $10 in the primary, $25 in the intermediate, $35 in the academic, and $45 in the collegiate departments. Boarding with private families was available for $15 per month for nonresidents. Instruction was offered, in addition to the customary subjects, in music, art, wax work, philosophy, ancient and modern languages, and calisthenics. In 1880 to 1881 the study of agriculture for boys was introduced. Although both boys and girls could attend the school, it kept them in separate departments, averring, apparently in keeping with the preference of its patrons, that it was NOT a coeducational institution. In 1883 it closed the school year with exercises, chiefly composed of musical entertainments and declamations provided by the student body of about 180, that ran for one full week. Three girls received diplomas on the last night of the festivities, which drew large crowds. Four years later the closing exercises were again elaborate and concluded with diplomas being awarded to two girls.

The Baptist school in Greenville, generally called the South Alabama Female Institute and the Greenville Male High School, provided strong competition to the Methodist one. Led by the redoubtable J. M. Thigpen and later by J. B. Little, at the times respectively, that they were also county superintendents of education, the Baptist institution was in reality one school, but in order to avoid being coeducational kept the boys in the theoretically separate Greenville Male High School. It was an outgrowth of the Herberts' Greenville Female School, established in 1846, but passed through various names and sponsorship. Its fees and curriculum were very similar, of necessity, to those of the Methodist Institute. The number of graduates, mostly girls, was also small, usually no more than two or three per year.

Several dozen other private schools existed in the county in the last third of the nineteenth century, but most of these had very short lives. Many were primary schools; a few called themselves "academies," but most of their instruction was at the primary and elementary level instead of the secondary level. One pair was born of Baptist and Methodist rivalry in the mid-1880s in the relatively affluent section of Forest Home. These were almost all established after the Civil War and had expired by the turn of the century. By 1917 to 1918 no private school for whites was left in Butler County.

Ironically, the only private schools left in Butler County by 1917 to 1918 were for blacks, the segment of the population least able to afford them. Like the white community in earlier decades, one was sponsored by Methodists and the other by Baptists. The Methodist, Lomax-Harron High and Industrial School, was by far the stronger. Founded in 1898, probably as a result of the diminishing educational opportunities for blacks in the county, by the African Methodist Episcopal Zion Church, it provided the only secondary level training for blacks in the county. In 1915 its enrollment (coeducational) was reported as 237, although when visited by a group representing the U.S. Bureau of Education, only 137 were in attendance of whom 113 were in one of the eight elementary grades and 24 were in the two secondary grades. The all-black staff included five women and three men, whose combined salaries amounted to

$1400. Nearly a third of the students boarded at the school. The Board of Education of the AME Zion Church provided nearly half the annual income for the maintenance of the school (then just over $4000), and tuition and fees made up nearly one fourth. The Lomax-Harron School was the only beneficiary in the county of outside philanthropy, having received in 1913 to 1914 $500 from the Julius Rosenwald Foundation. The school had a small library, a rarity for a school in Alabama for much of this period, estimated in value at $500. The visiting team, although pleased with the school as a whole, believed that the gardening and industrial training should be made more effective, that the limited domestic science equipment should be used for the girls' instruction, and that the school work in general should "be better adapted to the needs of the community." Whether this was simply an extension of the dominant view of the times that blacks should receive educations that fit them for farming and simple crafts instead of an education that would provide more vocational possibilities is impossible to determine.

By 1917 to 1918 Lomax-Harron had grown to 276, with twice as many girls in both the elementary and secondary division as boys. In the latter there were 16 boys and 32 girls. The boarding students had increased by more than 30 students, probably an indication that the school was rather well regarded among blacks in the Butler County vicinity. The number of teachers remained the same, eight.

The other black school in the county, South Alabama Baptist College, was supported by the local black Baptist association. The name was a grandiose title for "a poorly managed elementary day school" taught in 1914 to 1915 by the local Baptist pastor and his wife for 48 students at the elementary level. Its annual income for 1913 to 1914 was $578, most of which went for the teachers' salaries. It had little equipment and poor facilities in general. It offered no work in gardening or industrial training. By 1917 to 1918 it reported an enrollment of 146 students, five of whom (four girls and one boy) were at the secondary level. By that date it had added residential facilities and had 20 boarding students. Four women then composed the teaching staff.

To conclude discussions of education in Butler County with the pathetic South Alabama Baptist College, which offered no college work and very little at the secondary level, is to point to the desperate need in Alabama for both blacks and whites, but particularly for blacks, to have the government allocate more funds for education of the young of the state. A study by the Russell Sage Foundation in 1918 concluded that Alabama spent less local property taxes on its schools than any other state in the Union, a fact well known to any student of Alabama educational history. The study's conclusion however, was less familiar, namely that there was no doubt that Alabama was wealthy enough to raise its taxes—and increase its educational expenditures—if it wanted to. It wanted to, but only a little, and although Alabama's educational expenditures increased and consequently its school facilities improved in the the next decades, the position of Alabama relative to the rest of the nation did not change appreciably.

new york city, new york

J ohnson, Marquette, and Butler Counties differed in many ways, but they were united in one respect; each experienced some emigration of its rural residents to towns and cities in the late nineteenth and early twentieth centuries. The pull of the cities was strong, both for Americans and for emigrants from Europe, and many eagerly exchanged the green acres for the gray blocks in expectation of greater opportunities available in the city. For many this simply meant a better paying job, but among the wider range of activities of the cities were many distinctively educational ones. But in the city as in the rural areas and small towns the center of educational activity remained the school. Schools did not provide all the educational activities in the city, but to most urban dwellers, both children and adults, they were monumentally significant.

For the very large proportion of the city population who were either immigrants, or their children, the only social institution remotely competing with the school for educational attention was the social settlement. Its leaders were fond of speaking of their institution with the Marxist metaphor of the state, of its ultimate "withering away." Lillian Wald, founder of the Henry Street Settlement in New York, expressed her view: "The

143

stronghold of our democracy is the public school. This conviction lies deep in the hearts of the social enthusiasts who would keep the school free from the demoralization of cant and impure politics and restore it to the people, a shrine for education, a center for public uses." Her colleague at Hull House in Chicago, Jane Addams, shared this commitment to the centrality of the public school. Addams' work with John Dewey in Chicago in the 1890s intensified her zeal for schools.

The poverty and foreignness of city life with their attendant publicity were important factors in drawing attention to schools. The informal coalition of social workers and journalists who popularized these problems had a common faith in the power of the ideal school to remedy the evils they saw about them. Such a faith in education was typical of reformers who sought Band-Aid solutions to systemic infections. It led publicists to urge the schools to improve their programs so that the poor would be less poverty stricken and the immigrants less alien.

Many of these reformers believed that education was the solution to the stunning complex of problems urbanization, industrialization, and immigration presented. The school, an institution whose capacity heretofore had been limited to making some of its clientele literate, was expected to shoulder the burden of "Americanization." The school's business was to teach, to make children learn. To many concerned about the influx of foreigners, what children needed most was to learn to be Americans. The argument that this was the immigrant's greatest necessity obscured the more subtle and thorny problem of assimilation into an American society that was controlled largely by Anglo-Saxons and Protestants. Most new immigrants were neither Anglo-Saxon nor Protestant, but the dominant American ethos demanded that if they had not had those advantages of birth, at least they could be taught to act that way. The schools were to undertake this imposing assignment, working both with children in regular classes and with adults in evening programs. By turning over this difficult mission to the schools, other social institutions and individuals were exempt from wrestling with the extraordinarily delicate task of achieving a balance between preserving elements of the distinct cultural heritages being introduced to the United States while amalgamating diverse groups into a cohesive nation.

Much of the emphasis on the schools in cities resulted from the apparent but illusory ease with which reformers believed schools could be used to reach and influence children. They were right in believing that schools at least reached more children than any other known institution, but the question of influence was a thorny one. The eastern states, where the cities were concentrated, had been leaders in passing compulsory education laws. Some had even taken the additional step of making an effort to enforce these laws, particularly after the turn of the century. Even so, the truancy rates remained high in the cities, although lower than in many rural areas. In the city, unlike the farm or small town, the plight of the children who were not in school was fearfully apparent. The sight of tiny newsboys, inadequately clothed against the weather, was much more evident in a city, and hence more susceptible to public protest and subsequent correction, than was the comparably pathetic circumstance of a ten-year old helping his father clear the back forty for planting.

City residents, especially immigrants, recognized that the schools could be very useful for their children. The skills acquired in school were nearly indispensable in the city, but in the rest of the country men and women could support themselves without benefit of much formal education. To make one's living as a farmer required only minimal literacy; in fact, extensive schooling, many parents felt, only made the child more dissatisfied with the relatively restricted amusements available on the farm. In the cities, however, workers needed schooling to qualify for jobs in the new industries. Command of English also became a necessity, for although one might live in an ethnic ghetto and be able to shop and worship there, one could not move easily about the city, which was accessible even to the poor through inexpensive trolleys and streetcars, without some grasp of English. Adults might not acquire English, but they wished their children to become fluent.

The role of the schools in city life was also shaped by the widespread growth and acceptance of public education throughout the United States in the late nineteenth century, a movement in which many city schools had been leaders. City school systems were relatively well established when the massive waves of immigrants began arriving after 1890. The responses of these systems to the inundation of immigrants, largely Jews and Catholics from eastern and southern Europe, generally followed two main lines: (1) they endured reform at the hands of the Yankee, socially prestigious business and professional persons; (2) they centralized the operation of their schools, thus created a bureaucracy dominated by an emerging group of professional educators. Both developments insulated the immigrants from the schools, reducing the influence of the "patrons," as parents of schoolchildren were often called, on educational policy. Those kinds of decisions were made either by the professional educators who came to control the schools through the superintendency, principalships or various middle-range administrative jobs in the bureaucracy, or by the lay educational reformers. These reformers were likely to include patricians, such as Eliots or Lowells in Boston or Hewitts or Van Rensselaers in New York. The result was that the families whose children made up the majority of the public school population in the cities had their educational fates determined by others, many of whom did not send their own children to the public schools. This phenomenon existed in smaller communities as well, but there, where class structures were often less distinct, there was less isolation of the patrons.

Many of the school innovations of the reformers and administrators were not at variance with the wishes of the patrons. Often, however, the parents were not fully aware of the consequences of some of these programs for their children. This was particularly true of the vocational education programs, which often acted as a streaming device to move poor children into trades and not into academic courses that might lead to college. Much of what was institutionalized in the city schools was enthusiastically supported by parents. Many programs were simply organized expressions of the kinds of activities that went on informally in smaller communities, taken care of by parents, relatives, or neighbors. In the smaller areas living seemed less hectic than it was in cities and more *ad hoc* arrangements were possible. Urban life, on the other hand, seemed to exacerbate any difficulties, catapulting them into full-scale problems.

Many of these extended educational opportunities were simply responses to the demands of the frenetic environment. The need for a kindergarten, for example, in Johnson County, where the majority of the mothers were home with their children, was not nearly as acute as in the cities, where mothers might be away from home working to augment the meager family income. Even if they were home, there was little place for a child to play. A vacation school scarcely seemed necessary in Marquette where children were free to wander through the woods, fish the abundant streams, and take occasional dips in the frigid waters of Lake Superior, but in the cities, where such amusements were not available, they seemed essential. Little demand for school lunch programs arose in Butler County, where the children routinely carried their lunches, often the products of their own farms and gardens, but in the cities, public school officials and social workers believed the children desperately needed the nutritional value of a hot lunch. Hot lunches seemed even more important when the child's family eating habits were at variance with those of the school officials; hot lunches became crucial for children coming from a pasta or pickle cuisine. Once the city schools had added these programs, the small communities, who believed the city schools to be educational leaders, often followed suit.

These conditions prevailed generally among American cities in the late nineteenth and early twentieth centuries. No where were they more acute than in the largest American city, New York. The problems that New York presented were enormous. The city's population had grown from 1½ to 5 million in 1915. By 1910 there were more than twice as many residents who were foreign born than there were native born of native parents. There were nearly twice again as many who had either one or both parents born abroad. In short, it was an immigrant city, predominantly white with 2 percent nonwhite.

After consolidation in 1898 New York City consisted of five boroughs, two of which were separate islands, Manhattan and Staten Island, and two of which, Queens and Brooklyn, were part of a third island, Long Island. The fifth borough, the Bronx, was the southern tip of the mainland of the North American continent, contiguous with the rest of New York State. The boroughs differed dramatically in their economies, Manhattan initially having the most dense settlements and the principal concentration of industries. Staten Island was predominantly rural, with a few scattered settlements. Brooklyn grew rapidly in population after the turn of the century, as did the southern section of the Bronx. Queens remained bucolic and remote throughout this period, with isolated villages. The uneven distribution of the population was illustrated by the 1914 pattern of settlement in which 1/6 of the New York City population lived south of 14 Street in Manhattan on 1/82 of the city's land.

Much of New York thus displayed the characteristics of industrialized cities in America with their terrible tenement problem, which crowded large numbers of people in small areas, forcing multistory buildings and putting such a premium on land that it could rarely be economically used for anything but more tenements or businesses. Playgrounds and parks were unattainable luxuries for those neighborhoods, most of which were inhabited by persons who had formerly lived in rural areas, either in the United States or abroad. For them the adjustment to city life was difficult indeed.

Although New York exhibited the classic evidences of

urbanism, it tended to do so in a somewhat exaggerated manner. In New York situations often seemed just a little more extreme than they did in Chicago, Boston, or Philadelphia. Whether this was because New York always led in population or because its geographic location was advantageous for water traffic but difficult for human traffic, the result was that New York was perpetually *in extremis*, of both wealth and poverty, of beauty and sordidness, or comfort and distress. Such a wide spectrum characterized its educational offerings as well.

Schools date from the early seventeenth century in New York, that is, from the earliest settlement. The Collegiate School, founded in 1633 by the Dutch for the education of male children of members of the Dutch Reformed Church, is the oldest continuous school. Trinity School, established in 1710 for the education of young male Anglicans, reflected the triumph of the English over the Dutch in New Amsterdam a few decades earlier. By 1754 King's College was founded, also under British auspices, but changed its name after its Tory president had been run out of town by dissident students, the first of episodes that would figure prominently in its subsequent history under its new name, Columbia. Not till the early 1970s did either of the preparatory schools accept women students, and Columbia refused to become coeducational, leading to the founding of Barnard College in 1889.

By the early nineteenth century various kinds of privately supported schools served New York City, the only free school being one for black children established by the African School Society in 1794. In addition to the church-supported schools, of which the largest number even in the early nineteenth century were Roman Catholic, the Free School Society was organized in 1805 to provide schooling for poor children without religious affiliations. Three years later it extended its mandate to "all children who are the proper objects of a gratuitous education." In 1826 the Free School Society became the Public School Society, the institution that was the direct ancestor of the

Board of Education of New York City, which was officially established in 1853.

By 1865 the public schools in New York City, then consisting of Manhattan (the Bronx was added in 1874), were organized into seven school districts with a governing board of 21 members, three from each district. In addition, there were five trustees per ward and three inspectors in each district. This form of organization assured a decentralized school system that was quite responsive to the wishes of the people. It may be said that it was seriously threatened by political pull; typically, the daughter of a man politically active in his ward could be sure to get a job teaching school if she wanted one.

In 1866 the Free Academy, which had opened in 1849 to provide free education for boys at the postelementary level, became the College of the City of New York, but like most colleges of its time, its principal service was in providing high school training. It remained tuition free, even as a college, thus establishing the tradition of free higher education in New York City that has become such a hallowed line in New Yorkers' creed.

As early as 1866 New York was concerned about the many working people, particularly young ones, who wished to achieve economic and social mobility and hoped to do so by furthering their education. At that time 25 evening schools existed, 13 for men and 12 for women, further evidence that New Yorkers believed the sexes should be segregated, if possible, beyond the primary years. A normal school for women, the Saturday Normal School, had been organized in 1864.

An abortive effort to centralize the system by eliminating ward representation was attempted in 1871, but was defeated 2 years later, and the large number of ward trustees remained in effect in New York until the reform brought consolidation in 1898. By 1880 New York maintained 228 schools, slightly more than half at the primary level, and the remainder designated "grammar schools," although the distinction between upper primary and lower grammar work was by no means clear.

Most of the grammar schools, however, were single-sex schools, 46 for boys and 45 for girls, and only 14 (mostly in the Bronx) were coeducational. The single-sex educational tradition remained strong in the East throughout the nineteenth century and into the twentieth, particularly for youngsters in their teens. Most of the Ivy League colleges (Harvard, Yale, Princeton, Columbia, Brown, Dartmouth, Pennsylvania, and Cornell) for men and the Seven Sisters for women (Barnard, Bryn Mawr, Mt. Holyoke, Radcliffe, Smith, Vassar, and Wellesley) were all single sex until the midtwentieth century.

By the mid-1890s the problems that had been simmering in the educational sphere in New York for a decade or two, intimately involved as they were with political developments in the city, had begun to boil vigorously. A chief contributor to the debate was Joseph Mayer Rice, a former physician from Philadelphia who had studied psychology and pedagogy at Jena and Leipzig in the 1880s and returned to bring the German pedagogical message to American shores. Rice's interest in education was rather shortlived and somewhat specialized, but like so many successful publicists, his articles and subsequent book, *The Public School System of the United States* (1893) appeared at precisely the right moment, nearly coincident with Jacob Riis' *How the Other Half Lives* (1890) and *The Children of the Poor* (1892). His timing was superb, and his criticisms of city schools in America, and in particular, New York City, widely noted.

Rice argued that schools in America, based on his January to June 1892 tour from the east coast to the Midwest, had three principal failings: they were unscientific, they were tied to politics, and they neglected to consider the welfare of the child first. The first troubled him most, for he believed that if a school were conducted on "scientific" principles, by which he meant attention to the new developments in educational psychology, inevitably it could not be tied to politics (since it was tied to science), and the welfare of the child would irresistibly become foremost. In New York he observed that the public schools belonged "to a system conducted by laymen, thus providing that education is not recognized as a science in that city." Since lay control was a distinctively and universally American form of running the schools, Rice found much to criticize on his visits.

Like so many publicists Rice's work was picked up by others who quoted him to their own advantage. The educational reformers loved him, because he was intensely critical of the schools they sought to change. Some of their solutions, however, such as centralization of the school administration, were abhorrent to him. Furthermore, he had no firm alignment with immigrants. Of a Minneapolis school with a largely immigrant clientele, he patronizingly observed, "The Lincoln School, in my opinion, offers positive proof that when the teacher is competent it is not necessary to treat the children of poor immigrants with more severity than the children of refined American parents." The reformers were united behind teacher competence, and one plank in their platform was the elimination of ward appointments, to be replaced by ones based solely on merit.

In 1894 the Catholic-dominated, immigrant-oriented Democratic political machine in New York City, Tammany Hall, suffered one of its periodic overthrows at the hands of the largely Protestant, native-born Republicans. The 3-year ouster of Tammany was brief, but in that time major changes in public school administration and in the annexation of Brooklyn, Queens, and Staten Island occurred. By the time Tammany bounded back into City Hall in 1898, its supporters were expected to implement the decisions of the reformers.

The school crisis of the 1890s in New York, like most other controversies in that city, was deeply rooted in ethnic and religious divisions. In 1890 New York's population was about 1½ million, of whom 43 percent were foreign born and 80 percent either foreign born or of foreign parentage. Furthermore, the aliens were more and more coming from southern and eastern Europe, 10 percent in 1880, 23 percent in 1890, and

40 percent in 1900. A native-born Protestant New Yorker was likely to be concerned by such developments, particularly when he saw a school system, an institution he was likely to believe had great ameliorative powers, dominated through the ward trustees system by the Irish-Catholic immigrants of the previous generation.

Swinging into action after the defeat of Tammany and armed with the writings of Rice, Riis and others, Good Government Clubs sprang up about the city. One of them spun off a ladies' auxiliary that in 1895 became the Public Education Association, an organization committed to educational reform in the New York schools; it has remained active and influential to the present. Writing for *Harpers* at the center of the fight in 1895, Stephen Olin, one of the most active supporters and leaders in reform, noted Rice's earlier articles and adapted those arguments for his own use. "The fundamental vice," Olin wrote of the New York public schools, "is the division of power, and consequent destruction of responsibility." This became an argument for centralization and elimination of the locally-powerful ward system. "A grave defect in the school system," Olin continued, "is the weakness of the professional element in its general management." From this came the massive administrative apparatus of the Board of Education, complete with the Board of Examiners, instead of ward trustees, to select teachers. His debt to Rice clear, Olin observed, "Now, however, pedagogy has become a science, and the managing of public schools is an art." Finally, Olin noted, "It has been suggested that the Board of Education should consist of only a small number of commissioners, who should receive a salary." He recognized that from the point of "business efficiency," a modish reference at the time, that such a plan was meritorious, but he concluded that if that were the case the board "would become sooner or later a home for professional politicians."

Fundamental to the reformers' creed was that the schools should be "taken out of politics," but what they meant generally was that the schools should be left in the hands of professional administrators, overseen by a lay board of "statesmen." Such statesmen were presumed to be nonpolitical, but in fact were likely to be Republicans, like the man who probably more than any other was responsible for accomplishing the reform, Nicholas Murray Butler. What Butler and his colleagues were likely to mean by removing the schools from the political arena was that the persons making school decisions should not be obviously political, responding to individual requests in such matters as building contracts, and appointments. The schools inevitably were tied to politics with a lay board, particularly if it were both nonsalaried and hardworking. Only persons of wealth could be expected to serve on such a board, and financial affluence does not usually breed political indifference.

The school reorganization act, passed by the New York state legislature in 1896, was the work of Nicholas Murray Butler, former president of Teachers College, professor of philosophy, Dean and (after President Seth Low was elected mayor of New York in 190) President of Columbia University. If ever an educator were familiar with the political arena, it was Nicholas Murray Butler, chief apologist for keeping the schools out of politics. The supporters of the act had mostly been the Protestant reformers, a number of whom were in the Social Register, and others who believed the traditional Protestant morés should be inculcated in the public schools. Many of them clung to the notion that the public schools were really synonymous with "charity schools" and sent their own children to the exclusive and expensive day schools in the city or later to New England prep schools. The opponents of the bill tended to be the people most directly involved with the public schools: teachers, who correctly feared a decline in their own status if an administrative hierarchy developed; and neighborhood groups, who had had influence on local school policies in the days of ward trustees, and who rightly assumed they would lose this with central administration. Parents per se did not form a vocal political force, but many were represented in neighborhood groups.

The essential consequences of the school reorganization act, some of which did not come to pass for several years, were to remove the schools from the most overt political machinations, to centralize authority for the schools in a lay board, and to create an independent and increasingly powerful professional administration. The concentration of power in a responsible, small Board of Education did not occur until 1918. The overall goal of these moves was to bring order to a school system thought by some to be in chaos. The effort to establish reasonable control resulted in the creation of an educational bureaucracy in which order was rapidly replaced by rigidity. Thus the pedagogical ideal sought by Joseph Mayer Rice, in which the child was the center of the educational enterprise, instructed according to the newest scientific methods and aloof from political quarrels, did not come to pass in New York.

The protagonist in the New York school dramas from 1898 to 1918 was William Maxwell, an energetic, intelligent, and idealistic Scot whose family had emigrated to Brooklyn, where he had been active in school affairs. Not being able to secure their first choice for superintendent, the new consolidated Board of Education appointed Maxwell, who vigorously directed the fortunes of the massive school system. An admirer of William T. Harris, Maxwell was believed by many to be a reformer in his early years as superintendent, but his reluctance to introduce vocational training into the elementary grades, believing they should be reserved for liberal subjects, led to disagreements with the reformers during the last years of his tenure. Maxwell ardently supported the principle that children should not be forced into pedagogical regimes devised by teachers, but instead, that their own interests should be used as a base for instruction. Maxwell's educational rhetoric was superb, and doubtless he was also a sensitive and humane man who earnestly sought to remedy the vast assortment of ills the persons using the schools presented. Perhaps no one could have coped with the problems evident in the New York City schools in the first two decades of the twentieth century, particularly when so many necessary solutions could come only as a result of political compromise. In any case, Maxwell's strengths were those of a humanitarian pedagogue, not a politician, and many of the questions he faced, particularly the perennial issue of the overcrowded schools, depended on convincing the Board of Education and the Board of Estimate that additional schools were necessary and that more money must be spent. The lack of centralized control in the office of the superintendent caused many other problems, but, these, too, were only amenable to a political solution.

During these tumultous years the most immediate and pressing problem was that of too many children for the schools. Between 1900 and 1910 the city population grew by almost 40 percent, but the day school enrollment catapulted ahead by 60 percent. By 1910 over 62 percent of the children six to twenty years old in New York were attending school, and a decade later nearly 94 percent of the children seven to thirteen years old (those affected by the compulsory education law) were enrolled. Meanwhile, the new bureaucratic structure was reluctant to move quickly to authorize new buildings, so that in 1914 there were only 38 more schools than there had been in 1899, although there were 300,000 more pupils. In the fall of 1903 between 60,000 and 75,000 children were turned away because of the overcrowding, particularly in the densely popu-lated Lower East Side. By 1907 the pupil-teacher ratio for the city was 43 to 1, but this was lowered by the sparsely attended schools in outlying regions of New York. At that time the Lower East Side in Manhattan and in Brooklyn's Browns-ville had an average of 55 to 65 students per class. The following year it was estimated that more than one third of the school rooms had more than 46 children in attendance regularly, and that only one fifth of the schools had an adequate number of rooms. One way of coping with the overcrowding was to put the children on split sessions, and the number of part-time day students increased during the first two decades of the twentieth century. In 1903 nearly 90,000 children were attending for only a portion of the day, and by 1914 more than 107,000 were in school less than 5 hours per day.

The chief causes of the overcrowding of the New York schools were the massive immigration New York experienced in the first two decades of the twentieth century and the national tendency for more children to attend school separately and longer. In 1900 nearly half of New York's population was either German or Irish, but by 1920 the ethnic balance had shifted to Eastern Europeans, many of whom were Jews fleeing the pogroms, and Southern Europeans, of whom the largest group were Italians. The proportion of immigrants and children of immigrants in New York held relatively steady between two thirds and three fourths from the late nineteenth century through 1920. The school population reflected the shift in population quickly, as in 1908 over one third of the New York public school children were Jewish and over 10 percent were Italian, both groups clustered in grades two to four.

The much noted Jewish proclivity for academic achievement was observable in New York and elsewhere. Particularly when compared with fellow immigrants of the same period, the Jewish children demonstrated unusual intellectual prowess. For example, one author found that children of Eastern European parents, many of whom were Jewish, constituted a majority of the students at New York's free institutions of higher learning (City College and the Normal School) in 1900, a time when they made up only a fraction of the New York population. Such observations tended to make plausible Lewis Terman's conclusion in his *Genetic Studies of Genius*, published in 1925, that Russian Jews were the brightest group in America. One of the explanations given for the Jewish academic success was that relatively few Jews in the United States were illiterate (roughly 36 percent in 1900 and 14 percent in 1910). The proportion of Jewish males who were illiterate was much lower, and this facility with language was attributed to the religious studies required of all Jewish boys by their faith. The comparison with Italians, most of whom were Catholic, revealed a considerable discrepancy (65 percent of Italians in the United States in 1900 were illiterate and 43 percent in 1910). Despite the much vaunted Jewish academic facility, not every Jewish child vaulted smoothly over the academic hurdles. By 1910 most schools in the Lower East Side, which had heavily Jewish student bodies, also had classes for overage youngsters and for potential dropouts, indicating that Jewish children were not immune to the scholastic problems that beset other youngsters.

Expansion of Services

The result of the pressures applied to the schools by the tremendous overcrowding and the enormous influx of immigrants was an expansion of services, both vertically and horizontally. The vertical expansion involved adding both upper and lower grades to the traditional elementary program. The addition of the upper grades generally meant a high school program of some kind, either academic, commercial, or industrial. The lower grade was the kindergarten, which gained considerable popularity in the years after consolidation.

The horizontal expansion included the many activities that the school took over from the family, the church, and the smaller community. It was these, more than the tremendous burden of increased enrollments, that baffled school administrators, who had been trained to believe their job was to make children literate. Suddenly they were also supposed to make them well-nourished, clean, healthy, amused, and athletic. It was enough to make a strong man gasp.

These were the kinds of problems that Adele Marie Shaw noted in her 1903 article, "The True Character of the New York Public Schools," in *World's Work*. She observed "I chose New York City as the starting point in a study of the public schools of the United States because New York's problem is so difficult that once solved it would shed a calcium light upon the problems of other places. No other municipality had ever to meet a problem so difficult, so peculiar, and at the same time so all-embracing." She concluded her assessment of conditions in New York, "Under the present school administration it is doing wonderful work toward solving that problem. But conditions still exist that put the complete solution of the problem beyond the reach of any normal effort and expense." The only remedies she foresaw—and both were long in coming —were restriction of immigration and vast increases in expenditures, "larger than has yet been dreamed of." Later observers would note that even these remedies did not heal the ills of the New York schools.

Another peripheral issue in New York school administration was that the city was by no means a homogeneously urban, immigrant society with common concerns. Instead, as late as 1910, New York still included 1000 farms, totaling more than 21,500 acres. The schools serving these children bore marked resemblance to those of rural counties, and many on Staten Island were ungraded. Shortly after the turn of the century, annual per pupil expenditures for supplies in elementary schools ranged from $.11 in one Manhattan school to $14.75 in a Queens school.

The overage child was a clear and familiar source of concern to the New York school authorities, testifying as he did that the school system as it was then organized provided a most imperfect fit for many of the children who were subjected to it. In the years before graduation of classes became so widely accepted, children had less pressure to master a given amount of material during a 9-month period, year in and year out. In a school room with children ranging in age from six to sixteen and working on grade levels one to eight, it was much easier to accommodate the twelve-year old who still had difficulty reading. When such a child was consigned to a classroom filled mostly with six and seven-year olds, it was not surprising if he should become a discipline problem in class or, even more understandable, frequently truant. Either mode of behavior, though, was not inclined to advance his reading skill, and therefore, he was likely not to be promoted and would repeat the grade the following year with an even greater age discrepancy between him and many of his classmates.

Superintendent Maxwell reported in 1904 the following percentages of overage children in each of the elementary grades: grade one—23 percent; grade two—38 percent; grade three—45 percent; grade four—49 percent; grade five—49 percent; grade six—42 percent; grade seven—32 percent; and grade eight—25 percent. The cluster in the middle grades indicated that children were being retained there until age fourteen when they could legitimately leave school to work. Many found these figures shocking, and the school administrators began to attack the problem seriously. One solution was the creation on the Lower East Side of more than 150 special classes by 1908 for children who were overage. Additional classes were held in June after school was adjourned for the summer to help children make up work in which they had been deficient during the year so that they would not have to repeat the grade. The concern about the special arrangements necessary for the overage child led to considerable interest in the merit of homogeneous grouping of children by ability or achievement in the early years of the century. By 1910 the number of overage children in the grades had declined substantially, and school officials were inclined to believe that some of the special classes had contributed significantly to this reduction.

Among the other special classes for New York children after the turn of the century were the "C" classes, which provided intensive instruction in English for newcomers to the language. In cooperation with the Jewish social service agency, the Educational Alliance, the Board of Education gradually assumed responsibility for these classes. By 1905 more than 250 of these classes were functioning, no longer making it necessary to put a newly arrived immigrant child, regardless of age, in first gràde. Many children often spent no more than a month or two in the "C" classes before being able to join their age group in a regular class. The classes were concentrated on the Lower

East Side, the school district of the first Jewish district superintendent Julia Richman, who had earlier achieved the distinction of being the first female Jewish principal. Two Brooklyn neighborhoods with high immigrant populations, Brownsville and Williamsburg, badly needed but were slow in organizing such classes.

Other alphabetically designated classes, "D" and "E," illustrated the school system's effort, often inadequate, to diversify its offerings to meet the requirements of its exceedingly disparate clientele. The "D" classes were for children over fourteen with working papers, but who had not yet completed the fifth grade, as required by the compulsory education law in effect in the first years of the century. The "E" classes, also established in the first decade of the century, enrolled youngsters who were overage but who had unusual ability, allowing them to complete the ordinary curriculum more rapidly than would be possible in a regular class. Many of these youngsters were headed for eighth grade graduation certificates.

Classes for children with special handicaps (the blind, deaf, mentally retarded, crippled, tubercular, anemic, speech impaired, emotionally disturbed, and truant) also came into being during the first decade of the twentieth century. Some of these were the first public school classes of their kind in the country, and they illustrated again the way in which Superintendent Maxwell and his staff attempted to cope, administratively, with the variety of children to be served by the New York City schools. For the superintendent it was easier to create special classes or even a school for a special segment of the school population than it was to rearrange the ordinary classes to account for individual interests of the children composing it. In short, if a child were truly deviant in some noticeable way, there was a chance that New York might provide some special educational opportunity for him, but for the run-of-the-mill thousands without some obvious eccentricity, the usual curriculum was supposed to be adequate.

Even the ordinary curriculum was undergoing revision in the early twentieth century, particularly with the downward push to include the kindergarten, which, though never required, was in great demand. The first public kindergarten had been established in New York in 1893, and by 1899 more than 6500 children were enrolled in 101 classes, mostly in the Lower East Side where the kindergarten was thought to offer important compensatory opportunities to the poor, immigrant child. How valuable a kindergarten class of 65 children was could be debated, but there was no lack of enthusiasm in the neighborhoods. By 1914 more than 900 classes reached over 22,000 children, and the kindergartens were no longer concentrated in the poor neighborhoods. One alumna of a kindergarten in an upper-middle-class Brooklyn neighborhood of that period recalled its immense popularity with both children and parents and its use of Montessori materials in instruction.

The curricular extension at the other end of the school program was the high school, which New York had been slow in incorporating into its public school program. Prior to consolidation, Brooklyn had had four high schools and the other boroughs had had some high school work, although in populous Manhattan no regular high schools existed until 1897, when three opened. By 1899 there were nearly 14,000 public high school students in the city, and by 1914, almost 68,000, making the high school the most rapidly growing segment of the school system. Given the problems of constructing buildings in the city, New York concentrated on large buildings, to which children commuted on the trolleys and the new subways. By 1902 New York had 11 high schools, 7 with more than 1600 pupils, and 6 years later the number of high schools had increased to 19, 11 of which had more than 1600 pupils and 6 of which had more than 3000.

The enormous high schools were a persistent question to New York schoolmen, who wondered whether smaller specialized schools would be preferable. The administrative wisdom of the early twentieth century, however, favored the large school on the grounds of efficiency. Another concern was that specialized schools would be undemocratic, isolating the college preparatory students from the commercial or vocational ones. Gradually this later objection receded, particularly in the face of the vocational education movement, which reached its apogee in New York after the passage of the Smith-Hughes Act in 1918.

Although the greatest enthusiasm for vocational education came after World War I in New York with the creation of a number of specialized high schools to train students in particular skills, such as printing, design, and automotive trades, there was considerable agitation from the end of the nineteenth century on to include more practical studies in the school curriculum. Cooking classes were authorized for girls in the upper elementary grades in 1887. By 1910 nearly half of the seventh- and eighth-grade girls were enrolled in cooking and other household arts courses. Several model housekeeping apartments were acquired for the girls to learn about decorating, cleaning, and other domestic skills. In 1910 the Board of Education took over the Manual Trade School for Girls, which had operated under private auspices since 1902 for girls fourteen to seventeen, teaching them simple skills and helping them to find jobs where they could use these skills.

For boys most of the vocational training centered on learning trade skills, which Superintendent Maxwell argued in 1907 were particularly necessary in New York "because of its enormous foreign population." Maxwell wanted to confine this kind of instruction to the postelementary years, but there was considerable support for "prevocational" schools, grades seven and eight, for boys who would be unlikely to continue to high school. These were introduced in 1914 and gradually expanded.

The first free public day vocational school in the city opened in 1909. It was limited to boys and functioned with a factory routine, 11 months a year. Both trade and academic subjects were studied by boys who were at least fourteen and had either graduated from the eighth grade or passed an equivalency test. In 1910 its enrollment was 600 with an extensive waiting list of prospective students.

The teachers responsible for providing instruction in all these various classes had come under the Board of Examiners selection procedure after its creation in 1897. After 1902 further regulations required that teachers be appointed in chronological order from the lists of approved candidates prepared by the Board of Examiners. That decision, made in an effort to reduce political patronage in local districts, nonetheless did not prevent some ethnic match between teachers and students in some of the predominantly Jewish Lower East Side Schools. For example, P.S. 120 on Rivington Street was headed by a Jewish principal, and the assistant principal and 25 of the 68 teachers were Jewish. Nearby at P.S. 2 on Henry Street, 17 of the 57 teachers were Jewish. In the Italian neighborhood on Mott Street, P.S. 20 had an Italian principal. The overall ethnic background of the New York teachers in the early years of the century represented the pattern of earlier immigration; almost 20 percent were Irish, 8 percent German, and 6 percent Jewish.

Until 1904 no married women were permitted to teach in the New York City schools, and from then until 1920, only women who had married after having been appointed or married women who supported themselves because their husbands were incapacitated could join their spinster or widowed sisters in the classroom. The reason for the change, like so many affecting women in education, was not that such discrimination against women was recognized as wrong, but because there was a shortage of teachers during World War I, and married women seemed the only available source of instructors. The regulation prohibiting married women from appointment as teachers was suspended in 1918 and rescinded in 1920, the year after the suffrage amendment passed.

Women suffered severe discrimination in the New York City school, not only in conditions of appointment, but also in salary. Again, not until 1920 were men and women placed on the same salary scale. Previously men had consistently been paid about $200 more than women with equal qualifications. In 1912 an equalization effort had been made that had reduced men's salaries 20 percent and raised women's salaries 25 percent. In the early years of the century a female elementary school principal, responsible for 2500 children, was paid $750 less annually than a male high school department chairman and $150 less than a female high school assistant teacher. The discrimination worked at that time against both women and elementary personnel, a category largely populated by women, the men tending to congregate in the high school grades. In 1918 a minimum salary of $800 was set for kindergarten through grade six teachers, with a maximum of $1500. The minimum for upper grade teachers was $940 and the maximum, $1820.

One of the most important factors in understanding the schools' acceptance of additional responsibilities in the early years of the century was the panoply of philanthropic agencies that regularly initiated projects that they believed were necessary to the well-being of the children of the community and that they sought to turn over to the Board of Education once their worth had been proved. Neither the lay Board of Education nor the professional administrators had distinguished themselves as original and effective innovators, mostly because both were so bogged down by the crushing weight of the daily problems encountered in trying to keep the system going. Bureaucracies generally have not been noted for striking and effective proposals, and the New York school system was no exception. The private groups, on the other hand, had the immense advantage of being able to focus their attention on the problems that interested them and to attempt to solve them. As a result many of the programs for both children and adults that were subsequently hailed as "progressive innovations" of the New York schools originated with outside agencies.

New York was fortunate in having such private philanthropy apply itself to education. It may well be that the existence of welfare organizations that could provide a watchdog service to the schools was one of the most important factors determining educational opportunities in a community. Clearly one requisite for their existence was wealth within the community, and usually such money was limited to cities. Any evaluation of the urban schools must recognize the crucial role these agencies played in stimulating the schools to undertake various projects, ones that might have been ignored or considerably delayed if the school system had been left to its own devices, as most non-urban ones were.

Among the groups that sponsored projects subsequently adopted by the public schools were the Association for Improving the Condition of the Poor and Good Government Club E, which initiated vacation schools in 1894 and which the Board of Education took over in 1898. The Henry Street Settlement began vocational guidance services for young people around the turn of the century, a program gradually adopted throughout the New York City system by the 1920s. The Educational Alliance pioneered in English language classes in 1890, and by 1910 closed its classes, since the Board of Education was now offering a full array of such studies. The Association for the Aid of Crippled Children initiated classes for disabled children in 1899, and the Board of Education assumed responsibility for them in 1906.

The organization that led all others in spurring the school system to action was the Public Education Association, founded in 1895 with the intent of bringing about passage of the school bill subsequently passed in 1896. For the next 15 years it engaged in a shotgun approach to educational reform, supporting a great variety of low-budget programs, including boys' clubs and recreation centers on school grounds, instruction for boys incarcerated in the city jail, intermediate school vocational education, visiting teachers, and programs providing for greater art and aesthetic awareness in the schools. After a reorganization in 1911 and 1912 the PEA played a leading role in the school law reform, which was accomplished when the legislature passed a bill reducing the size of the New York City

Board of Education to seven, increasing the power of the City School Superintendent, and raising the city school appropriations. The principal prominence of the PEA in New York school affairs, however, occurred after World War I, especially in the 1920s.

Most of the programs initiated by the various philanthropic groups for subsequent adoption by the public schools involved nonacademic additions to the schools' activities, both for children and for adults. Examples of these for children were the school lunch program, initiated in the early years of the century, and by 1914 being served in 17 schools; the recreational playgrounds, organized in 1900 and totaling 197 by 1914; and the vacation schools, begun in 1894 and established in 36 schools by 1914. A variation on the vacation school was the summer day camp, which involved nearly 27,000 children in 1913. Evening recreation centers, designed for adolescents who were working and not regularly enrolled in day schools, were an extension of these kinds of activities, but not as popular as those for younger children. Until 1908 all were located on the Lower East Side, but after that date were extended throughout the city, reaching a total of 62 in 1914. Medical examinations were also given New York City schoolchildren beginning in a very small way in 1897 and emphasizing at that time isolation of children with communicable diseases. By 1902 school nurses, who could suggest treatment for common complaints, made an appearance in the schools, and 30 were appointed in 1903. In 1911 a report on the health of New York City schoolchildren found that 59 percent required dental attention, 11 percent needed corrective eyeglasses, and 2 percent suffered from tuberculosis.

The activities for adults tended to originate directly with the schools, although some were outgrowths of programs initiated by various social agencies. Among the most popular was the lecture series, which began in 1890 and attracted nearly 1 million New Yorkers in 1909. The city school administrators were equally enthusiastic about these lectures, too, because they reached many cheaply, the average cost for a lecture being a little more than $25 in 1911.

Popularized by Leo Rosten in *The Education of H*Y*M*A*N-K*A*P*L*A*N*, the English language classes for adults dominated the offerings of the evening schools, which had been a feature of New York public school life since the Civil War. Between 1898 and 1911 the number of evening schools nearly doubled, as did the attendance, with 119 schools in 1911 serving about 100,000 students. School officials regularly lamented the irregular attendance (ordinarily about 30 percent of enrollment) of the adults at these classes, attributing it to poor instruction and to their exhaustion at the end of the day. Social evenings were included in an effort to attract and keep the adult students. The English classes generally accounted for the largest portion of the students, the remainder being enrolled in homemaking courses, elementary trades, apprentice training, and the "common branches" (basic elementary school studies). In 1904 evening vocational schools opened in Brooklyn and Queens and in 1907 in Manhattan. The evening high schools offered trade courses, commercial programs, and traditional academic fare, including some college grade work.

Despite the persistently stated plea "to keep the schools out of politics," their administration remained a matter of interest to city politicians, many of whom believed they were too expensive. By the second decade of the twentieth century the call was for efficiency in administration, generally defined as getting a larger return for less money. Applied to the schools this meant an interest in streamlining the educational operation so that more students could be taught with a smaller budget. Two attempts to bring this about were the general inquiry into the New York schools, commissioned by the Board of Estimate and Apportionment, which allocated all school funds and would like to have allocated less. Concerned about what it considered the excessive expense of the New York schools, which accounted for almost 25 percent of the city budget, the Board of Estimate and Apportionment appointed a group of outside educators, headed by Paul Hanus of Harvard, to study the New York City schools from 1911 to 1913 and to report their findings to the Board. Hanus and his colleagues concluded that funds could not be substantially cut. This made their report unpopular with the Board of Estimate. Hanus also found that the course of study in the schools was too rigid and impractical and that the schools themselves too aloof. This antagonized the school administrators and teachers. Although the Hanus report met almost universal hostility, it provided a useful service by its telling indictment of an urban school system, attempting with limited success to make a predominantly immigrant population both literate and socially acceptable. The communittees' recommendations centered on ways in which the schools might be more sensitive and hospitable and humane to the pupils and the administration better informed so that school decisions could be made on a rational basis.

Another attempt to remedy New York's school problems was the abortive effort to institutionalize the Gary Plan. The essence of the Gary Plan, originated in the heavily immigrant steel town on the Indiana dunes 50 miles southeast of Chicago, was that children spent a long day in school during which, in addition to the usual academic subjects, they also studied vocational material. Time was allotted for physical training and for study halls. By having the children available for a full day instead of the customary short school day, the school could schedule many more children for classes and the facilities could be more widely utilized. The "platoon system," as it was called, was widely heralded as the ultimate in school efficiency, a topic of much interest in New York, where school buildings were estimated to be used only about 40 percent of the available working hours. The Gary Plan was formally adopted in New York in 1914, but according to its supporters was never properly implemented, the explanation that was given to account for the poor showing of the pupils in New York "Gary

Plan schools" in comparison with students in regular New York schools and in the prevocational ones. Although the schools following the Gary Plan ultimately could operate more efficiently than ordinary ones, a considerable initial expenditure was required to provide sufficient space and facilities for the full operation of the Gary program. Characteristically the Board of Estimate declined to appropriate adequate funds to convert properly the New York buildings participating in the Gary Plan. Thus supporters of the Gary Plan maintained it never had a fair trial in New York. After a vigorous mayoralty campaign in 1917 in which the Gary Plan was a major issue, Mayor John Purrroy Mitchel, who had supported the Plan, was defeated, and the Gary Plan discontinued in New York in 1918.

Religious Schools

The only other large school system in New York between 1865 and 1918 was that supervised by the Roman Catholic Archdiocese of New York, which included much of the Hudson Valley and the Diocese of Brooklyn, which included all of Long Island. The schools were born out of the 1840s to 1842 controversy that resulted in public aid being provided only to those schools not teaching any sectarian doctrine, but the parochial school system's spectacular growth came after the Third Plenary Council of Baltimore in 1884, which mandated a Catholic education for every Catholic child. New York did its best to concur, and between 1886 and 1890, 10 new parochial schools were established in New York, 5 more between 1890 and 1900, and 21 additional ones by 1908. Since this was a period of relative decline in the proportion of Catholics composing the New York population (although an increase in numbers), the record is eloquent testimony of the concern of Catholics for the education of their children under religious auspices. The following table gives the percentages of the New York City population divided by religious preference between 1890 and 1920:

	ROMAN CATHOLIC, %	PROTESTANT, %	JEWISH, %	EASTERN ORTHODOX, %
1890	39.2	48.8	12.0	0
1900	35.2	47.4	17.4	0
1910	35.1	37.4	26.3	1.2
1920	34.6	34.6	29.2	1.6

Intense acrimony characterized discussion between Catholics and others, mostly Protestants, on the school issue during the late nineteenth century. Catholics objected vigorously to paying taxes to support public schools, which many believed espoused Protestant doctrine. They held that this was especially unfair since they did not get tax relief for sending their children to parochial schools, the existence of which was a considerable financial saving to the taxpayers of the community. Protestants, on the other hand, frequently failed to see the argument of espousal of Protestantism in the public schools. For example, at one of the Boston Monday lectures a Protestant minister in 1888 addressed a presumably largely Protestant and extremely enthusiastic crowd, "We must teach in the common schools, in an unsectarian way, the broad, undisputed principles of morals and religion as to which good men agree, and thus stop the mouths of those who say that the American common school may be justly called godless." The bulk of his address, which was frequently interrupted by applause, was a violent denunciation of Catholics in America, particularly Jesuits, the nub of the argument being fear that the Pope would come to rule in America: "Roman Catholic parochial schools are intended to bring the whole Catholic population of the United States under the control of a few hundreds of ecclesiastics who are themselves virtually subjects of a foreign pontiff . . . . I believe that there are a few Jesuitical fathers so fanatical as to induce politicians and heedless young men in military organizations to combine under exclusively Roman Catholic auspices. I think it is done far more widely than the public generally supposes." Such speeches did not assure Catholics that their children would be welcomed in predominantly Protestant public schools.

The other major issue on which Catholics were attacked was their intimate alignment with the political machine, particularly Tammany in New York, and the resultant lucrative nature of that relationship. The Committee on Political Reform of the Union League Club reported in 1872, for example, that the Catholic Church had received nearly $5 million either in cash or its equivalent in public lands during the past 3 years through the machinations of the Tammany machine. Much of these proceeds had gone toward the establishment of parochial schools. Other religious groups were cited as well, but the Catholics caught the principal wrath of the committee.

Despite its critics, the Roman Catholic parochial school system grew rapidly after the 1884 Council. Between 1882 and 1891 the Catholic population of the United States increased by a little more than 26 percent, but the parochial school enroll-ments jumped by 64 percent. In 1891 it was estimated that 60 percent of Catholic children nationally were attending parochial schools. In New York the proportion was probably a little lower; in 1907, when Catholics accounted for about 35 percent of the city population, parochial schools enrolled a little less than 13 percent of the Manhattan school pupils. By 1920 the Catholic schools in New York City had grown to include over 20 percent of the enrolled pupils.

In New York as in most other communities instruction in the parochial schools was provided chiefly by members of religious orders. The Sisters of Charity, an American order, founded by a New Yorker, Elizabeth Seton, who was converted to Ca-tholicism in 1805, was the mainstay for the girls' schools. The German Ursulines (via St. Louis, and the French Religious of the Sacred Heart also opened girls' schools in the late nine-teenth century. The Ursulines' school eventually became the College of New Rochelle and the Religious of the Sacred Heart founded Manhattanville College. Both colleges originated as elementary schools for girls, progressed through the academy stage while still in New York City, and became colleges in northern suburbs in the twentieth century.

The two orders supplying most of the instructors for boys both originally came to New York from France, the Christian Brothers (Brothers of the Christian Schools) and the Jesuits. The former staffed many parochial schools (25 in 1908), most of which were elementary, while the latter, true to their aristocratic tradition, concentrated on higher studies. Having established St. John's College in 1841 (which became Fordam University), the Jesuits founded the academically rigorous and prestigious Regis High School in 1914.

Both other major religious groups in New York, Protestants and Jews, relied heavily on the public schools. Jews, however, frequently supplemented the secular fare their children received in the public school with additional instruction in the late afternoon and early evening hours at *heders*. Classes such as these were memorably described by Henry Roth in *Call It Sleep*. In 1903, 307 of these schools existed in the Lower East Side and enrolled almost 9000 boys but less than 400 girls, an indication of the greater importance placed upon spiritual training for males than females in the Jewish faith.

Private Schools

The other major group of schools in New York City were the private ones, some of which dated from prepublic school times. These, on the whole, offered a traditional curriculum to a homogeneously wealthy clientele. Most were predominantly Protestant, but a few had principally Jewish student bodies. In the late nineteenth and early twentieth century a distinctive feature of New York life was the preeminence of public schools. Except for Catholics, a handful of Jews, and the exceedingly socially prominent, all others sent their children to the public schools. This enthusiasm for public education did not last long in New York City.

In the second decade of the twentieth century a new type of private school emerged in New York, one that would subsequently be called "progressive." Frequently founded by women of the suffragette generation, these women directed their energies toward righting the pedagogical wrongs instead of the political ones.

The schools sprang up in the Greenwich Village neighborhood of New York and on the West Side, both areas that would soon attract "bohemian" and "intellectual" residents. These two groups provided many of the children for the City and Country School founded by Caroline Pratt in 1914, for the Walden School established by Margaret Naumburg in 1915, and later at the Little Red School House after Elisabeth Irwin was forced to leave P.S. 64, where her first educational experiments began in 1916. Each of these women came to teaching after earlier interests in social work.

Harriet Johnson pioneered with kindergartens at this time in the Village while Patty Smith Hill was laboring in the same vineyard at Teachers College on the Upper West Side. Her nursery and kindergarten work became part of the Lincoln School, organized in 1917. Meanwhile, Lucy Sprague Mitchell, who had begun working with Caroline Pratt but severed that connection in 1929 to join Elisabeth Irwin's staff, later founded an institution to train teachers to make them more receptive to the new ideas advocated in these schools. Mrs. Mitchell's institution was called the Bank Street College for Teachers, named for its Greenwich Village location where it resided until 1970, when it moved to Morningside Heights on the Upper West Side. Although Mrs. Mitchell believed that her school could better prepare teachers for the new classrooms, the founders of these progressive schools were by no means in total agreement on pedagogical principles. Walden focused its attention on children's psychological adjustment, City and Country (originally called The Play School) stressed learning through direct experience, and the Little Red School House emphasized homogeneous grouping. Helen Parkhurst founded the Dalton School in New York in 1919, basing it on the premise that children should have a chance to work at their own rate, hence "contracts" between student and teacher through which the child could make his way through the course of study at his own rate.

Despite their differing emphases the leaders of these schools were agreed on at least one point: the traditional schools were too rigid. Such might be a fitting epitaph for the New York schools in 1892 when Joseph Mayer Rice evaluated them or in 1918 when the new progressives viewed them. Observers today might even believe that the criticism still applies. The progressive schools in their halcyon days when they were new, small, and zealous at least avoided rigidity.

Another Educational Agency: The Library

Although the schools dominated the educational scene for residents of New York, one other institution, the library, competed in providing a vast array of education services. By the end of this period New York offered one of the finest library services of any area in the country to its residents, but this was not always the case. The New York Public Library, international triumph to bibliophilic skill, was formed in 1896 by a consolidation (as everything else seemed to be merging) of three libraries, the Astor, the Lenox, and the Tilden. All three were essentially research collections, the first specializing in history, humanities, and the classics, and the second and third primarily in rare books. In any case, none of these three was the kind of institution that would attract the great mass of New Yorkers away from the mundane pleasures of their neighborhoods.

The fundamental shift in the library fortunes of New York came in 1901 in two related events: the New York Free Circulating Library merged with the research collections that then composed the New York Public Library, and 2 months later, Andrew Carnegie offered the city a gift of more than $5 million to build and equip branch libraries (50 sites were authorized in 1902) if the city would provide the sites and maintenance. This was the beginning of the New York Public Library as a popular force in New York City.

The New York Free Circulating Library was an outgrowth of another ladies' philanthropic effort for the immigrant and poor in New York, in this case through the auspices of Grace Episcopal Church, whose ladies were appalled at the pulp magazines read by the girls attending the social service programs at the church. In 1878 the ladies decided to attempt to divert the girls from such unsuitable material and to the books that were provided in the new library. The *noblesse oblige* character of the library movement paralleled that of most social work and many educational efforts in New York in the late nineteenth and early twentieth centuries, but whatever the purposes or overtones of the beneficence, the result was that considerable reading material of wide variety circulated through many poor homes in New York that probably would not have had the opportunity for such books at all without the library.

In 1886 a report on the circulation of the New York Free Circulating Library revealed that its founders' aim of providing elevating literature for the neighborhoods had been realized. The leading volumes in terms of circulation (each having been borrowed more than 100 times during the year) were Alexander Dumas' *The Count of Monte Christo*, Harriet Beecher Stowe's *Uncle Tom's Cabin*, Charles Dickens' *David Copperfield*, *The Old Curiosity Shop*, *Oliver Twist*, and *Pickwick Papers*, Jules Verne's *20,000 Leagues under the Sea*, and finally a popular sentimental novel of the day, *Ethelyn's Mistake*. Three American history books were also in the category of books borrowed more than 100 times for the year, as was Huxley's *Elements of Physiology*. Throughout the 1880s and 1890s branches of the New York Free Circulating Library opened throughout Manhattan, including ones with collections especially suited to the ethnic neighborhood in which they were located. Of these the Ottendorfer branch, located in a German district on Second Avenue, was probably the best example, with its half-English and half German collection. At the time of its merger in 1901, the annual circulation among the 11 branches was more than 1,635,000 volumes.

The major other private libraries that offered free services to their patrons were sponsored either by religious denominations or by social settlements. Preeminent among the first was the Aguilar Library, founded in 1886 and located in the predominantly Jewish Lower East Side, but with branches as far north as 110 Street. Its collection included more than 1000 Russian volumes (indicating the national origin of many of the Jewish immigrants to New York) as well as nearly 1400 Hebrew volumes. It annual circulation in 1901 to 1902 was over 757,000 volumes. It became part of the New York Public Library in 1903.

Cathedral Library, founded in 1887 in connection with St. Patrick's Cathedral, was the principal Catholic Library in the city. By 1904, the date of its merger with the public system, its annual circulation was nearly 344,000. The Webster Free Library, organized by the Church Club of New York in 1892 and opened in 1894, provided a general collection for residents of the Upper East Side of Manhattan. In its first year of operation it had an annual circulation of about 20,000 volumes. Various settlement houses also established libraries, the best known being the University Settlement, which opened its collection in 1887 and maintained it until merger with the Public Library in 1904.

Subscription libraries also competed with the free libraries in New York, but by the last few decades of the nineteenth century, they were rapidly losing out to their cheaper competitors. The Harlem Library, founded in 1825, was one of the oldest and merged with the Public Library in 1903. The Washington Heights Library, located in an isolated neighborhood far to the north of the center of Manhattan activity, was organized in 1868 and became free to residents after 1883. It, too, ultimately merged with the city facility.

The tremendous gathering in of disparate libraries by the New York Public Library after the Carnegie grant in 1901 illustrated an effort on the part of New York to catch up to some of its urban neighbors in providing public library facilities for its residents. In 1901, for example, Boston, a city that New Yorkers reluctantly recognized as a center of American culture, was spending an average of $.50 per resident on public libraries, while the equivalent figure for New York City was less than $.09. Even that proverbial second city, upstart Chicago spent $.15½ per person on public libraries, and Buffalo, a community New Yorkers rarely even deigned to mention in connection with themselves, laid out $.41 per person for public libraries. Armed with these figures the supporters of the New York Public Library laid siege to the city administration for places to put the new Carnegie libraries. Reluctantly the city politicians acceded.

One of the explanations for the reluctance of the city to establish a library supported by city funds was that in New York private organizations had been active in the library field as in so many others in spurring the municipality to provide necessary services. Being astute politicians New York administrators observed that the New York Library association found 288 libraries to catalogue at the turn of the century, the vast majority of which were in private hands. City officials may well have wondered why a portion of the city budget should be allocated to a service that private groups seemed to be well on the road to providing.

To the reader, of course, whether the library was funded by the city or by private groups was immaterial, as long as he did not have to pay for the use of it. What most New Yorkers apparently sought in the libraries was a quiet and modestly comfortable place to read some of the many newspapers and periodicals in English and nearly every other language that were published in New York, a selection of materials that would bring enjoyment (serious fiction), edification (history and science), and escape (sentimental fiction). The New York Public Library provided this service to those who sought it, both young and old, thus becoming the quintessential voluntary educational organization in New York City.

from liberal arts college to university: princeton and wisconsin

The most significant determinant of educational opportunities in America from 1865 to 1918, the argument of this volume has been, was the place where one lived and the educational facilities that community offered. The major exception to this generalization was college. Ordinarily only for higher education would a person leave home for a specifically educational purpose. Sometimes, as in Johnson County, Marquette County, and New York City, it was not necessary to leave home in order to attend college, but for many Americans some travel was necessary. Travel seemed particularly necessary as the variety of educational institutions increased in the last quarter of the nineteenth century.

The diversification of higher educational institutions in the late nineteenth century occurred in two principal ways: in curriculum and in clientele. In 1865 nearly the only kind of higher educational institution was the liberal arts college, which usually enrolled only white men. By 1918 a multiplicity of institutions had appeared, and many seemed much more vital than most of the remaining liberal arts colleges. The colleges that persisted in 1918 in offering a set curriculum and admitting only men were typically Roman Catholic ones and definitely outside the mainstream of higher education in America. The colleges that had resisted the pulls to become universities had broadened their curriculums to include both a greater variety of courses and more opportunities for students to select among them. Many had either dropped or greatly reduced their Protestant denominational ties. Most west of the Alleghenies had begun to admit women, although many had reached this decision when low enrollments threatened their solvency.

During the last third of the nineteenth century new colleges were organized to serve groups of the population that had previously been denied access to higher education, particularly women and blacks. Another group that had grown enormously in the second half of the nineteenth century, Roman Catholics, were also establishing a number of colleges for both their sons and daughters, but the colleges for men and women were usually separate. Teachers colleges, of which the one in Marquette County is an example, also multiplied quickly.

The two most important institutions, however, were the research-oriented private university, specializing in the humanities, pure sciences, and the new social sciences and sometimes in the professions, and the state university, emphasizing research not only in the traditional areas but also on more immediately useful problems. Of these the former typically was an outgrowth of a moderately successful liberal arts college, and a paradigm of these is Princeton. The origins of the state universities are more mixed; some also were outgrowths of private, denominational liberal arts colleges while others were originally established as state-supported colleges or universities while still others were newly created by the states in response to the Morrill Act of 1862. The Morrill Act schools had federal funds alloted to them to provide for instruction and research in the three areas that the federal government in 1862 believed most essential to the national welfare: agriculture, the mechanic arts, and military tactics. Some states combined their earlier state college or university and their Morrill Act university, thereby concentrating the state's higher educational effort, and the University of Wisconsin is one of these.

Together with the colleges and universities discussed in earlier chapters, Princeton and Wisconsin exemplify the tremendous changes that took place in higher education in America during this period. By 1918 both had become regional educational centers, places for which students would deliberately leave home to attend, but neither had become the national center each now is. Both had also accepted specialization in disciplines as important for faculty and students. Both had immensely broadened their conceptions of what appropriate undergraduate educations should be, Wisconsin substantially more than Princeton. Postbaccalaureate students were an important, although numerically small, part of the university community. Both were much more secular and very much larger than they had been in 1865. Their resemblances to their 1865 existences as liberal arts colleges were limited indeed, and it was this transformation of higher education from 1865 to 1918 that was its most salient characteristic.

Princeton University

The College of New Jersey, unofficially known as Princeton because of its location in that south central New Jersey community, sought a replacement for President John Maclean upon his retirement in 1868. Although the institution was then over 100 years old, having been founded in 1746 partially in response to the Calvinist fervor associated with the Great Awakening, the College had fallen on hard times in the nineteenth century. With the outbreak of the Civil War it had lost its unique feature among American colleges, its national student body. It had contributed at least eight generals to the Confederacy and four to the Union forces. Probably even more important for Princeton postwar developments was the alienation that had occurred between the college and its formerly loyal clientele of Scotch Presbyterians in the border states.

Further evidence of Princeton's parochialism was President John Maclean's insistence on hiring only devout Presbyterians for the faculty. In 1866 he deliberately refused to appoint a New England Congregationalist to a professorship in Latin, and at his retirement in 1868 the faculty was composed of 10 men, 7 of whom were Presbyterian ministers and all reportedly "ardent Calvinists."

Another slight to Princeton was the decision of the New Jersey legislature in 1864 to designate Rutgers as the recipient of Morrill Act funds. Rutgers had also been founded before the Revolutionary War under denominational auspices, but as early as 1840 it had named a layman president. At least as important as its disengagement from religious involvements, however, was the effective lobbying of Rutgers spokesmen in the New Jersey legislature. Princeton's reputation for outstanding work in science, largely established during John Witherspoon's presidency from 1768 to 1794, would have made it a logical beneficiary of the Morrill Act funds, which were designed to promote research and teaching in the agricultural and mechanic arts. The selection of Rutgers for the federal assistance is simply additional evidence of the decline of Princeton during the first half of the nineteenth century. A final and crucial example of Princeton's difficulties was the loss of nearly one third of its over 300 students during the Civil War. For a college with Princeton's endowment of less than $500,000 in 1868, student fees provided the majority of the annual budget.

When the trustees met to consider a replacement for Maclean in 1868, they initially offered the position to a local candidate. After his refusal, they extended their search across the Atlantic to bring to Princeton James McCosh, a Scotsman who was then a professor of moral philosophy at Queen's College, Belfast. It is not clear if the trustees were aware that in choosing McCosh, they were in fact striking a profound blow at the provinciality that was engulfing the college. The effect of their action was to transform their institution from a hidebound Presbyterian college to one that by the end of McCosh's administration was a university in all but its official title. Still Presbyterian, even that cardinal feature of institutional character was diminishing.

Upon assuming the presidency at Princeton, McCosh immediately began to improve the academic quality of the college. In order to do so, he believed three steps were crucial. One dealt with the faculty, the second with the library, and the third, intimately related to the previous two, with the curriculum. He argued to the trustees that faculty salaries must be raised immediately and new professorships be created. He introduced the theme to which he (and many other educators) would return so often, that competition from other colleges was forcing Princeton to take on expensive projects. He was appalled that the Princeton library was open only 1 hour per week, accustomed as he was to European college libraries being available to students for several hours daily. He insisted that the library extend its regular hours and enlarge its collection, which then contained only about 14,000 volumes. McCosh also insisted that new scientific apparatus be acquired to improve instruction in that field.

Within the first 5 years of his presidency McCosh concentrated on making the college more academically rigorous and diverse. He saw to it that admission standards were raised, that modern languages were authorized for the curriculum, that fellowships in four fields for postgraduate students were created, and that a School of Science was organized. The School of Science was established primarily for students who were unable or unwilling to pursue the heavy requirements in classical languages in the "academic departments." By permitting the students to enroll in this program, similar to the Sheffield Scientific School at Yale and the Lawrence Scientific School at Harvard, Princeton was able to maintain a rather rigid, classically oriented curriculum for most of its students.

The issue of curriculum rigidity was one that McCosh faced throughout his presidency. Since he was always eager that Princeton be compared favorably with Harvard, Yale, and

Columbia, he was concerned when any of those institutions undertook changes in programs that might cause repercussions at Princeton. Probably the issue of electives was the most serious example of a step taken by one of these colleges, the reverberation of which swept up and down the eastern seaboard and west across the Alleghenies. On this question McCosh was characteristically firm, reporting to the Princeton Board of Trustees in 1884:

I hold that every branch of true learning should have a place in a thoroughly equipped college. But as life is short and young men differ in taste and capacity, it is not desirable, in fact it is not possible, to exact a deep knowledge of every kind of useful scholarship from every young man. So in all our higher colleges the studies are now divided into required and elective . . . I regard the proper distribution of the studies as about the most important point to be settled in our Colleges at this present time.

Some (not many) of the American colleges are seeking to draw students by giving them, younger as well as older, an almost unlimited choice of subjects through all the years of their course. This in my opinion is a fundamental mistake. Every one acquainted with College secrets knows that there are students who show uncommon skill in choosing among the Electives the subjects which require the least expenditure of thought and attention; and the Professors are tempted to give high grading marks without exacting rigid study . . . When such a state of things is allowed and encouraged, I hold that the education given, so far from being an advance upon that given to our fathers, is a retrogression, as in the older Colleges they required a solid knowledge of higher branches—which is true I may add of some of our smaller Colleges at this day. I hold that there are branches rudimentary and fundamental, which have stood the test of time, fitted to call forth the deeper and higher faculties of the mind and opening the way to farther knowledge, which all should be required to study. Such in Language are the classi-

cal tongues with certain European ones, and above all our own tongue, all of these with their literatures. Such in Science are Mathematics, Physics, Chemistry, and certain branches of Natural History. Such in Philosophy are the study of the human mind (psychology), logic, ethics and political economy. A young man is not literally educated who has been allowed to omit any of these; and certain of them should be required in every year of the course to keep the mind from being dissipated and wasted.

At the time of McCosh's 1884 statement Princeton permitted only juniors and seniors to choose electives, which constituted less than half of their programs in their upper 2 years. One of the trends at Princeton and elsewhere was toward a higher proportion of elective studies. Harvard, which had led the way in introducing elective programs for its undergraduates beginning in 1872 under President Charles William Eliot (and to whom many of McCosh's remarks were addressed), returned in 1910 to a position of limited electives with the retirement of Eliot and inauguration of A. Lawrence Lowell as president. From 1865 to 1918 Harvard led the colleges and universities in breaking the viselike grip of the classical studies on the curriculum. Eliot's endorsement and proselytyzing for the elective principle inclined other institutions to broaden their own curricula and permitted students to concentrate in the fields of study particularly interesting to them. The retrenchment at Harvard under Lowell in the twentieth century placed Harvard undergraduates in much the same position as students at other institutions that had never had free electives, that is, with some required subjects and with the necessity of concentrating in a specific field. Actually, only from 1897 to 1910 had Harvard students been able to choose their programs with no required courses other than a year of freshman rhetoric.

One of the obvious but very significant results of the movement toward election was the gap that rapidly widened between those colleges that were wealthy enough to broaden their curricula by adding new faculty members and were inclined to do so and those that either were not so wealthy or were not so inclined. New faculty members were an expensive addition to the college budget; more and more they were trained in Europe and joined the faculties with the intent of teaching only their specialty. Thus, it was no longer possible for a college to exist with three or four faculty members handling the entire curriculum for 75 or 100 students. Expansion and diversification of the curriculum, combined with the wish of significant portions of the faculty to emulate the style of their professors abroad, encouraged many colleges to consider transforming themselves into universities. Yale (and Princeton with it) had glorified the notion of the limited curriculum in its 1828 report, a document that many impecunious colleges had enthusiastically endorsed as a justification for their own constricted offerings. Until the end of the nineteenth century it was still possible to give a reasoned and spirited defense of the traditional curriculum, but the enormous expansion of knowledge, particularly in the sciences, which had been largely ignored in the old studies, made such a case increasingly difficult to argue. Although there were certain exceptions (largely in New England), in general those colleges that could financially support the broadening of their curricula did so, and the logical result of such an expansion was to become a university. The history of Princeton is such an example.

Princeton did not formally become a university until its sesquicentennial celebration in 1896 when it changed its official name from the College of New Jersey to Princeton University, but the real transition from provincial college to emerging university took place during the 1880s. The architect of the renovation was James McCosh, and practical Scot that he was, his reasons were largely pragmatic. He believed that Princeton could maintain itself as a leading institution (and there were some who believed that it was not a case of "maintaining" but "establishing") only if it followed the same path as the other northern colonial colleges (Harvard, Yale, Columbia,

Pennsylvania, Rutgers, Brown, and Dartmouth) and added graduate training. One of his earliest activities was to establish fellowships for graduates to enable them to continue their studies. By 1872 he reported to the Board of Trustees, "The Fellowship and Prizes have had a powerful influence not only on those who compete for them but on the better half of the students from the Sophomore Class upward." In McCosh's view these fellowships were having the dual effect of increasing the level of scholarly activity at Princeton and raising the academic tone of undergraduate life.

As the enrollment at the undergraduate level began to decline in the 1870s and again in the mid-1880s, McCosh worried a great deal. He attributed the decline substantially to the lack of "feeder" schools in the New Jersey area, noting that the New England colleges relied heavily on the preparatory schools, such as Andover and Exeter, to provide them with applicants and that the relatively youthful University of Michigan was located in a state where it was to be the pinnacle of the state public education system. Princeton was singularly unfortunate in having neither nearby private preparatory schools nor a well-established system of public high schools. Characteristically McCosh worked harder to organize a private preparatory school than he did to cooperate with the state in establishing a public school system. In 1873 he urged the trustees to support a New Jersey bill designed to aid secondary education, but he campaigned even more actively for funds to endow a preparatory school in connection with the College. This was indeed established, but did not flourish and was soon abandoned. Eventually Lawrenceville School was located within 15 miles of the college, partially as a result of McCosh's advice to the Board in 1880 that two or three "strategically-located academies" would be of greater benefit to Princeton than the public school system. He estimated that 60 percent of Harvard's freshmen class came from three prep schools. McCosh's vigorous and successful campaign for the first 15 years of his presidency to raise the admission standards for freshmen undoubtedly affected his opinion that the prep schools were more likely to produce suitable candidates for Princeton than the public high schools, which were then in their infancy.

By 1883 McCosh had become very concerned about the drop in the Princeton enrollment, which was most noticeable among the number of entering freshmen in the "academic department," the heart of the college. He attributed the decline to the further developments of local colleges, particularly in New York (Columbia, New York University, and City College of New York), Philadelphia (Pennsylvania and Temple), and Baltimore (Johns Hopkins); to the fact that Princeton was too expensive for the area it served; to the lack of feeder schools and possibly to excessively high admission standards given that absence; and finally, to Princeton's poor record in producing teachers who might recommend their college to their students.

In the mid-1880s McCosh faced problems at Princeton of at least equal magnitude of those that had confronted him on his arrival in the United States nearly 20 years before. Low enrollments combined with a dropout rate of nearly one third of the undergraduates and the pressure from the elective controversy convinced McCosh that the "great crisis in the higher education of America" that he had forecast had now come. To him, of equivalent importance with the declining numbers of students and the curriculum disputes, was Harvard's decision in 1885 to abandon both religious instruction and obligatory attendance at prayers in the college chapel. This diminution of the role of religion on the campus presaged a fundamental shift in academic life with which McCosh disagreed violently. Upon learning of Harvard's decision he announced to the Trustees, "I mean not only to defend but to fight for what I believe to be a fundamental principle with this college, that religion is not to be abandoned in college teaching." In many ways this was a reiteration of his statement nearly 10 years before: "I found it a Presbyterian College and mean to leave it so." There can be no doubt about McCosh's intent, nor indeed about his achievement, but with the various attacks to which McCosh and his views were being subjected, he recognized that inevitably he must face the issue of Princeton transforming itself into a university.

By June 1885 McCosh had faced the declining enrollment at Princeton, the abolition of required chapel at Harvard, and the enthusiasm for graduate study. He then reported to the trustees: "I have hitherto discouraged all proposals to make Princeton College a University. I am of the opinion, however, that the time has now come for considering the question." Shortly afterward, McCosh published his paper, "What an American University Should Be." During the next 2 years McCosh worked vigorously to secure public support for the university idea, especially from the alumni who formed a more and more important segment of the Princeton constituency. Canny Scot that he was, McCosh realized that the alumni were not supporting Princeton adequately financially and that in order for them to do so he believed a "new interest" must be awakened among them. By 1887 McCosh could report, "The great body of our alumni wish us to become a University," this view resulting at least in part from McCosh's assiduous cultivation of them during the previous 2 years. McCosh informed the Board that funds would not be forthcoming unless Princeton "were proclaimed a university." He added, "There is no difficulty in elevating a college into a university. They have done it at Harvard, they have done it at Yale, they are to do it at Columbia." His assertion illustrates the general uncertainty concerning just what, in fact, constituted a university.

The issue of competition from other institutions, never far from McCosh's consciousness, was heightened by the action of the most serious competitor of all, Harvard, when it celebrated its 250 anniversary in 1886 and no Princeton graduate received any of the 42 honorary degrees it awarded on that occasion. Furthermore, that quintessential New Englander Oliver Wendell Holmes named Yale, Amherst, Williams, and Bowdoin before mentioning Princeton in the Commemoration Ode prepared for the celebration. Such a slight disturbed

McCosh and undoubtedly spurred his efforts to bring Princeton to greater public notice, a feat he believed could be accomplished by making it a university.

The Trustees acquiesced in McCosh's pleas for expanding the institution and in 1887 sanctioned plans for awarding the degrees of Doctor of Philosophy (Ph. D.) and Doctor of Literature (Litt. D.). Such formal authorization provided the opportunity for postgraduate students, who had already been attending Princeton for some years, to follow a prescribed course of study and qualify for an additional degree. The organization of a formal "graduate college" was a much later and highly acrimonious issue, and not until its establishment in 1913 can Princeton be regarded as having fully become a university.

McCosh's retirement in 1888 necessitated a search by the trustees for a new president, an investigation that rather quickly—and disastrously—resulted in the appointment of a local minister and professor at the Theological Seminary, Francis L. Patton. Patton served 12 years before being removed by the trustees to a professorship of philosophy and later to assume the presidency of the Princeton Theological Seminary, which had no organic relation with the college. The years of Patton's presidency were ones of academic drift but of physical expansion. Technically the institution became a university at its sesquicentennial celebration in 1896 when the formal change in name to "Princeton University" occurred, but the crucial decision to shift from college to university had come under McCosh and the equally significant enactment of that decision, the creation of the graduate college, did not happen until 1913, 3 years after Woodrow Wilson resigned.

Patton assumed the presidency of a college that his predecessor had laboriously increased in enrollment from the 281 students in 1868 to over 600 students 20 years later. During Patton's custodianship family social expectations conspired with the increasing prominence of Princeton to more than double the college's enrollment by 1902. Other colleges were also experiencing significant increases in their enrollments in the 1890s. It continued to be a relatively expensive place to be educated, the tuition in the undergraduate academic department (science was more expensive) increasing from $75 to $100 in 1885, and to $150 in 1893 where it remained throughout the 1890s. Princeton estimated that the average funds (including tuition) required by a student ranged in 1892 from $680 annually for a freshman to $837 for a senior. By the turn of the century the amount had declined somewhat. At this time most professors on the faculty were being paid $3000 per year plus a house, more than half again as much as the average college professor in the United States. Given such expenses, it is not surprising that the number of Episcopal youth, many of whom came from more affluent families than the Scotch-Presbyterians whom McCosh had hoped to attract to the college in greater numbers, became a more and more significant part of the student body.

Although Princeton had no fraternities, the eating clubs began to assume considerable importance in the lives of the undergraduates. Beginning with Ivy in 1879 and Cottage in 1886, the clubs became self-perpetuating, selecting sophomores who retained membership in the club through graduation. For many students the club became the focus of undergraduate life. Eight more clubs were organized in the early 1890s, and gradually the vast majority of undergraduates joined a club. Eighty-seven percent of the upperclassmen were members in 1914. The effect of these organizations on undergraduate life, reflecting as they did a shift toward aristocratic allegiances and antiacademic attitudes at Princeton, developed into a major issue of Wilson's presidency. The growth in significance of the clubs at Princeton paralleled similar developments in fraternities and sororities at other institutions.

The most important academic development of Patton's presidency and one that exemplified to many his disdain for rigorous intellectual discipline was his reorganization of the curriculum so that more elective studies were available to undergraduates. The change affected both the "academic" and the science curricula, although the latter experienced the greater growth during this period, jumping from 16 percent of the student body at Patton's inauguration to 37 percent at his resignation. The growth is probably considerably more related to the absence of a Greek requirement in science and the lower Latin one than to a profound interest in the application of Newton's or Darwin's ideas. At a time when Harvard had nearly free election of courses, the Princeton undergraduate academic percentages of required and elective courses was as shown in the following table.

	1899-1900		1889-1890	
	REQUIRED, %	ELECTIVE, %	REQUIRED, %	ELECTIVE, %
Freshmen	100	0	100	0
Sophomores	75	25	75	25
Juniors	57	43	33	67
Seniors	36	64	0	100

In 1899, 64 professors and assistant professors and 22 instructors presided over the courses. Nine professors had Ph.D.'s from Germany.

Probably the most significant development in Patton's presidency was the organization of a college for women in Princeton for which both Patton and the dean of Princeton, James Murray signed the incorporation papers. The venture, Evelyn College, was principally the work of Joshua McIlvaine, a former Princeton professor of *belles-lettres* under President MacClean and later a Presbyterian minister in Newark. McIlvaine, who returned to Princeton in 1887 in his retirement, established the institution chiefly as a means of support for his two spinster daughters and without endowment, expecting incorrectly that tuition fees would be sufficient to operate the college at a profit.

Evelyn College's relationship with the other local educational institutions was a complex one. All but two of the original trustees of Evelyn were either faculty members or trustees of Princeton College or the Theological Seminary. Nearly the entire faculty of Evelyn were Princeton professors who supplemented their income by teaching at the nearby college, much as Harvard faculty members did at Radcliffe. The Princeton trustees had approved this use of their faculty and also permitted the Evelyn students to use the Princeton library and museums, thus obviating the need for Evelyn to provide such facilities for its own students. By the mid-1890s the Evelyn entrance requirements and Bachelor of Arts course of study were identical with those of Princeton, although Evelyn also offered a Bachelor of Letters degree, which was less rigorous, as was Princeton's Bachelor of Science degree. Both the latter two did not require the study of Greek.

McIlvaine died in 1897 and the college closed its doors a few months later. The demise of both the founder and the college in the same year is clearly related, but oversimplifies the cause of Evelyn's decline. McIlvaine's poor management was an obvious factor. This ineptitude, combined with the national financial difficulties in the 1890s, made it impossible for the college to continue. Parents were willing to make financial sacrifices to educate their sons, but most were less willing to do so for daughters. Although the enrollment was over 40 in the early 1890s, the number of students fell off precipitously after the panic of 1893. When the college closed in 1897, it had graduated only 15 young women.

Undoubtedly an equally important reason for Evelyn's demise was the inability of McIlvaine to establish a permanent accommodation with Princeton so that Evelyn could become formally the women's college of Princeton as at that moment Barnard College was becoming the women's undergraduate division of Columbia University, Radcliffe at Harvard, and Pembroke at Brown. Certainly women's colleges were much discussed in this period, but the two most conservative of the colonial colleges, Yale and Princeton, were unwilling to accept coordinate colleges or coeducation until 1969.

Princeton had documented its lack of enthusiasm for women's rights in 1866 when a talk by Lucy Stone, the well-known feminist and abolitionist, and her husband had been broken up "by boys and young men said to be students of the College of New Jersey." The account added, "We are assured that this is not an unusual occurrence in Princeton." Although the local newspaper had regretted the "disgraceful black-guardism at Mercer Hall," it had added, "such a population as that of Princeton could not be supposed to countenance the propriety of woman (sic) appearing on the rostrum to advocate political rights." The mood had not changed enormously 25 years later when a closer affiliation of the women's college was sought with Princeton. In addition to its political and academic conservatism, Princeton at this time was not suffering from a shortage of students and therefore undoubtedly felt less pressure to expand its student body than it might have if its enrollment been seriously declining.

Although Patton had served on the Evelyn board, he was not accustomed to leading the Princeton Board of Trustees in novel educational ventures particularly in the direction of what could have been a controversial issue. Woodrow Wilson, who became president after Evelyn's closing, but who played a leading role at Princeton in the 1890s, was not an enthusiast of coeducation, but he did recognize the inevitability of higher education for women. When deciding to accept his first teaching position at Bryn Mawr in 1884, he wrote to his fiancee, Ellen Axson, assuring her that he would not be serving under a woman (M. Carey Thomas, who was then Dean), but under Dr. James Rhoads, the president. He added, "I have none of the same objections to a school such as that to be opened at Bryn Mawr that I have to a *co-educational* institution." He concluded his comments on the Bryn Mawr appointment, "I should, of course, *prefer* to teach young men—and if I find that teaching at Bryn Mawr stands in the way of my teaching afterwards in some man's college, I shall of course withdraw."

In the face of Patton's apathy, Wilson's hostility, and Princeton's general conservatism, Evelyn was unable to achieve an affiliation and without it and without adequate funds was forced to close in 1897. Its closing left New Jersey without a single institution for the collegiate education of women. Two years later the Roman Catholic College of St. Elizabeth emerged from its former academy status, as did Mount St. Mary's in 1908. In 1915 Douglass College opened as the coordinate college for women of Rutgers, which remained all male.

The young political scientist who had opposed coeducation in principle became president of Princeton after Patton's departure in 1902. Woodrow Wilson diverged markedly from the policies of the Patton regime. Although his administration was a brief one, lasting only from 1902 until 1910, his influence on the university was enormous. Wilson's presidential career at Princeton presaged significantly the events of another 8-year period a decade later when he assumed another presidency, albeit one of greater responsibilities. In both Mercer County, New Jersey and in Washington, D.C., Wilson began his early years with a flourish, with important achievements, and with great popularity among his constituency. Somewhere after the midpoint of each career an occasion developed when compromise seemed appropriate to many observers, but Wilson remained adamant and termed it capitulation. To Wilson matters of principle, particularly ones involving "democracy" were not amenable to compromise. The final years of both the university and the national presidency terms were ones of losing the great fight, of parting with old friends, and of bitterness.

Born in Staunton, Virginia of a Presbyterian minister, Wilson was the first lay president of Princeton. Trained as a political scientist at Johns Hopkins University, Wilson introduced a major theme of his administration in his inaugural address in October 1902, "Princeton for the Nation's Service," thus establishing a nontheological and nonregional mission for the university. His predecessor, John Maclean, had deliberately rejected an outstanding Congregationalist for a faculty position. The more moderate James McCosh, who despite his ardent Presbyterianism had stated "that we should take at times an instructor belonging to another evangelical denomination, provided he be very eminent in his department." But Wilson in keeping with the national shift toward secularism made no specific religious demands on prospective faculty. Instead, he insisted on both gentility and scholarship, adding in keeping with the prevalent shift from piety, "If their qualities as gentlemen and scholars conflict, the former will win them the place." The ideal of "all-roundedness" at Amherst was replaced by gentility at Princeton. The transition from Calvinism to secular specialization was eased by passing through the way station of "gentlemanliness."

Three major issues confronted Wilson during his presidency, as they did most other college presidents of the early twentieth century. The first deal with a modification of the pattern and form of instruction, the second with the excessively non-academic tenor of undergraduate life, and the third with graduate education. The first was a triumph for Wilson, the latter two, both of which Wilson attempted to link to his crusade for social democracy, were personal failures.

One of the most obvious problems at Princeton in 1902 was the haphazard character of the curriculum and the quality of instruction. Now enrolling over 1300 students, the institution had gradually shifted from the recitation to the lecture method in many of the large classes required for freshmen and sophomores. Meanwhile, the juniors and seniors often sought elective courses that tended to have very few students and did not necessarily form a coherent sequence. Wilson believed that new young faculty, equipped with the requisite gentility and scholarship, should be brought to Princeton in significant numbers to supplement the large lectures with small sections for discussion. These would form the basis of the preceptorial system. Second, Wilson believed that the college should determine the courses for freshmen, that sophomores should choose among certain "fundamental" courses, and that juniors and seniors should select disciplines in which they wished to "concentrate." This approach to the old conflict between a prescribed and elective curriculum was similar to that introduced at Bryn Mawr when Wilson taught there and gradually became widely adopted as the standard curriculum of required general education for lower classmen with a choice of majors and minors for upperclassmen.

When the preceptorial method and the new curriculum were introduced in the fall of 1905, Wilson was nearing the summit of his popularity at Princeton. Despite the tremendous expense of the new additions to the faculty, the Princeton trustees were pleased with their choice. After the academic aimlessness of the Patton era, the university had clearly entered a period of vigorous presidential leadership.

Wilson himself recognized his unusual popularity with the trustees and with the Princeton community generally. He decided to press for another major reform at Princeton, one that he considered more crucial than the development of the graduate college. Wilson was much troubled by what he considered the stranglehold the eating clubs had on the lives of the undergraduates. To counteract this he introduced to the trustees in the spring of 1907 a "Quad Plan," which would have housed faculty and students together in new quadrangle types of dormitories where they would also have taken their meals. The purpose of these was to develop a loyalty among the undergraduates to a university unit more hospitable to academic ventures than the eating clubs, many of which were luxuriously furnished houses adjacent to the main campus that made no pretense of academic interests.

Wilson's concern about the excessive importance of the clubs was amply demonstrated by the tremendous furor among the alumni that his quad plan precipitated. One anonymous alumnus issued a pamphlet entitled "The Phantom Ship of The Quad System," in which he admitted the universality of the problem of student preference for the "relaxational" instead of the educational, but opposed the Wilson plan on the grounds that it was impractical, prohibitively expensive, and would repel students from Princeton. Wilson's principal biographer,

Arthur S. Link, has argued that here Wilson made a major tactical error by advocating his own quad plan and not attacking the clubs directly on the issue of social democracy, which was Wilson's real concern and on which they were obviously vulnerable. By lacing himself to the mast of his quad plan, Wilson refused to accept a compromise reform of the club system and thoroughly antagonized the alumni, who would not have objected violently to some restrictions being placed on the clubs. The indignant alumni reaction to the proposed quads indeed proved Wilson's contention that the clubs had usurped the undergraduate loyalty that was due the college. The action of the alumni also illustrated how they had replaced the Presbyterian clerics as a determining faction with whom a president must contend. As usual in these matters, financial considerations were all-important. Since the alumni had become the principal sources for outside funds for the institution, their endorsement of new plans was essential. Without it there could be no quad. Thus, Wilson's quad plan sank as a "phantom ship" in early 1908.

The squabble over the quad plan had seriously damaged Wilson's enormous popularity and had also obscured another potentially more serious controversy gathering steam at Princeton. This was the issue of the graduate college in which Wilson found himself locked in battle with Andrew West, the dean of the foundering graduate school, who had enlisted important allies among the trustees, alumni, and potential benefactors. West saw the creation of a graduate college principally as a necessity of high priority at Princeton for which he had raised money and to which he had given most of his time for nearly 10 years. He had had the majority responsibility for administering the entire institution during the lackadasical presidency of Patton and had been dispatched to England by Wilson in 1903 to study Oxford and Cambridge as possible models of graduate education. When he returned Wilson wrote an appreciative introduction to West's report, stating that the development of a graduate college was indeed a matter of urgency for Princeton. By the fall of 1906, Wilson had still not turned his attention to the graduate college, and when West was offered the presidency of Massachusetts Institute of Technology, he seriously considered accepting it, since he feared that Wilson did not indeed wish to proceed rapidly to implement plans for the graduate college. For some inexplicable reason, Wilson urged him to remain at Princeton and promised to move ahead with the graduate college. When Wilson then undertook the quad plan fight, West was naturally unhappy.

Although there were many maneuvers in the fight between West and Wilson, the final battle, fought from 1909 to 1910, was over the donor's condition for the location of the graduate college, a site about a mile from the central campus, which West supported and to which Wilson objected. Characteristically, Wilson saw this as an issue of social democracy, arguing that the isolation of the graduate students in their own college would contribute to their feeling superior to the undergraduates. In speeches to the Princeton alumni in New York and Pittsburgh in early spring 1910, Wilson reiterated the theme that separation of graduates from undergraduates was "undemocratic" and thus "unAmerican." "Seclude a man, separate him from the rough and tumble of college life, from all the contacts of every sort and condition of men, and you have done a thing which America will rank with contemptuous disapproval," Wilson told the Pittsburgh alumni in April 1910.

Wilson's argument for democracy in education, for an abolition of class distinctions, and for unified approaches to learning reflects the dominant mood of American progressive thought. This is the theme that John Dewey developed much more fully in *Democracy and Education* in 1916. The irony is that Wilson should take this stand at Princeton, which had been moving steadily toward an more aristocratic undergraduate student body since the days James McCosh had pleaded for inexpensive dormitories so more sons of impecunious Presbyterian clergy could attend to balance the growing numbers of wealthy Episcopalians. Certainly the socially homogeneous Princeton undergraduates were not likely to supply the graduate students with "all the contacts of every sort and condition of men" that Wilson deemed essential. The notion that *graduate* students would become a social elite at Princeton, despite their separation from the campus and their elegant accommodations, simply flew in the face of what an intelligent observer of Princeton or any of the other major eastern universities could see. The academic demands on undergraduates then were not taxing, giving them ample leisure to pursue their social activities. The clubs, which Wilson had unsuccessfully tried to curb, had gained such strength that by 1914 about 87 percent of the eligible undergraduates were members.

The separation of the graduate students from the undergraduates may produce problems, but not the ones Wilson enumerated. Instead by leaving the graduate students in seclusion, they would have little contact with the undergraduates and, therefore, could not be expected to exert a significant academic influence on the campus to counter the prevailing antiintellectual one. McCosh had recognized the value of the presence of graduate fellows on campus for this purpose beginning in the late 1860s. Therefore, the issue of social democracy was indeed germane to the controversy, but not for the reasons Wilson expressed. By having the graduate students apart, the undergraduates could continue their postprep school life-style, unaffected by the graduate students whose academic interests were presumably more intense.

The issue came to a head in mid-1910, again because of money. A new generous bequest made possible the building of the graduate college on the golf links apart from the main campus, precisely what West wanted. By this time Wilson had antagonized a substantial group on the board of trustees, the same board that 4 years earlier had been calling Wilson "Princeton's greatest asset," as well as many of the alumni and faculty. Some of the rhetoric that upset the board also caught the attention of the Democratic politicians of New Jersey, who were looking for a high-principled candidate for governor, who would brighten their tarnished image. Wilson agreed to be nominated, trading the academic political arena for the state and, 2 years later, the national political arena, where he would repeat the cycle of early victories and later defeats.

The major events in Princeton's history for the period 1865 to 1918 had occurred when Wilson departed in 1910. The university, which had undergone a thorough renovation of its undergraduate academic life with the introduction of the preceptorial system in 1905, had been wracked by the bitter disputes accompanying the quad plan in 1907, now observed the opening of the much debated separate graduate college in 1913. Clearly it was time for a respite from controversy and bold action.

By 1918 Princeton was no longer the parochial, pious college it had been in 1865. Within a few years it would be immortalized by F. Scott Fitzgerald in *This Side of Paradise*, and many years later George Kennan would present a minority but not contradictory point of view in his *Memoirs*. Although one was a fictional representation and the other was an autobiographical reflection, both described Princeton as an institution that has lost all significant Presbyterian connections, where piety was passé. Undergraduate life was dominated by club life, although for the rare student like Kennan who did not join a club, study was dominant. By this time Princeton had lost its academic provinciality, although it had certainly not attained the great democratic ideal of Wilson. It had become one of the major American universities. Harvard could no longer ignore Princeton as it had in 1886.

The University of Wisconsin

Like Princeton, the University of Wisconsin is a paradigm of its class. Its class, however, was different from Princeton's; at Wisconsin and at the other state universities the aim was to provide service on a total basis, to students through teaching, to knowledge through research, and to the populace through service. No issue was exempt from legitimate examination; no resident with a high school diploma ineligible for admission.

Princeton's purview was much less ambitious, but Wisconsin attempted to do everything for everybody and, to an astonishing degree, it succeeded.

The success of Wisconsin lies in the leadership of two university presidents, the willingness of the legislature to provide the resources for a great university, and perhaps most important, to the pioneer and often immigrant residents of the state who attended the university, benefitted from its research, and supported the legislators' appropriations.

Two presidents of Wisconsin between 1865 and 1918 emerge as major figures in shaping that university; they are also representative of the kind of leaders who built state universities throughout the nation. They were John Bascom, who was president from 1874 to 1887, and Charles R. Van Hise, who was president from 1903 to 1918. Bascom was a New Englander, educated at Williams College in Massachusetts and two theological seminaries, Auburn and Andover. Prior to coming to Wisconsin he had taught at Williams under a former Wisconsin president, Paul Chadbourne (1867 to 1870), who had recommended Bascom for the Wisconsin position at least partly because he recognized that Bascom's talents were better suited to an emerging educational institution than to a more traditional, pedagogically conservative one. Bascom's gifts were not political, and for this reason his tenure was relatively short because he resigned after difficulties with the governing group of the university, the Board of Regents. However, Bascom brought to the university what it then needed more than administrative skill, educational vision. Bascom was a man of wide intellectual interests, and he gave Wisconsin a desirability of broad knowledge. He was interested in many kinds of questions and believed the university should be too.

From the opening of Wisconsin's doors in 1850 the university had suffered the usual vicissitudes of state universities: insufficient funds, inadequate presidents, collapsing enrollments during the Civil War, and a tentative new breath of life with Morrill Act funds. After the war Paul Chadbourne, who had steadfastly refused to come to Wisconsin unless it modified its coeducation provision, permitting women students to attend only if they were housed and recited completely separately from the men, presided over the university. The struggling and rather pathetic campus in Madison gradually began to show some prospects of vitality. In 1867 one man received a B.A. and four received B. Phil. (Bachelor of Philosophy), and in 1868 two received B.A.'s and seven received B.Phil's. Chadbourne's departure in 1870 opened the way for full participation of women as undergraduates. The lack of preparatory schools in Wisconsin (neither private nor public high schools existed in significant number) necessitated both a preparatory department and woefully low admission standards. The preparatory department was abolished between 1882 and 1883, partially as an inducement to the development of public high schools. Entrance to the law school, for example, required only the ability to demonstrate some competence in English and evidence of good moral character. Sometimes students were even admitted there when they failed to pass the exam for entrance into the preparatory department.

Another step in the movement toward elevating academic standards occurred in 1871 when classroom grading became based solely on academic performance and not on deportment. Shortly before Bascom's arrival the university approved an alternative for the bachelor's degree to the totally prescribed classical course common to nearly all colleges in the nation. The alternative led to a bachelor of letter's degree and permitted substitution of modern languages for classical ones. During the first year of its existence six students chose the modern classical course and nine chose the ancient, these figures providing an index both of preferences of the students and of their numbers.

Bascom's arrival in Madison in the spring of 1874 precipitated the changes that would permit the University of Wisconsin to offer not only a traditional liberal arts course of good quality, but also alternatives to it comparable in academic quality although different in emphasis. Bascom believed in permitting students in the College of Letters to select programs at the University that built on their own interests, chiefly their linguistic and scientific preferences. He also recognized that the preparation offered in the growing but scattered high schools in the state precluded advanced foreign language study for many college freshmen. Convinced as he was that students should be broadly trained, Bascom provided for three alternative courses of study in the College of Letters, each with extensive coverage in various disciplines of the liberal arts but with varying emphasis in science and languages.

Other students could enroll in the College of Arts, which emphasized primarily scientific courses. This had a more practical orientation. During much of this time the College of Arts also included what little work existed in engineering and agriculture. The science courses in the College of Arts attracted more students than the ancient and modern classical courses in the College of Letters, either because their precollege training prepared them more adequately or because the students, many of whose parents had not had extensive classical educations, believed these studies more appropriate for the lives they would lead.

Bascom had a sense of the vital role that the university could play in the state, preserving the best of the traditional liberal arts program, but still adapting other college courses to assist in the more immediate needs of the state. Bascom was one of the last major figures among the state university leaders who firmly believed that the goal of an undergraduate education was to produce "the well-rounded man." His own writing covered a great many disciplines and his conception of education was familiarity or competence in most of the major branches of human knowledge. He was too advanced for his time at Williams in advocating parity of various disciplines, in lacking theological orthodoxy, and in championing of coeducation. These were all qualities that stood him in good stead at Wisconsin where he combined these views with his belief that the most inclusive test of any educational system was the extent of and character of its service to the state. In his valedictory statement to the Wisconsin community Bascom said, "The

University of Wisconsin will be permanently great in the degree in which it understands the conditions of the property and peace of the people, and helps to provide them; in the degree in which it enters into the revelation of truth, the law of righteousness, and the love of man, all gathered up and held firm in the constitution of the human soul and the counsel of God concerning it." In Bascom's characteristic nineteenth-century rhetoric, this statement foreshadowed the more precise implementation of this doctrine by Charles Van Hise in the "Wisconsin Idea" in the early twentieth century. Bascom thus sowed the seeds that germinated under Van Hise a quarter of a century later.

The intervening years between Bascom and Van Hise (1887 to 1903) included a number of changes in the university that permitted Van Hise to reap the fruits of his predecessors' labors and allowed Wisconsin to emerge in the early twentieth century as one of the two or three leading state universities and among the top dozen universities in the country. In keeping with the secularism becoming characteristic of academic life in general and state universities in particular, the succeeding presidents were all laymen and two of the three were scientists (Thomas Chamberlin, 1887 to 1892 and Charles R. Van Hise, 1903 to 1918). The third, Charles Kendall Adams (1892 to 1902), was an historian.

In these interim years Wisconsin made its peace with the dominant academic issue of the day, the elective system. Not going as far as Harvard in abandoning all requirements but rhetoric for students, Wisconsin nonetheless affirmed the essential position, already tentatively advanced under Bascom, of an equality among studies. President Chamberlin urged a program for the first 2 years of "basal studies" that would provide an introduction to the major academic disciplines that could serve later as a basis for the student's decision for his specialization. The emphasis at Wisconsin in the College of Letters was on the social sciences, often at the expense of the classics, which between 1891 and 1892 enrolled only 10 percent of the students in Greek. This compared with 21 percent at Minnesota, 25 percent at Michigan, 36 percent at Northwestern, and 23 to 60 percent at the various denominational schools in Wisconsin.

The decade of Adams' presidency, 1892 to 1902, was one in which the university was adjusting to its unprecedented growth both in personnel and in academic offerings. In 1887 the faculty numbered 40; in 1896 it numbered 113. With these new faculty members came a variety of new academic demands. One of the most pronounced of these was the library. In 1868 the library budget was $300. Six years later there were just over 5500 volumes in the library. By 1892 the library acquisition budget was $3000 and the following year (Adams' first) this amount was trebled. By 1895 the holdings had nearly doubled the 1889 number (approximately 33,000 volumes), but even these new books brought the total to barely that or less than the libraries of Minnesota, Kansas, Iowa, Northwestern, and Illinois, universities frequently regarded as less distinguished than Wisconsin.

Another major development of the last decade was the healthy growth—at last—of the engineering and agriculture departments, for which the Morrill Act funds had originally been appropriated. Their hesitant development had been speeded by the additional appropriations available under the Hatch Act of 1887 and the Morrill Act of 1890, but at least as important was the passage of time necessary for persons to acquire the knowledge that would make them competent teachers and researchers. In the agricultural sphere at Wisconsin the winter short courses, adopted by the Regents in 1885, and two fundamental discoveries in dairying, one an easy test for the butterfat content of milk and another dealing with the manufacture of cheese, convinced the farmers of the state that the university did indeed have information that would be useful for them. Attendance in both the regular agricultural curriculum in the college and in the special winter short courses for farmers increased dramatically. Between 1898 and 1903 agriculture enrollments increased 66 percent and engineering increased 158 percent. The corresponding rise in the College of Letters and Science was 18 percent.

Probably the most significant accomplishment of the Adams' years was the firm establishment of graduate study. After graduating from the University of Wisconsin himself, Adams had traveled to Germany, as so many of his generation did. The encounter of these men with the European tradition of lectures, seminars, and independent research had an important effect on American colleges and universities, then undergoing such a variety of changes. Particularly as new subjects moved into the curriculum, it became necessary to move from the standard *explication du texte* into a more expansive approach to the subject. During this period the undergraduate teaching began to shift from recitation sessions to lectures, and the accompanying graduate instruction to seminars and guided research.

Although nearly all state universities would eventually move to extensive programs of graduate study, Wisconsin was one of the first, and this was in large part because of President Chamberlin, a committed researcher in geology, and President Adams, the historian. Many of the new faculty whom they assembled in Madison were imbued with the research emphasis, a substantial number having studied at John Hopkins University, the seat of American scholarship in the last 20 years of the nineteenth century. The historian Frederick Jackson Turner, who became renown for his frontier thesis, taught at Wisconsin, having taken a year off at Chamberlin's insistence to complete a doctorate at Johns Hopkins. In 1891 he was joined by Charles Homer Haskins, destined to be one of America's finest renaissance scholars. Both subsequently joined the Harvard faculty (Turner in 1910 and Haskins in 1902) at a time when Harvard was again assuming its preeminent position in American education, a fact that made it somewhat easier for Wisconsin to let them go.

Turner, and to a lesser degree, Haskins, were instrumental in persuading their former professor in political economy at Johns Hopkins, Richard T. Ely, to join them at Wisconsin in 1892. Ely's appointment marks the beginning of Wisconsin's position as an institution providing opportunities for serious graduate work and for supporting faculties in their own research. Ely came to Wisconsin with requirements that foreshadowed those of his academic descendants of the mid-twentieth century. He demanded that a special division within the University be created for him with its own budget. He wished additional appointments to be made at junior levels in his field so that he would not be intellectually isolated. And, finally that precursor of midtwentieth-century academic problems, he refused to teach undergraduates, preferring instead to devote his time to his own research and to a limited number of graduate students. In classic fashion Ely believed he could make these demands of Wisconsin at least in part because he was leaving a position at a university with great academic prestige to come to an institution considerably less well-known academically. For its part Wisconsin was trying to establish itself as an outstanding university, and this was clearly one way to do it.

One of the basic facts that was soon apparent to all connected with the management of the university was that the movement away from undergraduate class recitations to greater diversity of course offerings, and especially to graduate instruction, was very expensive. Although the citizens of Wisconsin, through their legislature, had been willing to support the university at a level barely adequate for an ordinary undergraduate program, and the federal government assisted with the engineering and agricultural programs, it remained to be seen whether the state would support programs of research in the liberal arts fields, particularly when the subjects probably had no immediate application. In this respect, as in so many others, Wisconsin came out considerably ahead of the other state universities, but it was always a problem to convince legislators—and sometimes even the administrators within the institution—that research without utilitarian benefit should be aided.

The principle research contributions of the state universities have been in scientific fields where both the theoretical and technological achievements have been immense. Although the social sciences have fared reasonably well, particularly when expertise could be applied to government and business, research in the humanities often had not prospered at the same rate. One of the salvations of the humanities was that research in those fields was not as expensive as in others. Apparatus was not needed, and in some cases even library demands were minimal. This was fortunate, because the president of a state university pleading for his budget before a committee of the state legislature generally found it much easier to convince the legislators of the benefit to the state of research in dairying instead of in philosophy.

A president capable of dealing with a legislature was Charles Van Hise, Adams' successor at Wisconsin. Although the Regents showed some reluctance in appointing him, partly because he so obviously wanted the job and eagerness is often a great handicap to selection, Van Hise was ideally suited to bring Wisconsin to public recognition in the La Follette years. Much of the fabled "Wisconsin Idea," the notion that the University should be a repository of services of all kinds for the state, was a legacy Van Hise inherited, but he brought it to the self-consciousness of the state and to the attention of the nation. For Van Hise this was largely a matter of recounting his own past. Born to a pioneer family in Wisconsin, he entered the University in John Bascom's last year as president, going on to receive in 1892 its first Ph.D. Like President Chamberlin, Van Hise was a scientist, therefore one of the new breed of academic men, and like Chamberlin, he was also a geologist. Van Hise was a man of varied interests and abilities, not the least of which was his flexibility. His genuine commitment to investigation in geology did not preclude fascination with university administration or prevent his writing one of the early definitive books on conservation.

Van Hise's administration from 1903 until his death a week after the armistice of 1918 brought Wisconsin into the mainstream of modern American academic life. Van Hise's tremendous concern for the University's involvement with the state became for many major American universities later in this mobile century a similar involvement with the nation. Efficiency of operation, about which Van Hise was so concerned, persists as a continuing tension, although the primitive school and university surveys of his time so indebted to Taylorism have been replaced by somewhat more sophisticated analyses today.

Van Hise and his friend Governor Robert M. La Follette combined their administrative and political skills and, following the canons of Progressivism of the early twentieth century, attempted to put the university at the service of the state. Van Hise was candid in explaining that the university's primary responsibilities were to the students and to the people of Wisconsin. His concern with students, however, did not lead him to value teaching highly. Instead, he insisted rigorously on research from his faculty, some of whom believed that he was not adequately appreciative of their service to the institution. He also encouraged them to serve the state as experts in their fields, and in 1908 over 40 were so involved. The ground was thus prepared for the midcentury battle regarding the professor's time and allegiances: to teach undergraduates, to do research, or to consult in his specialty. The pendulum swung a full arc for professors, who in Bascom's days at Williams spent their time reviewing standard texts with undergraduates, but with Van Hise at Wisconsin concentrated their energies on empirical investigations, the fruits of which should be of use to the state.

In both his commitment to faculty research and to efficient university management, Van Hise expressed views of many other presidents. His sense of the obligation of the university to the state, a corporate noblesse oblige, however, is more characteristic of the state universities than of the private ones. Even in this respect, however, the state universities were not unique; Johns Hopkins, the exemplar of the research-oriented private universities, had assisted the city of Baltimore and the state of Maryland in preparing tax laws. Other universities frequently performed services to their society and especially to the areas in which they were located, so the distinction must not be too sharp. It would be fair, however, to point to the increased responsibility to the agency that funded them, which the state universities invariably felt.

At Wisconsin the obligation was fulfilled in many ways, most of them initiated by Van Hise's predecessors, but popularized by Van Hise. The faculty experts who served on various legislative panels were one example. The research of professors in the School of Agriculture on topics of greatest concern to Wisconsin farmers was another. The establishment of the Agriculture Experimental Station with county agents serving as liaisons between the farmer and university was still a third. The extension program by which faculty members of the university lectured in various communities throughout the state on topics of their particular interest was yet another.

Perhaps the most encompassing of all the efforts of the university to assist throughout the state was in its decision to accredit high schools and preparatory schools so that their graduates could attend the university without taking an examination. By assuming this responsibility the university achieved tremendous influence over the state's schools. Inevitably there were objections from the schools to this practice, since the school administrators correctly pointed out that by no means all students in the high school expected to attend college, but in the spirit of the N.E.A. Committee of 10 (1894), the university was not dissuaded from its efforts to standardize work in the state schools. Since the school must pay the expenses of the professor, it often asked him to give a public lecture on the evening of his visit so that admission might be charged. Although this may have been another way of bringing the university to the people, it was not an altogether satisfactory one from the point of view of the professor, who found the trips arduous and the schools often discouragingly poor.

This service of the university to the state received wide attention for several reasons. One was Van Hise himself, who with his keen sense of publicity, encouraged many articles about it. Second, Charles McCarthy's book of 1912 describing the "Wisconsin Idea" found numerous readers. Finally, the coincidence of Van Hise's presidency and the political progressivism of La Follette made broad coverage inevitable. McCarthy, like the good public relations man he was, called the plan of service to the state the "Wisconsin Idea," but what happened at Wisconsin occurred at the other state universities as well. At Wisconsin, as in so many other educational matters, it was done a little better.

Van Hise was fond of saying that the university existed for the students, and, indeed, he was correct in pointing to the necessity of understanding a university through the persons educated there. The most obvious fact about the students in the beginning of this period was their scarcity. During the Civil War years the university had been forced to suspend operations for lack of students and later had accepted the principle of women undergraduates, at least in part, in order to fill the vacant classrooms. During the winter of 1862 to 1863, only 12 students of college grade were enrolled in the classical course and 17 were enrolled in the new scientific course. The following year when the teacher training division (the normal department) opened and included women, 119 of the 162 students were women. Here the curriculum was quite similar to that of a high school. It was abolished in 1868, and teachers could either be prepared in normal schools scattered throughout the state, which offered work at approximately a high school level, or they could attend the university in a regular bachelor degree program in which they could prepare to teach secondary school. In June 1874, bachelor's degrees were awarded to 15 women and 23 men in the liberal arts courses, 2 men in engineering, and 19 men in law. That fall the number of entering freshmen had increased to 82, 32 of whom were graduates of graded high schools of the state. The growth of the high schools was an important development for the university, since it meant that the university could eventually disband its preparatory department.

In an effort to aid the enrollments the Regents recommended in 1870 and the state legislature passed an act in 1872 allowing graduates of Wisconsin high schools to enter the university without payment of tuition. A similar policy was in effect in Michigan, Minnesota, Missouri, and Iowa, and although the university did not charge these students tuition, it did levy fees for matriculation, incidentals, and laboratory and library usage, the effect of which was to keep revenue coming into the university from enrolled students but to make apparent to Wisconsin residents advantages accruing to graduates of Wisconsin schools. The contrast between Wisconsin's method of solving the problem of inadequate enrollments, common to nearly all colleges in the last third of the nineteenth century, and Princeton's approach is striking. Wisconsin worked very hard to achieve a working relationship with the public schools in the state, encouraging their growth among other reasons so that they could supply the state university with prospective students. Princeton, the private institution, concentrated on establishing private "feeder" prep schools when similarly faced with this difficulty. Franklin College, of course, enjoyed the support of the local editor, who urged closing the public high school and sending those students interested in education beyond the grades to the college's preparatory department at public expense.

President Bascom was eager to drop the subfreshmen, since he believed that not only would this force the development of the high schools of the state, but also it would improve the quality of student life by making it more serious and academic. The admissions' standards in the precollege group were rising. To be admitted to the preparatory department in 1870 a person had to be 12 years of age and prepared to study such subjects as English, arithmetic, and geography. By 1873 prospective students to the preparatory department were examined in reading, spelling, penmanship, arithmetic, civil and descriptive geography, English grammar, and United States history. Bascom was able to gain the Regents' approval to abolish the preparatory department. In 1882 the university opened with only 369 students, but all of them in the college courses.

By the end of the 1880s the slump in enrollments at Wisconsin (as well as elsewhere) had begun to improve. In 1886 to 1887 (Bascom's last year) there were 549 students, and 6 years later the number was nearly double. By the turn of the century Wisconsin was enrolling nearly 2500 students and in 1903 to 1904, the first year of Van Hise's presidency, over 3000 students. The increase was accounted for partly by the large jump in population of the state, which in 1900 had over 2 million residents, and partly by the greater availability of high school preparations and the absence of a debilitating economic recession. The most significant cause, however, was the increasing conviction that a college education was beneficial, that something of value could be learned in college.

With the increase in numbers came some changes also in the character of the student body. In the senior class of 1872 eight members of the class of less than 40 had been born outside the United States, while the majority were natives of Wisconsin. Five years later all were native born and a substantial majority were from Wisconsin. Religious preferences among both groups were divided among various Protestant sects and Roman Catholics, none having more than a handful of supporters. In both years by far the largest group of students expressed no denominational preference. By the end of the century the overwhelming majority still came from Wisconsin, and a bare majority were children of business and professional parents. Geography within Wisconsin continued to play an important role, with more students attending from Dane County, in which the university was located, than any other county in the state.

Perhaps the most noticeable shift in the student body in the early twentieth century was in the substantial increase in the number of children of farmers and of immigrants. The children of immigrants had doubled the persistence rate in college of the children of American-born families. Children of immigrants had begun to appear at the university in appreciable numbers in the 1880s, but by 1907 30 percent of the entering class and 60 percent of the graduating class were of foreign parentage. Half the foreign fathers in 1907 came from Germany while Norway and the British Isles were the next two major sources of emigration.

By the mid-1870s the presence of women in the student body was no longer regarded as the simple economic necessity it had been during the Civil War or even the Midwestern educational aberration President Chadbourne had regarded it as in the late 1860s. The Wisconsin citizenry, as early as 1866 (11 years after Iowa had opened as a coeducational institution), apparently favored coeducation. One of the few accomplishments of President Twombly's brief tenure had been to permit women full participation in the undergraduate life of the college. "In our University," he stated in 1872, "young ladies have shown themselves fully competent to pursue the higher studies with young men." The following year he observed that the admissions standards for the Ladies' College were higher than in the all-male College of Arts, a circumstance that remains common today in many coeducational institutions. An indication of the academic excellence of the women students was the award of the prize for the best commencement essay to a woman during Bascom's second year. Between 1870 and 1892 12 percent of the women and 16 percent of the men who entered as freshmen graduated. By the turn of the century the rates were nearly equivalent, 18.4 percent of the women and 19 percent of the men. The proportion of women in the College of Letters and Science had also increased from 29 percent in 1887 to 45.9 percent in 1908, a higher proportion than the present proportion of women undergraduates in the United States. In the professional schools the women throughout this period were a very small minority.

Despite the success of the women at the university and the

equalitarian sentiments of most Wisconsin residents on the subject of coeducation, periodically critics would appear and warn the university of the possible dangers to the women's health of having them pursue such a rigorous program of studies. For example, in 1877 President Bascom found it necessary to reply to the Board of Visitors' allegation that the female students were suffering ill health, as evidenced by their appearance of paleness. Bascom observed that there were 397 students in the collegiate and dependent departments, of whom 25 percent were then women, but that the men had three times higher absence rates for medical reasons than the women. Furthermore, the women's absence rate declined the longer they stayed in college, thereby attesting to the beneficial effect of the college environment.

Another threat to full and equal coeducation appeared in 1908 when President Van Hise urged separate sections in various courses for men and women. For Van Hise the proposal was simply one designed to promote more economical utilization of the university's facilities and did not imply any attitude on the nature of women. The debate quickly became fraught with ideological overtones, of which the statement of the head of the Department of Education, a well-known psychologist, Michael V. O'Shea, was one of the most inflammatory. O'Shea argued that the inherent physical and psychological differences of women, especially girls during adolescence, made it inadvisable to subject them to the same type of education provided for boys. His own daughter, however, was one of the early women Ph.D.'s. Despite the testimony of the expert and his own notions of efficiency, Van Hise yielded to the considerable outcry both in Madison and outside it, and women remained as regular members of all classes.

For the students at Wisconsin, both male and female, the attractions of the university were by no means limited to the curriculum. In the early days of the university when the studies were largely prescribed and dealt with traditional subjects, the students enlivened their programs by avid participation in the literary societies, where topics of contemporary interest were discussed with enthusiasm. A principal outgrowth of the literary societies that flourished at Wisconsin into the twentieth century, considerably longer than at most universities, was the joint debate, again an intellectual exercise into which the students entered with vast enthusiasm. Among the topics of the debate were regulation of railroad rates, immigration restriction, prohibition, free coinage of silver, and the efficacy of the capitalist system.

Gradually student enthusiasm for the literary societies and the joint debates declined, partly because the curriculum itself was shifting to fulfill some of the functions formerly served by the debates. Many of the early topics had dealt with essential political, social, and economic questions of the day, and now these same issues could be explored in the classes of Richard T. Ely, E. A. Ross, and others. Furthermore, the nation as a whole by the turn of the century seemed less interested in arduous self-improvement of the sort fostered by the debates. The peak enthusiasm for the home reading courses of the Chautauqua Circles coincided with the popularity of debates and also declined swiftly and steadily in the new century.

The decades surrounding the turn of the century marked a significant shift in the nation's tastes in entertainments, and this was reflected on the college campuses. At Wisconsin the focus of amusements in the 1890s became athletics. At Wisconsin the teams were often coached by Princeton men, an acknowledgment of the earlier interest of the East in these pursuits. The annual football game with the University of Minnesota became one of the most significant events of the year in the lives of the university undergraduates and even the alumni. President Adams fostered this enthusiasm for sports, to the consternation of his faculty, and the athletic mania continued unchecked into Van Hise's administration.

Several abortive attempts in the early twentieth century finally led to the formation of the Big Ten Athletic league in the 1890s. The league tried establish uniform regulations for players on teams and to achieve some standardization of the game. Nearly all the other members were state universities comparable to Wisconsin: Michigan, Minnesota, Iowa, Indiana, Purdue, Illinois, and Ohio State. In addition, Northwestern University and the University of Chicago were included to complete the ten. For several decades the Big Ten dominated interscholastic football, and universities whose scholarly eminince might be questionable could achieve a national reputation on the football field.

The other major undergraduate diversion in the late nineteenth and during the twentieth century was fraternity and sorority life. These organizations, which were secret, generally Christian and preferably Protestant, dominated the social and extracurricular life at Wisconsin from the 1890s until well after World War II. In part, they were a reaction to the expansion of the student body and the inability or unwillingness of the university to provide dormitory space for students. More significantly, though, they were an expression of the new social emphasis at the university. Beginning with many laudable notions of social service, the fraternities and sororities soon became exclusively devoted to providing pleasant living and dining accommodations, suitable social contacts, and entries into the social life of the campus for their members. Beginning with the established Midwestern fraternities, the Miami Triad, made up of Sigma Chi, Phi Delta Theta, and Beta Theta Pi, the "Greeks," as they were known to distinguish them from the nonfraternity members, known as "barbs" (barbarians), came to dominate student political life by the 1890s, despite the small fraction of the student body they enrolled. The girls organized themselves into sororities in much the same ways, Kappa Kappa Gamma, Delta Gamma, and Gamma Phi Beta all being established by 1885. The resentment created by this minority rule led President Adams to believe that the solution lay in establishing more fraternities so that fraternity membership itself would be less exclusive. Ultimately this was the solution, and a number of other well-known groups, but also predominantly Jewish and Roman Catholic houses, were established at Wisconsin. The Jewish ones were much more numerous, since the Christian ritual of the fraternities and sororities did not officially preclude Roman Catholics.

The fraternities and sororities were yet another manifestation of the ostensibly secular but predominantly Protestant character of the University of Wisconsin and the other state universities. Throughout the 1860s and into the 1870s the leaders of the university were trained as theologians (Chadbourne, Twombly, and Bascom), and Twombly himself was a Methodist minister. In this period "Evidences of Christianity" was taught to the women students, "free from sectarian bias," the instructor assured the Regents. Despite its Protestant overtones Wisconsin moved more swiftly than other universities in becoming secularized. Chapel attendance was made voluntary in 1868 (compared with the University of Minnesota in 1887, Illinois in 1890, and Missouri in 1896) and was dropped entirely in 1885. This led to criticism from some Wisconsin residents and a reluctance to send their children to such a godless institution. On the other hand, Roman Catholics, believing that the secular-Protestant university was inadequate for Catholic young people, established in 1880 an undergraduate Catholic Club, an ancestor of the Newman Clubs of the twentieth century. By the turn of the century the official university policy had become decidedly secular, so much so that the College of Letters and Science successfully resisted establishing a nonsectarian but essentially religious course in ethics. The University of Wisconsin remained a bastion of secular learning, a result of the difficult tension between religion and other studies that characterized much of the history of American education from the midnineteenth to the late nineteenth century.

Conclusion

The optimistic sentiment dies hard in Americans, and it is appropriate, therefore, to end this book on education in

America from the Civil War to World War I with a discussion of the University of Wisconsin where, more than at most places, the American dream of what education should be became a reality. There the democracy in education, of which Woodrow Wilson spoke and John Dewey wrote, came close to actuality; there education was tied to life and access to formal education was broadly available to the populace. In Wisconsin higher education—and crucially, the *best* higher education in the state—was publicly supported and available to all graduates of the state's public high schools. In Wisconsin there was no major competition with the state university from other older, more prestigious colleges or universities, as was true of much of the East and South. The state university, furthermore, had made an effort to expand the state's high school system so that the high schools reached a substantial portion of the eligible population. At Wisconsin relatively little hierarchy existed among subjects. Unlike Princeton and the great private universities, where technical subjects stood second best (if at all) to humanities and sciences, at Wisconsin in 1918 subjects such as agriculture, home economics, and engineering were an accepted part of the curriculum. Students studying them had at least the illusion that their studies were on a par with the best of the traditional colleges and universities.

At Wisconsin, too, secularism had asserted itself by 1918. No formal or informal religious tests existed for students, and there were no formal ones for faculty, although one suspects that Jewish and Roman Catholic faculty members were rare. Qualifications for academic positions were defined in terms of scholarly and pedagogic quality, and presumably it was simply an accident that such excellence failed to occur in Jewish and Catholic males. That they should be found among women, of whatever religious persuasion, rarely occurred to anyone. Similarly, blacks, who at that time indeed did have a very small educated group, were not represented on faculties of predominantly white colleges either, although the explanation for their absence (when any was given) was much the same as for the women: they were needed to teach their own kind.

In 1918 the University of Wisconsin was probably the most distinguished state university in the nation. It had defined its responsibilities in terms of the population of its state and, given that definition, one can only argue that it had served the population well. It provided them with opportunities for mobility, although in America at that time mobility always was thought of as "up," never "down." It had offered classes on a variety of subjects, some that were immediately useful to the citizens and others that belonged to the traditional studies. In both kinds its faculty included leaders in their fields. It had admitted women as well as men students, and it had minimized overt prejudice against women undergraduates. It had admitted immigrants, and by 1918 they were continuing in course at a rate nearly double that of the children of native-born Americans. In short, the University of Wisconsin had done much to democratize education in the way that Wilson's rhetoric had pointed but which he had never been able to accomplish in either of his presidencies, of Princeton or of the United States.

Critics could observe that the University of Wisconsin had made this remarkable achievement in the best of circumstances, and they would, of course, be right. Like Johnson County, Indiana, where public education at the elementary and secondary levels flourished in the late nineteenth and early twentieth centuries, so it did at the University of Wisconsin in the early twentieth century. Some of the explanations for success were the same. In neither place was there any well-established private institution competing with the public institutions. Both had small but weak competition, but neither had to deal seriously with strong private educational forces, as did the state universities in the East or the public high schools in such cities as New York. Although the state of Wisconsin inevitably did not have as homogeneous a population as Johnson County, both were much less hetereogeneous than the nation as a whole. Neither had large black populations and neither had large groups of new immigrants from southern and eastern Europe. Wisconsin, of course, had a significant immigrant population in 1918, but it was chiefly from northern and western Europe, with cultural traditions that merged more easily with early twentieth-century America than those of the newly arrived southern and eastern Europeans. Even the Catholic population was largely German and, therefore, less suspect than the Irish, who dominated the Church's hierarchy, or the more recently emigrated Italians and Poles.

Finally, Wisconsin and Indiana were both significantly without the wealthy, established aristocracy, which existed in greater numbers and power in the East. As educators from Horace Mann on had noted, this group tended to educate their children in separate, private schools and to persist in thinking of public education as something for "others." When the aristocracy was too small, or too ill-defined to establish separate schools for its children, then it tended to support the public schools. This was the case in Marquette and was also the case for whites in Butler County after 1892. Furthermore, the absence of a well-defined aristocracy created opportunities for intelligent and hard-working young men that were sometimes more difficult to achieve in communities with clearer class lines. Undoubtedly this was more true in education than in any other sphere. Where the best education was public, open to all, and relatively cheap, possibilities for ambitious young men were considerable. In 1900 if one had one's choice (which, of course, one never did) it would still be best for one's future social and economic success to have been born the son of Philadelphia Main Liners or Boston Brahmins and gone to Princeton or Harvard. If that were not available, as indeed it was not to nearly all Americans, an excellent second choice would have been to have been born a white male in Johnson County, Indiana and to have moved with the family before college age to Wisconsin.

Educational opportunities for the population at large were simply much greater from 1865 to 1918 in relatively homogeneous Midwestern, small communities. There the school board was characteristically composed of the most prominent men in the community, and they wanted good schools for their children. When the only schools available in the community were the ones their children attended, they were likely to be good. Elsewhere, such as Butler County, Alabama or New York City, areas of the country in which the population most deviated from what much of the nation liked to think was "true Americanism," the offerings were more spotty, sometimes excellent, but often not. In those regions the circumstances of one's birth—sex, race, religion, parents' birthplaces, and family social and economic status—weighed heavily in determining educational opportunities.

bibliographic essay

the intent of this book has been to look carefully at the educational opportunities available to representative segments of the citizenry. For most of the populace, both young and old, where one lived was a fundamentally significant determinant of one's educational opportunities. This conviction about the importance of residence has determined the format of this book, that of focusing on individual communities to illustrate the educational undertakings current from 1865 to 1918. On the assumption that only for college would individuals leave their local communities specifically for an educational activity, the final chapter deals with the kinds of higher education generally open to persons during this period.

The decision to write a book on the history of American education in the late nineteenth and early twentieth centuries that concentrated on specific communities entailed research of a considerably different kind than that which would have resulted from a book dealing with the nation as a whole. Obviously the first questions were which communities and on what rationale they would be chosen. The places finally selected reflect the national patterns of that period. Three of the four are predominantly rural, although each has a county seat that dominates local educational, cultural, and commercial life. The fourth is a growing urban area (New York City) with a diverse population reflecting the ethnic, religious, and racial diversity that characterized many cities. One of the counties (Johnson) is homogeneously white, Protestant, and middle class. Another (Marquette) illustrates those predominantly nonfarming rural areas with large immigrant populations and with a high proportion of Roman Catholics. The third (Butler) is populated by a large group of poor blacks living in a southern farming county where most of their white neighbors are only slightly more affluent than they.

The higher educational institutions exemplify the two largest groups of colleges and universities, Princeton enrolling only men, and chiefly white, Protestant, upper-middle-class ones. The University of Wisconsin, on the other hand, welcomed a more diverse student body, one that included women, children of immigrants, and non-Protestants as well as the ubiquitous white, middle-class, multigeneration-American males.

No New England community has been included, partly because educational activities in that region have been better chronicled by other historians than those in any other part of the nation, and partly because New England no longer presented a distinctive educational climate. Furthermore, the population center of the United States was moving rapidly west between 1865 and 1918. By 1910 the population of New England was less than that of either the Middle Atlantic states or the East North Central region. Doubtless one reason for this extensive research on New England is the obvious one that it led the nation in establishing schools and school systems, and scholars have been legitimately interested in the problems of origins. Undoubtedly another factor that has led to the relatively heavy emphasis on New England has been the accessibility or records there and the proximity to major universities whose scholars, particularly in recent years, have found it more pleasant and convenient to pursue a topic within easy commuting distance of Boston.

Relatively little has been written on the history of American education from the Civil War to World War I, although this has been a period of considerable interest to American social and intellectual historians. Robert Wiebe's *The Search for Order* (New York: Hill and Wang, 1967) is an example of this genre; it includes an excellent bibliography. Most of the writing in American educational history in this period until quite recently has been taken up with the progressive education movement, of which Lawrence A. Cremin's *The Transformation of the School* (New York: Knopf, 1961) set the standard. More recently historians of education have been concerned with education's futile efforts to bring about social change in this era. Specific examples of these efforts are Henry Perkinson, *The Imperfect Panacea* (New York: Random House, 1968); Michael Katz, *Class, Bureaucracy, and the Schools* (New York: Praeger, 1971); Marvin Lazerson, *Origins of the Urban School* (Cambridge: Harvard University Press, 1971); Timothy L. Smith, "Native Blacks and Foreign whites; Varying Responses to Educational Opportunity in America" in *Perspectives in American History, VI* (1972): 309-338. Colin Greer, *The Great School Legend* (New York: Basic Books, 1972). An excellent compendium is the series "Urban Education," *History of Education Quarterly IX* (1969): 281-328. Somewhat earlier examples of books that dealt with the establishment and role of schools at this time are Edward A. Krug, *The Shaping of the American High School, 1880-1920* (New York: Harper and Row, 1964) and Theodore Sizer, *Secondary Schools at the Turn of the Century* (New Haven: Yale University Press, 1964).

Although these interpretive accounts were of interest and help in preparing this volume, of far greater direct assistance were the materials dealing with the particular communities and colleges. Preeminent among these were the United States Bureau of the Census reports, for which the thirteenth census, taken in 1910, (Washington, United States Government Printing Office, 1913) with its various abstracts and state supplements with their breakdowns by counties was most helpful. Among the contemporary accounts of education in America in these years the most useful were Adele Marie Shaw's series in *The World's Work VII* (1903-1904): 4204-4221, 4460-4466, 4540-4553; *VIII* (1904): 4795-4798, 4883-4894, 4996-5004, 5244-5254, 5405-5414; *IX* (1904-1905): 5480-5485; the "Phases of Modern Education" series in *Education* from September 1905 to June 1906 (14-26, 65-70, 129-136, 191-202, 253-259, 315-323, 385-392, 447-461, 509-518, and 571-583). Three contemporary book-length accounts of school conditions in the United States were also useful: Joseph Mayer Rice, *The Public School System of the United States* (New York: The Century Co., 1893); Scott Nearing, *The New Education* (New York: Row, Peterson and Co, 1915); and John and Evelyn Dewey, *Schools of To-Morrow* (New York; Dutton, 1915). The annual yearbooks of the National Herbart Society (beginning in 1895) and becoming the National Society for the Study of Education in 1902 gave a picture of current issues in American education. Ellwood Patterson Cubberley, *Public Education in the United States* (Boston: Houghton-Mifflin, 1919) was the standard text in the history of American education. Cubberley's professor, Paul Monroe, prepared a supplementary volume, *Founding of the American Public School System, From the Early Settlements to the Close of the Civil War Period* (New York: Macmillan, 1940).

Johnson County sources

General histories of Indiana are John D. Barnhart and Donald F. Carmony, *Indiana, from Frontier to Industrial Commonwealth* (New York: Lewis Historical Publishing Co., 1954) and William Wilson, *Indiana, A History* (Bloomington: Indiana University Press, 1966). Richard G. Boone, *A History of Education in Indiana* (New York: D. Appleton and Co., 1892; reprinted in Indianapolis; Indiana Historical Bureau, 1941) is a first-rate state history and places educational developments in Indiana in a national context. Fassett Allen Cotton, *Educa-*

tion in Indiana, 1793-1934 (Bluffton, Ind.: Progress, 1934) is less successful.

The two standard sources on the history of Johnson County were prepared by eminent residents of the county, David D. Banta, *Historical Sketches of Johnson County, Indiana* (Chicago: J. H. Beers Co., 1881); David D. Banta, *History of Johnson County, Indiana* (Chicago: Brant and Fuller, 1888); and Elba Branigin, *History of Johnson County, Indiana* (Indianapolis: B. F. Bower Co., 1913). Banta was a local judge, who became dean of the Indiana University Law School, and Branigin was a member of a prominent farming and political family. Both histories are essentially eulogistic and anecdotal, but each contains some useful information, particularly about informal educational arrangements in ephemeral schools and churches. Branigin's is superior to Banta's more personnal assessment.

Of greatest help in determining the routine activities of the community were the weekly local newspapers, especially the Franklin *Democrat*, which began as the *Herald-Democrat* on July 4, 1879. The Franklin *Jeffersonian* also began in 1879 and was succeeded by the *Republican* in 1886, which ran continuously until 1894. Sporadic issues are available after that date. Beginning in June 4, 1912 a daily appeared, *The Franklin Evening Star*, which published throughout the period.

The principal source on particular school activities were the minute books of the Board of School Trustees for the city of Franklin for 1866 to 1918, which were available in the Superintendent of School's office. They were remarkably complete, including class rolls, attendance records, and grades. Of special value was the Johnson County Schools Exposition Materials, prepared in 1904, which included the handwritten daily lesson plans of all the teachers for the fall term, the detailed curriculum for each grade, the qualifications of each teacher in the system, and some additional local historical material. Other records preserved in the Superintendent's office included the ranking of the Franklin schools relative to other comparable

Indiana communities. An additional course of study for the Franklin schools has been preserved; this is the one prepared by Superintendent Arnold Tompkins, *A Graded Course of Study for the Franklin Public Schools* (Franklin: n.p., 1883). Since this was Tompkins' prescription for the Franklin schools, it is interesting as a guide but less reliable as an indication of what actually occurred in the classrooms than the later teacher-prepared materials. Less systematic accounts of school life in Johnson County are found in the "The Story of Hopewell Schools, 1829-1884, (no author) in the Mock collection of the Indiana State Library and the Demaree-Shuck letters given by Vincent Akers to the Indiana State Library.

Other useful materials on education in Johnson County are H. D. Vories, "Young People's Reading Circle," *Independent School Journal XXXIV* (1889): 654-656, which is an account of Vories' work as Superintendent of Schools in Franklin with the Reading Circle, and Charles A. Deppe, "Autobiography," (Franklin: n.p., 1956), an anecdotal and amusing account of his early education. This mimeographed paper is on deposit in the Franklin College Library.

One of the superintendents of Franklin schools subsequently became a well-known American educator, Arnold Tompkins. His work is described by W. P. Krolikowski, "Arnold Tompkins: Midwest Philosopher and Educator," doctoral dissertation, University of Illinois, 1965. Krolikowski deals principally with Tompkins after he left Franklin. Most of the material here about Tompkins at Franklin comes either from the local newspapers or from the School Board minutes.

The principal historian of Franklin College has been John F. Cady, who wrote *The Centennial History of Franklin College* (Franklin: n.p., 1934) and *The Origin and Development of the Missionary Baptist Church in Indiana* (Franklin: n.p., 1942). Earlier materials on the history of the college include President W. T. Stott, "History of Franklin College, A Brief Sketch" (Indianapolis: n.p., 1874) and "Jubilee Exercises, First Half Century of Franklin College" (Franklin: n.p., 1884). These materials are all available in the Franklin College Library. The

Robert Y. and Hester H. Coward, *Catalogue of the David Demaree Banta Indiana Collection* (Franklin: Franklin College, 2nd ed., 1965) is an excellent guide to the Banta collection, which includes a number of useful materials for the historian of Indiana. By coincidence David Banta also spent part of the summer of 1890 traveling along the southern shore of Lake Superior, including Marquette County, and he related his experiences in a series of articles in the *Indianapolis News* in the winter of 1890 to 1891. The clippings are in the Banta collection.

Marquette County sources

Two early volumes deal with educational questions in Michigan: Daniel Putnam, *The Development of Primary and Secondary Public Education in Michigan* (Ann Arbor: George Wahr Publisher, 1904) and Arthur Raymond Mead, *The Development of Free Schools in the United States as Illustrated by Connecticut and Michigan* (New York: Teachers College, Columbia University, 1918). Three of the four-volume history of education in Michigan have appeared, and these three concern the pre-World War I era. They are Floyd R. Dain, *Education in the Wilderness* (Lansing: Michigan Historical Commission, 1968); Charles R. Starring and James O. Knauss, *The Michigan Search for Educational Standards* (Lansing: Michigan Historical Commission, 1969), and Donald W. Disbrow, *Schools for an Urban Society* (Lansing: Michigan Historical Commission, 1968). On the whole these books concentrate on developments in public education to the exclusion of private or parochial schools. Furthermore, they tend to view Michigan's problems and successes in the context of the lower peninsula of the state, which was much wealthier and more industrial than the poverty-stricken upper peninsula, which was isolated from the remainder of the state, sharing no border with it. Since Marquette County was in the upper peninsula, these books are of rather limited value for an understanding of it.

The Marquette County Historical Society was the principal

source of information about Marquette County, and the existence of the Society and its John Longyear Research Library was an important reason for selecting Marquette County. A wealth of pamphlet material on education in the county is available there, including the 1878 Catalogue of the Marquette Public Schools and a 1903 list of the high school alumni. The Columbia Exposition Educational Exhibit for Grade Schools and High Schools, 1892-1893, is a valuable source.

Despite the work of the Society, less material is available on Marquette than on Johnson County. The *History of the Upper Peninsula of Michigan* (Chicago: Western Historical Publishing Co., 1893), pp. 379-472 is the principal published history of the area. The *Inventory of the County Archives of Michigan* (Detroit: WPA, Michigan Historical Records Survey, 1940, No. 52) for Marquette County is also helpful.

One of the major contributions of the Historical Society is its index of the *Mining Journal*, the local Marquette newspaper, which is available for this period in nearly a complete run. Its predecessor, *Lake Superior Journal*, survives only in scattered copies in 1858 and 1860 editions.

For educational matters the most comprehensive sources are the School Board Minutes of the Marquette City School Board, which were available in the City School Superintendent's office from 1885 through 1918. Since the Baraga School had just closed when work on this book began, the Baraga records had been transferred to the offices of the Marquette-Alger Intermediate School District, and it was possible to examine the Records of Reports for 1917 and the Tuition and Record Books for 1916 and 1917.

Graduate student papers for history of education courses at Northern Michigan University, Marquette were a tremendous help in locating additional material on specific topics. Particularly useful were Paul LaBreche, "A History of Catholic Parochial School Facilities in Marquette, Michigan" (1969); Grace M. Richtmeyer, "A History of the John D. Pierce School" (1969); James V. Kalamajka, "History of Negaunee St. Paul High School and Events Which Led to its Closing" (1969); Gary

L. Buchschacher, "A Short History of the Development of Marquette County Schools" (1968?); Judith Soine and Bryan Ogea, "The History of Education in the Champion-Humboldt Schools" (1964); Gerald Erickson, "The History of Bessemer's Public Education" (1969); and Alan D. Johnson, "A Brief History of Marquette's Public Schools to 1927" (1969).

Material about Roman Catholic education in Marquette County is rather spotty, particularly since Catholic activities were not given much prominence in the local newspaper. Antoine Ivan Rezek's *History of the Diocese of Sault Ste. Marie and Marquette* (Houghton, Michigan: n.p., 1906, 1907, 2 vols.) is an enthusiastic account of early Catholic churches and clergy in the region. Since the first Catholic bishop of the Diocese of Northern Michigan, Frederic Baraga, is now being considered for canonization, a group of concerned clergy and laymen has organized a center for collection of material about Bishop Baraga's life and work. This is called "Cause of Bishop Frederic Baraga" and is located in Marquette. Since its collection is about Baraga, there is not as much material about Catholic life in the area as a scholar might wish, but it is still a useful place. Choyastom Verwyst, O.S.F. wrote the Standard biography of Baraga in English, *Life and Labors of Rt. Rev. Frederic Baraga* (Milwaukee: M.H. Wiltzuis Co., 1900). Two books about orders that sent nuns to teach in Marquette contain helpful material: Mary L. Savage, *The Congregation of St. Joseph of Carondelet* (St. Louis: B. Herber Book Co., 2nd ed., 1923) and Mother M. St. Paul, O.S.U., *From Decenzano to "The Pines"* (Toronto: Macmillan, 1941). *Our Sunday Visitor*, Centennial Issue, Northern Michigan edition, August 20, 1953 contains much anecdotal material about Catholic life.

More general information about Catholic education in America, which provides a useful perspective for viewing the Marquette experience as well as that of New York City, can be found in such books as Robert Cross, *The Emergence of Liberal Catholicism in America* (Cambridge: Harvard University Press, 1958), especially Chapter VII, "The Question of Schools." Cross's article, "Origins of the Catholic Parochial Schools in

America," *The American Benedictine Review XVI* (1965): 194-209, is the best analysis of that question available. Neil G. Mc-Cluskey, S. J. has edited a good collection of documents, *Catholic Education in America: A Documentary History* (New York: Teachers College Press, 1964). Philip Gleason has an excellent interpretive essay, "American Catholic Higher Education: A Historical Perspective," in Robert Hassenger, ed., *The Shape of Catholic Higher Education.* Vincent Lannie is currently doing very interesting work on Catholic education as his mimeographed paper "Church and School Triumphant: The Sources of American Catholic Educational Historiography" (1973), demonstrates.

The standard sources on the history of the Catholic education in America for this period are James A. Burns, *The Growth and Development of the Catholic School System in the United States* (New York: Benziger Brothers, 1912); John Gilmary Shea, *A History of the Catholic Church within the Limits of the United States* (Rahway, N.J.; Mershon Co. Press, Vol. I, 1890; Vol. II, 1892), and more recently, James A. Burns and Bernard Kohlbrenner, *A History of Catholic Education in the United States* (New York: Benziger Brothers, 1937) and Edward J. Power, *A History of Catholic Higher Education in the United States* (Milwaukee: Bruce Publishing Co., 1958). The section on Catholic higher education (Chapter IX, "Catholics and their Colleges") in Christopher Jencks and David Riesman, *The Academic Revolution* (Garden City, N.Y.: Doubleday, 1968) is a useful analysis.

Butler County sources

Two recent books illustrate the dilemmas Alabama faced in the post-Reconstruction years: Sheldon Hackney, *Populism to Progressivism in Alabama* (Princeton: Princeton University Press, 1969) and William W. Rogers, *The One-Galloused Rebellion: Agrarianism in Alabama* (Baton Rouge: Louisiana State University Press, 1970). Both supplement and are much more critical than the standard Alabama eulogistic history, Thomas McAdory Owen, *History of Alabama and Dictionary of Alabama Biography* (Chicago: S. J. Clark Publishing Co., 1921, 4 vols.). Charles Spurgeon Johnson, *Statistical Atlas of Southern Counties* (Chapel Hill: University of North Carolina Press, 1941) supplies a wealth of data about southern counties, and it was critical in determining which Alabama county should be selected as representative of the south.

Charles Dabney, *Universal Education in the South* (Chapel Hill: University of North Carolina Press, 1936, 2 vols.) and Edgar W. Knight, *Public Education in the South* (Boston: Ginn and Co., 1922) are the classic histories of education in the South, and both concentrate on education of whites. Henry Allen Bullock, *A History of Negro Education in the South, from 1619 to the Present* (Cambridge: Harvard University Press, 1967) attempts to present the difficulties facing blacks after Reconstruction but devotes most of his attention to the efforts of northern philanthropists to improve schools for blacks. Considerably superior to Bullock are Horace Mann Bond's two volumes on black education: *The Education of the Negro in the American Social Order* (New York: Prentice Hall, 1934) and *Negro Education in Alabama* (Washington, D.C.: Association Publishers, 1939). Louis M. Harlan, *Separate and Unequal* (Chapel Hill: University of North Carolina Press, 1958) and C. Vann Woodward, *The Strange Career of Jim Crow* (New York: Oxford University Press, 1955) are also helpful. James M. McPherson, "White Liberals and Black Power in Negro Education," *American Historical Review, LXXV* (1970): 1357-1386 is a first-rate summary of black participation in higher education in the South in the late nineteenth and early twentieth centuries. Allen B. Ballard, *The Education of Black Folks* (New York: Harper and Row, 1973) contains useful material.

Probably the best contemporary survey of educational opportunities for blacks is *Negro Education: A Study of the Private and Higher Schools for Colored People in the United*

States (Washington, D.C.: U.S. Bureau of Education Bulletins No. 38, 39, 1916). Since this study was done just before World War I it encompassed most of the results of the Jim Crow movement in the south. W. E. B. DuBois, *The Negro Common School* (Atlanta: Atlanta University Publications, 1901) is an earlier work which gives more attention to public education.

Histories of education in Alabama deal principally with educational opportunities for whites. The standard ones are Willis G. Clark, *History of Education in Alabama, 1702-1889* (Washington, D.C.: Government Printing Office, 1889), which deals in the nineteenth century chiefly with Mobile; William F. Perry, "The Genesis of Public Education in Alabama," *Transactions of the Alabama Historical Society, II* (1897-1898): 14-27, which is autobiographical; Stephen B. Weeks, *History of Public School Education in Alabama* (Washington, D.C.: U.S. Bureau of Education Bulletin No. 12, 1915), which relies heavily on Clark; and Oscar W. Hyatt, *The Development of Secondary Education in Alabama Prior to 1920* (Nashville: George Peabody College for Teachers Publishers, 1933), which, given the topic, is understandably rather sketchy.

Several master's essays include useful information on Alabama educational history, preeminent among them Shirley Garrett Schoonover, "Alabama's Quest for Social Justice During the Progressive Era," M. S. thesis, Auburn University, Auburn, Alabama, 1970. Also helpful is Peter M. Hoar, "A History of Public Education in Alabama, 1865-1875," M. A. thesis, Auburn University, Auburn, Alabama, 1956. Useful bibliographic aids are Rhoda Coleman Ellison, *History and Bibliography of Alabama Newspapers in the 19th Century* (Tuscaloosa: University of Alabama Press, 1954) and Allen W. Jones, "Theses and Dissertations in Alabama History," *The Alabama Review* (July 1969): 208-229.

Since Alabama had a highly centralized public school system with most funds being provided by the state and not by local communities, the Alabama State Archives and History collection in Montgomery under the directorship of Milo Howard,

Jr. (and formerly under the leadership of Thomas McAdory Owen and Marie Bankhead Owen) is a mine of information of local Alabama educational history. The letter books of the Superintendent of Education from the 1870s through the 1890s are there, as well as the county reports (with many missing) to the state requesting payment for teachers based on the number of pupils and days taught. Clearly there was some misrepresentation of these local reports in the immediate post-Civil War period, but it is still interesting to look at them. At the Archives and History are also found a nearly complete set of the State Department of Education Annual Reports with data on each county (if it reported), beginning with 1868 to 1869. Also there is a report issued by the State Department of Education, Montgomery "Alabama's Country Schools and Their Relation to Country Life," Bulletin No. 33, 1913 (no author), which includes much useful information about the rural schools, about which very little was written. The Archives and History have a fairly complete set, which is complemented by the Auburn University collection, of the Proceedings of the Alabama Education Association, beginning in 1884.

Material on Butler County is available both at the Archives and History and at Auburn University Library. By far the most valuable source is the local newspaper, the *Greenville Advocate*, which began publishing January 9, 1867 and of which the Archives and History has nearly a full run of the weekly. Its existence was a major reason for studying Butler County. It is a marvellous newspaper for local historians, since in the nineteenth and early twentieth centuries it was much more interested in Butler County activities than in national ones, although it virtually excluded mention of any of the 40 percent or more in the population who were black. Forney E. Thomas, "Greenville Life as Revealed by the Greenville *Advocate*, 1867-1877," M. S. thesis, Auburn University, Auburn, 1935 and Paul G. Blacketor, "The Policy of the Greenville *Advocate*, 1877-1892," M. A. thesis, Auburn University, Auburn, 1955, summarize much that appeared in the newspaper.

The publications of the Butler County Historical Society, which began in March 1965, are also helpful, but few deal with educational topics. The Crenshaw family letters of the 1860s and 1870s in the possession of Myra Ware Crenshaw add useful data. The history of Butler County, John B. Little, *The History of Butler County, Alabama from 1815 to 1885* (Cincinnati, n.p., 1885) is a compendium of the author's observations on his community, and since he was an active educator in the area is particularly helpful to the educational historian. Other newspapers are preserved in isolated numbers or limited series at the Archives and History and are helpful as supplements to the *Advocate*. They include *The South Alabamian*, which has scattered issues extant from 1869 to 1876; *The Living Truth*, a Populist paper published in Greenville from the early 1890s until 1916; *The Butler County News*, published in Georgiana, a small town in Butler County from 1911 to 1916, of which only a few issues from 1914 and 1916 are available in the Archives and History; and *The Greenville Ledger*, which began publication in 1915 as a competitor to the *Advocate*.

Denominational histories are another source for Butler County educational and cultural life. Particularly helpful are J. W. Joyner's manuscript at the Archives and History, *A History of the Baptists of Butler County, Alabama*, 1819-1957; B. R. Riley, *A Memorial History of the Baptists of Alabama* (Philadelphia: Judson Press, 1923); Avery Hamilton Reid, *Baptists in Alabama: Their Organization and Witness* (Montgomery: Alabama Baptist State Convention, 1967); Marion Elias Lazenby, *History of Methodism in Alabama and West Florida* (n.p., 1960); James Williams Marshall, *The Presbyterian Church in Alabama* (unpublished manuscript in Archives and History); Walter C. Whitaker, *History of the Protestant Episcopal Church in Alabama, 1763-1891* (Birmingham: Roberts and Son, 1898).

New York City sources

Unlike the other counties studied where materials were difficult to locate, New York City presented quite a different problem. For New York the task was to isolate and condense from the mass of data the material that was germane to the educational history of the locality. The general works on urban history cited earlier are, of course, valuable. Unfortunately no first-rate history of New York City in the period exists, so one is forced to rely on the local newspapers, especially *The New York Times*.

Walter Laidlaw, *Population of the City of New York, 1890-1932* (New York: Cities Census Committee, 1932) has much useful information. Moses Rischin, *The Promised City: New York's Jews, 1870-1914* (Cambridge: Harvard University Press, 1962) is a model of its kind for an ethnic history of a group within a city.

The history of public education in New York City for 1865 to 1918 is found in the many reports of the New York City Board of Education during that period, most of which are preserved at the Teachers College, Columbia University Library. The report of Paul Harus, Committee on School Inquiry, 1911-1913, is crucial. Particularly helpful summaries are A. Emerson Palmer, *The New York Public School, Being a History of Free Education in New York* (New York: Macmillan, 1905) and Harold W. McCormick, *The First Fifty Years, New York Superintendent of School Report, 1898-1914* (New York: New York City Board of Education, 1948). Diane Ravitch's forthcoming study of the New York city school wars will undoubtedly shed additional light and much-needed interpretation on these complicated events. David Hammack, "The Centralization of New York City's Public School System, 1896: A Social Analysis of a Decision," M. A. thesis, Columbia University, New York, 1969 is a useful and provocative guide to that complicated time.

Selma Cantor Berrol, "Immigrants at School: New York City, 1898-1914," PhD dissertation, City University of New York, New York, 1969 focuses on Jewish and Italian immigrants in New York City and includes a very extensive bibliography. A good study of blacks is Frances Blascoer, *Colored Schoolchildren in New York* (New York: Public Education Association, 1915) Herbert Shapiro, "Reorganization of the New York

City Public School System, 1890-1910," Doctoral thesis, Yeshiva University, New York City, 1967, is less analytical than either Hammack or Berrol but has several useful sources. Sol Cohen, *Progressives and Urban School Reform: The Public Education Association of New York City* (New York: Teachers College Press, 1964) adds helpful material about the PEA's educational work. *New York Learns* (Washington, D.C.: Federal Works Agency, 1939) is a compilation and brief history of educational institutions in New York City. Richard Whittemore, *Nicholas Murray Butler and Public Education, 1862-1911* (New York: Teachers College Press, 1970) recounts that phenomenal man's involvement with the New York schools and concludes that he was a crucial figure, particularly at turn of the century.

Contemporary accounts of New York schools of special interest are Adele Marie Shaw, "The True Character of New York Public Schools," *World's Work, VII* (1903): 4204-4221; Joseph Mayer Rice, "The Public Schools of New York City" (two-part article) and "Need School be a Blight to Child Life?" *Forum, XII* (1891): 529-535 *Epoch, IX* (1891): 390-391 and 406-408; Stephen H. Olin, "Public School Reform in New York City," *Educational Review, VIII* (1894): 1-6; W. H. Maxwell, "Stories of the Lives of Real Teachers," *World's Work, XVIII* (1909): 11877-11880; and Burton J. Hendrick, "Six Thousand Girls at School," *McClure's XLI* (1913): 46-57.

Material about the Roman Catholic parochial schools is found in Michael Lucey, "The Parochial Schools of New York City," M. A. thesis, Columbia University, New York City, 1908; Sr. Margy Agnes O'Brien, S.C., "History and Development of Catholic Secondary Education in Archdiocese of New York," PhD Dissertation, Columbia University, New York City, 1949; n.a. *The Parish Schools of New York* (New York: Columbus Press, 1905); and Rev. Joseph Cook, "Roman Catholic Parochial Schools," *Boston Monday Lecture Series* (Boston: n.p., 1888), pp. 117-128.

Particular information about the New York Public Library system and its predecessor library collections is meticulously collected in Harry Lydenburg, *History of the New York Public Library* (New York: New York Public Library, 1923) and Phyllis Dain's more evaluative volume, *The New York Public Library* (New York: New York Public Library, 1972). A contemporary account of the libraries is n.a., *Libraries of Greater New York* (New York: New York Library Club, 1902). Catha Grace Rambusch's compilation, "Museums and Other Collections in New York City, 1790-1870," (n.p., n.d.) is available at the New York Historical Society.

Princeton and Wisconsin sources

The standard histories of higher education in America against which the stories of Princeton and Wisconsin must be seen are Richard Hofstadter and Walter Metzger, *The Development of Academic Freedom in the United States* (New York: Columbia University Press, 1955): Frederick Rudolph, *The American College and University: A History* (New York: Knopf, 1962) and Laurence Veysey, *The Emergence of the American University* (Chicago: University of Chicago Press, 1965).

Thomas Wertenbaker has written the standard history of Princeton, and it abounds with the customary eulogies to the institution as well as some outsanding omissions, particularly no mention of the existence of Evelyn College. *Princeton, 1746-1896* (Princeton: Princeton University Press, 1946). Other histories of the university include Varnum Lansing Collins, *Princeton* (New York: Oxford University Press, 1914); Edwin Mark Norris, *The Story of Princeton* (Boston: Little, Brown and Co., 1917); and George P. Schmidt, *Princeton and Rutgers. The Two Colonial Colleges of New Jersey* (Princeton: Van Nostrand and Co., 1964). Of some incidental value are James W. Alexander, *Princeton—Old and New, Recollections of Undergraduate Life* (New York: Scribner's, 1898). Willard Thorp, ed., *The Lives of 18 from Princeton* (Princeton: Princeton University Press, 1946); John Rogers Williams, *The Handbook of Princeton* (New York: Grafton Press, 1905); George R. Wallace, *Princeton*

Sketches. The Story of Nassau Hall (New York: Putnam's, 1893); John Frelinghuysen Hagerman, *History of Princeton* Vol. II (Philadelphia: Lippincott, 1879); and William M. Sloane, "Princeton," in Edwin Slosson, ed., *Four American Universities* (New York: Harper, 1895).

By far the most valuable source on the history of Princeton are the Princeton University Archives at the Princeton University Library. There the President's Reports to the Board of Trustees are the most useful contemporary summary of events at the institution. Also available in the Archives and of immense significance for an understanding of the graduate school controversy is Andrew F. West's "A Narrative of the Graduate College of Princeton University from Its Proposal in 1896 until its Dedication in 1913," whose preface states that it was written in 1920 and revised in 1929. Of special interest to the history of Princeton is the account of the abortive effort to establish a women's college in Princeton with some kind of coordinate status with the men's institution; this is described in Frances P. Healey, "A History of Evelyn College for Women, Princeton, New Jersey," Doctoral dissertation, Ohio State University, Columbus, 1967. A contemporay account is Adelaide Stirling, "Evelyn College," *Harper's Bazaar*, XXIX (1896): 806-807.

The presidency of Woodrow Wilson was a crucial time for Princeton, and Wilson's years have been well studied, particularly by Arthur S. Link, who is editing Wilson's papers. Link's *The Road to the White House* (Princeton: Princeton University Press, 1947) deals with Wilson's Princeton years, as do Henry Braydon, *Woodrow Wilson: The Academic Years* (Cambridge: Harvard University Press, 1967) and Hardin Craig, *Woodrow Wilson at Princeton* (Norman: University of Oklahoma Press, 1960). The opposing position to Wilson's is set forth in a pamphlet by an anonymous alumnus, "The Phantom Ship, or the Quad System, Some Discussion of its Merits; Also of the Effect of its Continual Agitation upon Princeton University," (n.p., 1911?), which is located in the University Archives.

One of the best university histories is Merle Curti and Vernon

Carstensen, *The University of Wisconsin, A History* (Madison: The University of Wisconsin Press, 1949, 2 vols.) Although it is a long history, it is not merely an accumulation of facts about the university. It is interpretive, and it also attempts to place developments at Wisconsin within the context of the other major midwestern state universities. Less sophisticated histories of the university are J. F. A. Pyre, *Wisconsin* (New York: Oxford University Press, 1920) and C. W. Butterfield, *History of the University of Wisconsin* (Madison: University Publishing Co., 1879). Helen Olin, *The Women of a State University* (New York: Putnam, 1909) is a excellent example of a rare genre: the history of the coeducation movement. Much useful material is found in biographies of two leading members of the university community, Richard T. Ely, the economist whose moderately iconoclastic views prompted an academic freedom case, and Charles R. VanHise, the president who led Wisconsin in the early twentieth century. Benjamin G. Rader, *The Academic Mind and Reform, The Influence of Richard T. Ely in American Life* (Lexington University of Kentucky Press, 1966) provides much background information on Wisconsin in the 1890s. Maurice M. Vance, *Charles Richard VanHise: Scientist Progressive* (Madison: State Historical Society of Wisconsin, 1960) illumines the life of the president who probably did more than any other in this century to make the university distinguished. Charles McCarthy, *The Wisconsin Idea* (New York: Macmillan, 1912) is a contemporary account of VanHise's efforts to make the university serve the state.

The most helpful materials for this period in the University Archives are the Regents Reports, Volume B, beginning 1866, and the Proceedings of the Regents, beginning 1866, Volume C. Of the two the Reports are more interesting, since they are the accounts of Committee Reports presented to the Regents for their action. The Proceedings simply report actions of the Regents and give less indication of debates within the group.

index

7